Singing
through the Night

Singing
through the Night

Courageous Stories of Faith from
Women in the Persecuted Church

Anneke Companjen

Revell
Grand Rapids, Michigan

© 2007 by Open Doors International

Published by Fleming H. Revell
a division of Baker Publishing Group
P.O. Box 6287, Grand Rapids, MI 49516-6287
www.revellbooks.com

Printed in the United States of America

Library of Congress Cataloging-in-Publication Data
Companjen, Anneke.
  Singing through the night : courageous stories of faith from women in
the persecuted church / Anneke Companjen.
    p. cm.
  Includes bibliographical references.
  ISBN 10: 0-8007-3198-0 (pbk.)
  ISBN 978-0-8007-3198-4 (pbk.)
  1. Christian women—Religious life. 2. Persecution. 3. Suffering—Religious aspects—Christianity. I. Title.
BV4527.C634 2007
272′.90922—dc22   𝟹𝟼𝟻𝟽𝟸𝟼𝟸𝟻 𝟷𝟶/𝟶𝟽   2006039144

Song on pages 147–48 used by permission of Gilbert Hovsepian.
Song on pages 247–48 used by permission of Graham Kendrick.

To my dear mother who kept singing
through the dark night of widowhood.
Despite deteriorating health and increasing
dementia, she still has a "song in the night."
I am fortunate to have had such a mother!

Contents

Foreword

More than twelve years ago, our family suffered a devastating blow. My husband, Haik, was killed as a direct result of his obedience to Jesus Christ. He was a leading pastor in Tehran, Iran, and he refused to comply with the rules of the Islamic government concerning the freedom of Iranian churches. Although he was the superintendent of the Iranian Protestant churches, the authorities ordered him not to share the gospel with Muslims. Many Iranian Muslims were hungry to hear the message of Christ, and Christians like my husband couldn't ignore them. But the price some of them paid for disobeying the regime was very high indeed.

After our oldest son, Joseph, was asked to go and identify his martyred father's body, I cried out to God in pain and wondered how He could allow this to happen to our family. I needed my husband; our children needed their father. God seemed to answer that I had to leave the "why" with Him, because He was in full control, and one day He would use my testimony to touch others. In hindsight that is exactly what happened.

When my story was told in Anneke Companjen's first book, *Hidden Sorrow, Lasting Joy,* and I saw it in print for the first time, I was deeply touched. I cried as I read it, even though it was my own testimony. I was encouraged to see the way God had worked in my life, to realize the many lessons He had taught me. When I heard that other women, after reading my story, were encouraged to forgive and to turn over their grief to God, I saw how God was fulfilling His promise to me. When I shared my testimony in different countries and saw hearts being touched, I thanked God because my suffering had not been in vain.

This, Anneke's second book, will encourage the women of the Persecuted Church. I know they will be uplifted when they read these stories, because they will see that they are not the only ones who are suffering. I have experienced that myself. I would like to say to them that if I could make it through the valley, they can make it too. If God could do it for me, He can do it for them. God knows just how much we can handle, and He does not give us more than we can carry, even though at times it may seem otherwise.

Even those who are not facing hardship now may encounter difficulties later. Most of us will pass through dark nights at some stage in our lives. The women who are featured in this book can teach all of us valuable lessons about how to persevere when life gets tough.

In the dark, despondent days after Haik's martyrdom, some young girls from our church in Tehran sometimes came to our house and sang to us. At that time I found it hard to sing. Whenever I tried, I choked and out came the tears. The girls' songs really ministered to me. Though I found it hard to keep my voice steady, my heart was in tune with what they sang.

My children and I discovered that not only is it possible to sing through the night, but it is enormously uplifting. Our sons are very talented musically. One of them, Gilbert, found an outlet for his grief in composing eloquent songs after the death of his father. His songs ministered to all of us.

Eventually our family began to minister in song at various church meetings, and this encouraged many other Christians to see that

God gave us peace in the midst of our sad circumstances. Worship is indeed a powerful tool in overcoming hardship, but so are reading the Word of God, help from other believers, the empathy of people who visit or phone, and the love of brothers and sisters from around the world expressed in cards and letters. Many things helped me through, but most of all it was the grace of our loving heavenly Father who walked with us through the valley.

I have often shared how, in the years after Haik's death, I felt as though I studied in God's university. He taught me to trust Him 100 percent and to hand over my life to Him completely. He asked me to forgive my enemies, to allow Him to replace my anger toward the murderers of my husband with His love, to obey Him in order to grow spiritually. I had to choose to stay in His school; He did not force me. I could have become bitter because of what happened. Instead, I chose to obey.

Today I can testify that through God's help our family is well. We stayed in Iran for five years after Haik's death. Then for the sake of the children, I made the difficult choice to move to America. It proved to be the right thing to do. Now, through modern media like video, satellite TV, and films, our children are involved in reaching Iranian people across the world, including inside Iran, with the gospel of Jesus Christ. The oldest three are married, all four of them follow the Lord, and I am the proud grandmother of four grandchildren.

If I have learned one thing through my ordeal, it is that God has the final say and He is in full control. That is why I am so glad to recommend this book. May you be encouraged as you read the stories Anneke has written about women who face persecution for their faith. Following Jesus involves taking up our cross, but God makes it up to us in so many ways. I would not choose any other way than His.

Takoosh Hovsepian
California, USA

Acknowledgments

I am greatly indebted to . . .

The women who were willing to tell me their stories and allowed me to include them in this book. They encouraged and challenged me and taught me valuable lessons.

Our program directors and field workers who made it possible for me to meet many of the women featured in this book. Apart from reading the stories with special focus on factual correctness and security issues, some of them helped me find appropriate songs.

Ron Boyd-MacMillan for allowing me to use one of his stories.

Graham Kendrick and Gilbert Hovsepian for giving me permission to use their songs.

May, Maria, and Esther for reading the first few stories. Their comments gave me confidence to go ahead with the project.

Trich for reading the first drafts of most chapters. Her questions and comments helped me rewrite and correct many of the stories.

Lela Gilbert, whose professionalism taught me a lot; as with my first book, her skillfulness turned my manuscript into a readable and publishable book.

Anneke, Esther, Jane, Jenny, Jo, Helen, and Nelie who were willing to read the manuscript and answer my questions. Their comments were of great help to Lela Gilbert and me in finalizing the text.

Al Janssen, Open Doors' "writer in residence," for his helpful comments and advice on many occasions.

Jo Janssen for her willingness to write the questions to add to the chapters and her sensitivity to the guidance of the Holy Spirit while she worked.

The women I met in many different countries who read my first book, *Hidden Sorrow, Lasting Joy.* Their comments, their prayers for the Persecuted Church, and their requests for more stories kept me going during days when the writing was tough.

Last but not least, Johan and our three wonderful children, without whose love and support I never could have written another book. May God bless them for their willingness to be included in some of my personal testimonies.

Introduction

The battle is not yours, but God's. . . . You will not have to fight this battle. Take up your positions; stand firm and see the deliverance the LORD will give you. . . . After consulting the people, Jehoshaphat appointed men to sing to the LORD and to praise him for the splendor of his holiness as they went out at the head of the army, saying: "Give thanks to the LORD, for his love endures forever." As they began to sing and praise, the LORD set ambushes.

2 Chronicles 20:15, 17, 21–22

June 7, 1996, was a sad day in our family. I spent the afternoon in a hospital, sitting at my father's bedside. He had suffered a stroke four days earlier; he could not talk, was partially paralyzed, and was being fed through a tube. My mother and sister had sat with him through the morning, and I arrived to be there in the afternoon. I will never forget watching my mother, clasping his limp hand, stroking it, and telling him again how much she loved him. She left the room not realizing it was the last time she would see him alive.

I can only describe the rest of the afternoon as a battle. It was a physical battle for my dad, as his temperature soared and he gradually lost his fight for life. But it was also a spiritual battle for me. It was as if the devil—the Bible calls him "our last foe"—was trying to show me his power.

I prayed and read Scripture, proclaiming out loud that the battle was already won. My father had given his life to Christ when he was a young man. His sins were forgiven by the blood of Jesus, and Satan no longer had power over him because of Christ's victory won at the cross. Now, all that was left for me to do was to pray and wait. Hours later, after my husband, Johan, and my brother and his wife arrived, my father passed away peacefully.

Later that evening, I held my weeping mother in my arms. "I would have so much liked to have him with me a bit longer," she sobbed. "But I don't complain. We had such a good life together, and after all, not many reach the age of eighty like your dad."

The next day it was my turn to cry. While my mother was busying herself in the kitchen, I heard her alto voice singing one of her favorite songs, "Count your blessings, name them one by one, and it will surprise you what the Lord has done."

That week, I realize in retrospect, part of my mother died as well. Now ten years later, she is suffering from dementia and receives good care in a nursing home. Despite the frequent visits of friends and loved ones, she gets lonely, and she realizes she is losing control over her life. But the principles she lived by still work. Many times over the last few years, she has told me, "I felt very lonely last night, but I sang and it helped!"

My mother is not the only one who relies on singing in times of struggle and pain. As I have traveled with my husband to meet persecuted Christians around the world, I have heard countless believers who share her experience: it helps to sing through the night.

I remember one evening during a visit to Central Asia. After dinner our young host picked up his guitar and began to sing. There were only eight of us present, all seated on the floor. A young boy, Olav, sat across from me. Although his face was radiant, I knew that his life was far from easy. He was paying a high price for following Jesus. Often his own mother physically abused him to, in her words, "beat the Russian God out of you!" That evening, during one of the purest worship meetings I have ever attended, Jesus was there at the center, as we focused on Him. And in the process, like young Olav, we were all lifted above our circumstances.

Several years ago when I first visited Ethiopia, I noticed the important role worship and choirs play in some of the churches. After young people come to a personal belief in Christ, they are often excommunicated from the Orthodox Church. As a result, many of their parents throw their children—often still teenagers—out of their homes into the street with only the clothes on their backs. Afterward, they treat them as if they were dead. These young people, who are severely persecuted by both family and society, continue to worship God, singing His praises with a volume and a vigor that initially struck me—a stiff Northern European with a Calvinist background—as a bit "over the top." But I soon came to see that worship is a lifeline for them. They need continually to remind their souls of the truth of God's love, a truth that is freely expressed in the words they sing. At the same time, their praise serves as a means of overcoming the powers of evil that surround them. Each choir composes its own songs, which are filled with biblical messages. These Christians understand the miracle that happened among the people of Israel in 2 Chronicles 20, the passage I've quoted above. Worship is stronger than weapons.

In Afghanistan in the fall of 2001, a group of eight international volunteer workers spent three months in dark, dirty prisons. Before they had been abducted, they were in the habit of beginning each day with a time of singing and praying. During their captivity they continued this habit.[1] Worshiping God, despite their inhumane and frightening circumstances, helped them focus on the One they trusted for deliverance.

When I hear South Korean Christians worship, I often just listen. Because of their great harmonic skills, their singing is especially beautiful; in fact, I sometimes wonder if God has given every one of them the voice of a soloist. Recently, however, when my husband and I visited them, the music made me sad as my thoughts wandered to North Korea. For more than fifty years, our Christian brothers and sisters in the north have not been able to sing praises openly to our God. Apart from a few government-ruled churches that are open for tourists, there are no public places of worship in North Korea. And when Christians take the risk to come together in twos or threes, they only dare "sing" by moving their lips. Meanwhile, untold thousands of Christians have died in North Korea's brutal prison camps, often with a song on their lips, to the chagrin of their torturers.

After the service, I shared my feelings with a South Korean friend, and he told me a story he heard about an old North Korean couple. This elderly husband and wife often walked far into the mountains, acting as if they were searching for herbs. Instead, they would enter as far as they could go into a deep cave. When they were sure no one but God could possibly hear them, they lifted their voices to heaven, singing all the Christian songs they could remember.

The songs of believers, often sung in times of great darkness and tumult, have always inspired me. And now, six years since the publication of my first book, *Hidden Sorrow, Lasting Joy*,[2] at the request of readers from all around the world, I have the opportunity to share more stories of women who have faced persecution for their Christian faith. This time I have focused on the lessons they have learned during their times of hardship.

I have met many of the women whose stories you will find in the pages that follow. And those I have not personally met, I have heard about through our colleagues at Open Doors, the organization founded by Brother Andrew and with which my husband, Johan, and I have been involved for more than thirty years. Open Doors works with all of the women mentioned, in a few cases simply by asking for prayers and advocacy, but more often by active support through programs in their countries.

There are a few important issues that I want to point out. First of all, you will notice that some of the stories are short while others are longer. The length of a story has no relevance to the intensity of the suffering or the importance of the person. Also some countries where Christians are persecuted and where Open Doors is involved are not represented. And in most cases, to protect the identity of a person, names have been changed and locations withheld.

Persecution is painful, and in the face of it, perseverance is accompanied by blood, sweat, and tears. Although there are lessons to be learned through suffering, in no way do I have the intention of making persecution sound easy. There are no simple methods for endurance. Nonetheless, I have learned from these women. Their lives are not hopeless, because Jesus is with them. And they have learned to praise Him in the midst of their circumstances.

As I travel, I am aware that pain and suffering are not exclusive to women who live in countries where they suffer because of their faith in Jesus. Wherever we live on this planet, our Enemy is the same. Satan wants us to give up, to become bitter and useless, so we can no longer be involved in building the kingdom of God. In some areas his weapon is persecution coming from governments, extreme elements within religions, terrorism, family members, and others. But in the Western world, challenges created by materialism and secularism have caused many to waver or even give up their faith.

Christians around the world need each other, and we can learn from each other. Even women who live in affluent, free countries have to deal with pain and suffering, and the women of the Persecuted Church have much to teach us. This is the reason the stories in each chapter are grouped together according to the important lessons these women have learned. Of course there are many other lessons for us all as well. Looking beyond the present, giving thanks in all things, not looking at our circumstances but fixing our eyes on Jesus, and retaining a sense of humor in the midst of persecution are just a few I would have added if it had been possible.

As Paul wrote, if one part of Christ's body suffers, the whole body suffers (1 Cor. 12:26). Likewise, when we help carry the load of others, their burden becomes lighter. One of the questions I am often asked as I speak and write on behalf of these women is, "What can I do to help?" Since the publication of *Hidden Sorrow, Lasting Joy,* Open Doors has increased its number of projects for women in both free and restricted countries. So there is something you can do. Involvement starts with gaining information, and at the end of this book, you will find ways in which you can keep yourself informed on a regular basis. You will also find information on how you can support these women and get involved in assisting them. They do not ask for our pity. They ask for our prayers. Let's join our voices with theirs, not only in prayer but in praise and thanksgiving to Jesus, whose grace is all-sufficient in the midst of our darkest hours.

Singing through the Night

On August 16, 2005, Alan Yuan passed into the presence of the Lord. During his life, he had spent twenty-one years and eight months in Chinese jails because he refused to comply with rules the government imposed on churches. He told many of his visitors that during the long years in jail, two songs continued to encourage him. One was Psalm 27 set to music and the other was "The Old Rugged Cross." The prisoners worked nine hours a day with only one break, but during that break Alan Yuan stood outside and sang those two songs over and over again. "I found the Chinese version of 'The Old Rugged Cross' better than the English one," he later told a friend. "In Chinese it tells us to be faithful servants and to follow the cross, which was what I wanted to do."

On a hill far away stood an old rugged cross,
The emblem of suffering and shame;
And I love that old cross where the dearest and best
For a world of lost sinners was slain.

So I'll cherish the old rugged cross,
Till my trophies at last I lay down;
I will cling to the old rugged cross,
And exchange it some day for a crown.

O that old rugged cross, so despised by the world,
Has a wondrous attraction for me;
For the dear Lamb of God left His glory above
To bear it to dark Calvary.

In the old rugged cross stained with blood so divine,
A wondrous beauty I see;
For 'twas on that old cross Jesus suffered and died
To pardon and sanctify me.

To the old rugged cross I will ever be true,
Its shame and reproach gladly bear;
Then He'll call me some day to my home far away,
Where His glory forever I'll share.

George Bennard (1873–1958)

在各各他山上

1. 在各各他山上，孤立十字寶架，這乃是羞辱痛苦記號；
   聖子耶穌基督，為世人被釘死，這十架為我最愛最寶。
2. 在世人眼光中，十字架是羞辱，於我卻是為榮耀徽號；
   神愛子主耶穌，離開天堂榮華，背此苦架走向各各他。
3. 各各他的十架，雖然滿有血跡，我仍看此架為美為聖；
   因在此寶架上，救主為我捨命，擔我眾罪使我蒙拯救。
4. 故我樂意背負，榮耀十字寶架，甘願受世人輕視辱罵；
   他日救主再臨，迎接我同昇天，永遠分享榮耀在天家。

   故我高聲稱頌主十架，直到在主台前見主面，
   我一生要背負十字架，十字架可換公義冠冕。副歌

China: Mrs. Yang

One of our Open Doors colleagues, Ron Boyd-MacMillan, has traveled extensively in China. One day he met a believer named Mrs. Yang, one of many female evangelists who play a vital role in the enormous growth of China's church. Her simple lifestyle and Christian zeal intrigued Ron.

At that time people often walked into the hills to have their morning devotions. One day, when Ron was spending time in prayer in the hills, he saw Mrs. Yang a short distance away. He noticed that she began her day with about twenty minutes on her knees in prayer. Then she got up from the damp, rocky ground and started to walk around, singing as she went. Then she read her Bible, making notes, evidently planning the day's sermons. Finally, once again before she returned home, she sang for another half hour.

As she walked back toward the village, Ron caught up with her. "Mrs. Yang," he said. "I hope you don't mind, but I saw you as you had your quiet time this morning. May I ask you something?"

She tilted her head to look up at him. "Of course. What do you want to know?"

"Why do you sing so exuberantly when you are by yourself?"

Mrs. Yang tried to answer his question as best as she could. "My father once taught me that one of the sweet things about the Christian life is that believers do things simply because they are commanded to. Singing is a command. In the Psalms we're constantly exhorted to sing praises to our God."

Making mental notes of her words, Ron quietly walked beside the slightly stooped lady, who went on, "I didn't really understand the power of worshiping God and singing His praises until I was arrested and sent to prison. There I prayed and read Scripture, but nothing raised my spirits like singing. Maybe it's because singing somehow concentrates the whole body on the praise of God.

I have found it essential in my Christian life. To keep a positive spirit, I *need* to sing."

Ron could sense that she wanted to say more, but she seemed hesitant to go on. "Were you about to say something else?" he asked.

"Well, it's just that an old lady once told me something that really sums up the main reason I sing. She said, 'Our spirits are like flowers, and song is the sun. Just as flowers open only when the sun shines, so our spirits blossom only when we sing.' I believe that is true. Since my prison cell, I cannot do without song. As God's Word says, 'And in the night his song shall be with me'" (Ps. 42:8 KJV).

"Thank you, Mrs. Yang," Ron said. "That really is an important lesson."

But Mrs. Yang wasn't finished. As they neared the village, she went on to tell Ron about her fears for the future of China's Christians as the country opened up and the churches got more organized. "I fear that the day will come when we're going to leave the singing to the professionals. I think that would be terrible. The only way a Christian can have a full blossoming spirit is to sing to the Lord."

Before he left China the following day, Ron saw a vivid example of the power of worship and song in the lives of Mrs. Yang and of Chinese Christians.

A discouraged and downcast woman, who was another full-time preacher, came to visit Mrs. Yang. She wanted to buy a tape player for her ministry, but she had no money. Mrs. Yang listened as her friend unburdened her heart; then she began to sing to her. Her elderly voice was deep and scratchy, but although the tune was barely discernable, the words were simple and lovely:

> I am a wanderer, my home is heaven.
> Life is fleeting.
> Our home is in heaven.

In this world we have many trials,
And sadness and sickness.
True happiness is not in this world.
But in heaven.

Mrs. Yang seemed to be singing to the Lord. Every word poured out from her heart with total conviction. Tears rolled down her cheeks, one hand was clenched in the air, and she beat time on her hip with the other. Soon the visiting preacher joined in the song. Ron watched in amazement as they sang the hymn together, smiles wreathing their faces. The preacher left, still with no money for her longed-for tape player, but refreshed and encouraged nonetheless.

I am not sure if it's my age or my personality, but these days I seem prone to lying awake at night. During those dark, sleepless hours, it is tempting to start worrying, so I have to make a decision. Will I worry or worship? I know all too well that worry takes me on a downward spiral, while worship lifts me up. On many occasions, especially when there were real reasons to be worried about our children, my husband, or the ministry, I have had to make that choice. Do I concentrate on the circumstances, or do I fix my eyes on Jesus? Like our courageous Chinese Christian sisters, I have found that it helps to sing through the night.

I met Han, another of these heroic Chinese women, while her husband, Ning, was in prison. She too found that her spirit was lifted above her present circumstances when she began to sing God's praises.

China: Han

Restless and anxious, Han tossed and turned in bed. As much as she tried, she could not shake off the nagging feeling that something was wrong with her husband. Her thoughts were like raging rivers, bursting through time and space, churning incidents from the past with those of the present as she tried to imagine where Ning might be.

She remembered the evening in 2000 when she had learned that he had been arrested. Caught in the possession of Christian literature that had been printed without government permission, he had been taken to the Public Security Bureau (PSB)—the Chinese government's policing arm. That night, like this one, Han had been unable to sleep. She had spent most of the night worrying about Ning and praying for him. And then, unexpectedly, he had turned up the next morning. The story he told her sounded as though it had been drawn straight from the book of Acts.

"The officers who were supposed to guard me fell asleep, and I was hungry so I tried to find some food," he said. "When I found that the door to the police station was unlocked, I just walked out."

To their amazement, Ning was not immediately rearrested. It seemed as if the PSB had more pressing matters at hand. The crackdown on the religious sect Falun Gong took up most of their energy, which lifted some of the pressure off the house churches. As a result, the church Ning was pastoring at the time hadn't been under much police scrutiny.

But now Han had reason to be worried. Despite his previous arrest, Ning continued his "secret" ministry, and Han knew it might very well get him into trouble again.

Sweet Beginnings

As she lay there in the darkness thinking of her husband, Han remembered the happy times they had shared together. She would never forget the memorable evening when she'd first met Ning. Already a pastor at the time, Ning came to her mother's house to preach. Their living room was packed with people eager to hear the young man's words. Sitting on a stool in a back corner of the dimly lit room, Han could not keep her eyes off Ning, who spoke so eloquently and with such enthusiasm about his faith.

Ning returned again and again to preach, and the more he came, the fonder Han became of him. His frequent visits quickly became a highlight in her life.

Han was barely out of her teens when Ning told her mother that he was interested in marrying her daughter. An orphan, he longed to have his own family. "It won't be easy," Ning warned Han. "You know I am a preacher, so I'll probably be away from home a lot. The work of the Lord has to come first—before anything or anyone else in my life. But if you can accept that, I would love to spend the rest of my life with you." Han barely heard what he said—she was going to marry Ning, and nothing could spoil her joy!

In the years that followed, she was not disappointed. Unlike many Chinese men she knew, Ning was a good husband, and Han helped him as much as she could. She kept a small vegetable garden that provided them with fresh produce in the summer. She worked on their plot of land and rented part of their allotment to the church, providing additional income to free Ning for his pastoral duties. And she faithfully went about her duties as a pastor's wife, leading the women's meetings, attending prayer meetings, and visiting people.

To their great joy, Han gave birth to two children—first a girl and then a boy. Because her daughter, Yulong, was born first, they were allowed to have a second child, despite China's one-child policy. When Wang, their son, was born three years later, Han considered herself rich. Sons are more highly esteemed than daughters in China, but she was very grateful to have both.

The Need for Bibles

Not long after Wang was born, Ning became involved in a new secret ministry. At that time the Chinese government permitted the printing of an average of 2.6 million copies of the Bible per year on the Amity Press in the coastal city of Nanjing. This amount was not nearly enough to meet the great need for God's Word among the millions of new believers in the rural areas of China. Cults cause confusion and havoc all over China, leading many new believers astray. The best way to combat their influence has always been to teach new believers directly from the Word of God. They need their own Bibles to read what Jesus really says and to understand the principles of Christianity. Ning knew that the government considered it illegal to distribute "unofficially acquired" Bibles to the house churches without registering one's name at an official Three-Self distribution center (government approved centers and therefore potentially unsafe for house-church members), but Ning saw the urgency to make more Bibles available. More to the point, he was willing to take the risk.

Ning would not allow danger to hold him back, nor would he let fear paralyze him. As a loyal wife and Christian, Han shared his burden. Although many Chinese Christian leaders left their families behind for most of the year, Ning invited her to go with him on some of his trips. Han's mother lived with them and was happy to take care of the children; Yulong and Wang were good friends and played well together, which made it easier for Han to leave them behind.

After that first frightful night when Ning was taken to the police station, Han and Ning discussed their ministry. Han voiced her fears. "I'm afraid that one day they won't let you go so easily."

"That could well be the case. You and I both know how many Christians in our country are serving time in labor camps for their activities. We have no guarantee we won't have to suffer. And I'm prepared to pay the price for being obedient," Ning answered.

Ning was convinced he was doing the right thing, and Han's fears would not change his mind. Han knew it would not help to protest—in the Chinese culture, women are expected to follow their husbands, who make the major decisions. So Han decided to keep quiet and continue performing the duties that were required of her as a pastor's wife. Despite her fears, she too was willing to follow Jesus all the way.

After several years of secretly distributing Bibles, Ning announced to Han that he was going to make a long trip, and it would take him many days to reach his destination.

"I wish you would stay home!" Han objected. "The children and I need you. You've been away so much lately—do you really have to go?"

"You can come with me, if you like," he offered, but Han felt the children needed her more. So Ning left on his own, loaded with heavy bags full of "Good News."

"I'll pray for you—you know I will!" Han said as she waved good-bye.

The Arrest

Several weeks passed. A few times during Ning's trip, he had called Han on his cell phone to say all was well, but then the calls stopped. Too much time passed, and Han began to worry again. One night she was awake for hours, fretting about her husband's situation. Had Ning been arrested? Had something worse happened? What if she never saw him again? How could she live without him?

"Lord, please help me!" she interrupted her own thoughts. "Help me to fix my eyes on you instead of drown in my worries. You are the One in control. You promised to be with us always. Please, Lord, be with Ning wherever he is. Please, Father, give him strength. Help him to glorify your name whatever his circumstances may be."

29

Finally she fell asleep for a short while, but when she woke up at the crack of dawn, anxiety fell on her again. Something was wrong—she could sense it.

Wearily Han dragged herself out of bed, combed her long hair, and tied it into a ponytail. Her chubby cheeks had lost their usual rosy color, and the dark circles beneath her eyes revealed how tired she really was. She could only hope that the children didn't notice she had been crying.

As part of her morning routine, Han helped her children, now teenagers, pack their bags for school. Shortly after they left, the screech of tires and the slamming of car doors outside killed the glimmer of hope she was so desperately trying to grasp.

Three policemen marched into the house without knocking. "We have orders to search this place," one of them snapped. "Stay out of the way!"

As if she were nailed to the floor, Han stood still and tried not to show her fear. She watched as the angry-looking men in uniforms searched through all her possessions, turning drawers upside down and emptying the contents onto the floor. They pounded their fists against the walls, searched for hiding places behind the cabinets, and looked under the bed. When the men finally found some Bibles under a loose tile covering an opening in the floor, they were thrilled. Embracing their confiscated treasure, they headed for the door.

"Your husband won't be home for a while," their spokesman told Han. "Don't bother to wait up for him tonight."

Now she knew. Ning had indeed been arrested, and Han felt as though her heart was going to beat out of her chest. A number of possible scenarios spun through her mind, but it made no sense to try to figure out what may have happened. The truth was that Ning was in custody, and Han didn't know when he would be back. Sinking into a chair, she held her face in her hands and wept.

Now Han had to tell her children the news. She had not shared her worries with them before they went to school that morning. When they got home, she would have to tell them everything. Then there was the church to care for—who would lead in Ning's absence? It was likely that Ning would not be back for a while, so others would need to fill his place. And Ning—what about Ning? Would she be able to see him? Where was he? To which prison would they send him? Would he get a fair trial? All these questions raced through her mind.

Suddenly her thoughts were interrupted by a familiar sound.

"Han, what happened? Why was the PSB here?" Shu's high-pitched voice announced her arrival even before she got to the door. As a trusted friend and faithful church member for years, Shu's presence brought Han a much needed sense of relief.

Shu listened intently as Han poured out her concerns for Ning. "How will I tell the kids their father may not be coming home for a long time?" she asked Shu. "How can I cope without him?"

"One thing at a time, Han," Shu advised. "Like the old hymn says, 'Step by step our Savior leads us.' Let's worry about the children first, and the rest will come later. Your friends from the church will be here to help. You won't have to go through this alone."

But Han couldn't bring herself to tell her children the sad news. Reserved and reticent by nature, it was hard for her to express openly the truth with them. Trying to protect them from grief, she withdrew and kept silent about their father's arrest. Finally Han's mother informed her grandson about the situation. "Be a good son now, Wang," she told the seventeen-year-old boy. "Your mother needs your help."

Immediately, Wang went and told his sister what had happened. Yulong cried quietly in her pillow all that night, unable to understand why her mother had not told her the sad news herself. It took time for the children's bruised feelings to heal, making Han's heart ache more than ever.

For months it was unclear where the authorities had taken Ning or what kind of punishment he would receive. Eventually Han learned that he had been placed in a labor camp far away and would soon be sentenced.

Well aware that Christians are treated unfairly in China, Han feared the worst for Ning and refused to be hopeful. Possession of "unauthorized religious literature" was considered a criminal offense. Some Christians had received heavy fines when caught with Bibles, while others had been sentenced to two to three years in prison. When the day of judgment came, Han braced herself for the worst.

And the worst happened. Ning was sentenced to five and a half years in prison. Han nearly fainted when she heard the terrible verdict. How could the authorities give her husband such a long sentence—more than five years in prison simply for distributing the Word of God? Ning was a good citizen who had never done anything but try to help people.

For Han, another series of restless and tearful nights followed. But in the midst of this very dark cloud, there was a small ray of light—she was advised that Ning was about to be moved from the distant labor camp to a prison within their own province. Soon she would see him again.

Visiting Ning in Prison

As soon as Han received permission, she went to the prison, about a half day's journey away. Separated by iron bars, she and Ning were able to talk but unable to touch one other. To Han's relief, Ning didn't look terrible; he seemed reasonably clean and healthy, although she could see that he had lost weight.

At first, neither of them knew what to say. They simply sat in strained silence with racing minds. "How are the children?" Ning finally began. "How have they taken my arrest?"

Han told him that they were past the initial shock and seemed to be coping now, although Wang still seemed a bit withdrawn. She promised she would bring them as soon as they were allowed to come.

"But how about you? Is it hard for you?" she asked. She had to weigh her words; a guard stood nearby, watching and listening.

"Well, they make me string badminton rackets all day," he said, looking as upbeat as possible for his wife. "It's hard work and the days are long, but overall I'd say I'm doing all right."

After his work in the badminton-racket factory, Ning was given a job in the prison laundry ironing clothes all day. As time went by, he was transferred to the kitchen where he helped cook the prisoners' food. Then Han was allowed to meet her husband in the prison canteen, and they were able to talk more privately.

"I have a surprise for you," Han whispered to Ning on one of her visits, her face beaming with joy. She looked around to make sure nobody was watching them. Then she reached under her blouse and produced a small Chinese Bible.

Ning could hardly believe his eyes. He caressed the precious gift. "Thank you so much—nothing you could bring me would have made me happier," he told his wife. "You have a lot of courage, Han."

On Han's next visit, Ning seemed radiant with happiness. He admitted that his cell was still damp and cold, his wooden bed hard, and his blanket dirty. But he joyfully told Han, "I get up at five in the morning to have my quiet time alone with the Lord. It's so wonderful to have a Bible again—I spend all my spare time reading and praying." Han could see with her own eyes the change the Word of God had made in him.

His prison job had also improved. Ning chuckled. "I'm now the chief of the kitchen, so I don't have to work so hard. I'm also doing some administrative work for the prison. Really, my life is a lot easier now compared to what it was like before. I have plenty of free time to study my Bible."

As usual, a guard motioned for Han to leave long before she was ready to go, but the visit was uplifting and she left in good spirits.

Biweekly visits to the prison became a routine in Han's life. The children always looked forward to their scheduled visits, but seeing their father behind bars was still somewhat traumatic for them. As time passed, church members were allowed occasional visits too. Only two things were absolutely forbidden during these visits: crying and praying. But despite these restrictions, all his visitors brought great encouragement to Ning.

"Pray that I'll be like Joseph, Han," Ning said one day, reminding her of the biblical patriarch in the book of Genesis. "Pray that God will use me more after I get out of prison than before I went in. I'm learning so much while I'm here. Finally I have time to study His Word—I never had this much time before. God is using my stay in prison for good. I am sure of it!"

While Ning was doing better, Han and the children sometimes found life very difficult. Non-Christian neighbors looked down on them. Who would want to be friends with the family of a prisoner?

At first, since their school was in a nearby town and not in their own village, the children managed to hide their family situation from their classmates. But as time went by, Yulong began to have problems. It became known that she was the daughter of a "counterrevolutionary." Eventually Han had to remove her daughter from school and send her to a city far away from home where no one knew about Ning.

Yulong missed her father terribly and often cried for hours after returning from a visit to the prison. "I wish I knew how to help her," Han confided in her friend Shu. She felt helpless at the sight of her daughter's tears. "All I can do is pray for her," Han continued. "But do you know what she said to me the other day? She told me, 'I want to be like Dad. I want to be involved in the work he was doing.'"

A faint smile formed on Han's lips. "I am so glad she doesn't blame him. She's proud of him, instead."

The members of Ning and Han's house church continued to provide plenty of support to Han and the children. They all missed Ning's leadership, but during his absence, their faith continued to grow. They divided his jobs between them, with Han even taking on the task of preaching—something she never would have dared do before Ning's arrest.

During one Sunday service, she shared her personal feelings with the group. "Ning used to be like my big tree," she told the congregation. They understood very well this figure of speech, commonly used in the Chinese countryside. "I could hide under Ning's strong branches. He always protected me from the hardships of life, but now I feel so exposed. I could lean against him, and he supported me. As his wife, I also loved for him to lead me. He was my guide and my protector. He was always the strong one in our family, but things are different now. It feels like my sturdy, leafy tree has been cut down, and I miss his shelter."

In her heart, Han knew that she was learning a difficult lesson. Her husband could not be her primary support. As much as she loved Ning, only God deserved that place. God was always there; no one could ever take Him away from her. He had promised in His Word that He would never leave her or forsake her (Heb. 13:5).

A Special Visit

Not only did God help Han, but other Christians helped her as well. A few years after Ning was imprisoned, she had an opportunity to visit Beijing. She had heard about the hardship some of China's beloved Christian leaders had endured during Mao Tse-tung's regime, especially at the time of the Cultural Revolution. Christians around the world have treasured the testimonies of Wang Ming Dao, Samuel Lamb, and Alan Yuan, but they were cherished even more by a younger generation of Christians in China. When Han heard that Alan and Alice Yuan were still alive in Beijing, she decided to pay them a visit. They had been separated from each other for twenty-two years because of Alan's imprisonment, and Han was sure they would be able to provide her with sound advice and encouragement.

Like everyone else who visited the old couple, Han received a warm welcome. Alice busied herself providing tea and snacks, while Alan listened to Han's story and shared with her some valuable lessons he and Alice learned during their years of hardship and separation. "God knows about your circumstances, Han," he told her as their conversation came to a close. "Keep fixing your eyes on Jesus. Your help comes from Him. He will use this difficult time in your life, even if you don't see it now. God has the final say—not the devil."

These words reminded Han of something she had learned when her own parents had embraced the truth of Christianity: "Take up your cross and follow Jesus," they had told her. She also recalled another Scripture that seemed especially appropriate to China's beleaguered Christians, including Ning and herself: "Everyone who wants to live a godly life in Christ Jesus will be persecuted" (2 Tim. 3:12).

It lifted Han's heart to see that even in the Yuans' old age, after everything they had suffered, they were still standing strong. Alan gave her a book about his prison experience and how he had learned to cope, which provided extra encouragement to Han in the months that followed.

Before they said good-bye, Alan prayed. And Han offered a brief prayer of thanks as well. "Thank you, Lord, for Your strength," she said quietly. "What you did for Alan and Alice, I am confident you will do for Ning and me. After all, what is five and a half years compared to the twenty-two years Alan and Alice were separated? You are the same yesterday, today, and forever."

Joy in the Midst of Sorrow

Even after her visit to Alan and Alice, Han had her ups and downs. Sometimes she felt terribly lonely and discouraged. "I miss Ning," Han told Shu one afternoon. "Especially at night, when I find myself alone in the dark—sometimes I'm just overwhelmed by loneliness."

Before Shu could reply, Han went on, "But last night I had a wonderful experience," she smiled. "I was really sad, feeling worse than ever. Then all at once I started thinking about Paul and Silas, and how they found themselves in prison in Philippi. Remember how in the middle of the night they sang together? It occurred to me that singing might be good for me too. It must have been the Holy Spirit who prompted me, Shu, because it really helped."

Then Han quietly began to sing. Shu recognized the song immediately as one of Xiaomin's *Canaan Hymns*, which they often sang together in their house fellowship. Xiaomin's story was known all over China. Although she was an ordinary and uneducated peasant girl, through the inspiration of the Lord, she had composed hundreds of beautiful songs. Her words and music were born in blood and tears, written in the midst of the darkness she had passed through herself.

> Can't stop the tears of gratitude.
> Can't stop the words from deep within.
> Hands marked with the imprints of nails
> Open the doors long shut.
> We know this is a path of the cross—
> A painful path with violent storms.
> But the loving hands of the Lord
> Hold our heads all the time.
> There's no reason
> Not to follow the Lord Jesus.
>
> *Canaan Hymns*, 303

"While I was singing there in the darkness, I began to feel up-lifted. Somehow the pain began to diminish. I just sang and sang and sang until I fell asleep."

"We heard the same thing from those evangelists who came to our church not so long ago," Shu smiled. "Remember?"

"Yes, and now I know what they were talking about," Han nod-ded. "I've experienced it for myself. Singing to God makes all the difference between pain and joy. In fact, it works even better when I don't feel like singing at all!"

New Beginnings

Han was willing to praise the Lord in the midst of her pain, but after her conversation with Shu, more lonely nights followed. Often she had to remind herself to sing away her sadness. Then came the greatest heartache of all, and strange as it seems, it came when Ning was released from prison some years later.

One day Han received a phone call from a church elder. "Han?" The voice on the other end of the line was full of excitement. "Ning is here! He's been released from prison and he's here thanking us for our support and prayers!"

Han could hardly speak. When she finally did, she was unable to mask her disappointment. "He went to see you first?" she asked quietly. "He went there before he came here? Before he came to see the children and me?"

The person on the other end of the line was speechless. But Han wasn't finished. She grew more agitated and emotional with every word. "Doesn't his family mean anything to him at all? And why should you be the one to tell me he's free? Couldn't he tell me himself?"

Han slammed down the receiver and fell apart. Overcome by disappointment and sorrow, she told herself she did not deserve this. For five long years she had supported her husband. She had visited him every time she could. She had run their house single-handedly and had supported the church in his absence. Weak as she often felt, she had tried to be strong for their children. During her visits with Ning she had felt close to him, and she had thought he loved and appreciated her. Yet now she felt nothing but rejection.[3] When Ning finally came home, their reunion was not at all the happy occasion Han had envisioned. And in the months that followed, the distance between them increased. The wound in Han's heart was deep, and her pain was relentless.

Meanwhile, Ning couldn't begin to understand his wife's feelings. He was unable to grasp what he had done wrong. In his mind he was trying to be obedient by not loving anyone or anything more than Jesus (Matt. 10:37). What was Han's problem? Not only did he resent her chilly response to him, but he was also offended by the cold shoulder she had given their co-workers who had helped her so much during his absence. She acted as if it was their fault he hadn't come directly home.

One day a Christian couple came to visit Han and Ning. They had attended several seminars on biblical teaching about marriage and family life, and their own eyes had been opened. Among other things, they had learned that it was not unspiritual for a Christian leader to spend time with his wife and children. On the contrary, in Ephesians 5:25 they read that a husband should love his wife as Christ loves the church.

This godly couple tried their best to help Ning and Han come together again. The woman took Han aside and talked to her quietly while her husband spoke to Ning. Han was encouraged when the visitor did not condemn her for her feelings. She felt safe enough to allow her pain to come to the surface, and after months of suppressed feelings, at last her tears flowed freely.

Ning found help too. The husband listened to Ning's frustrations, then tried gently to help him see the situation from Han's perspective.

All of them knew that the rift between Han and Ning could not be bridged during one visit. But before they left, the visitors suggested that Han and Ning attend a marriage seminar. "It would be so helpful for both of you. What you are going through isn't at all unusual in China. And we've seen for ourselves that with God's help your wounds can be healed."

But it was not meant to be.

Before Han and Ning could work out their problems, Ning was rearrested and sentenced to two years in prison. He was accused of not cooperating with the Public Security Bureau after his release and of overseeing house-church meetings in his network again. The accusations were false, but in China it is impossible to argue with the authorities.

Once again, Han faced the many extra responsibilities she had shouldered during Ning's previous imprisonment. But this time it was much harder. She felt helpless and tired and very much alone. The worst part of all was coping with the resentment in her heart. Darkness seemed to envelop her.

Not long after Ning's second sentencing, another Christian couple arrived to see how Han was doing. In years past they had helped the family, and they wanted to know if they could be of assistance now. Han was overwhelmed by their kindness. She broke down sobbing. Finally, when she was able to control her tears, she began to describe the sad events of the previous weeks. "Please ask people to pray for us!" she cried. "We need it more than ever!"

The couple did their best to encourage Han, and before they left, they prayed with her. "O Lord, once again, please give Han a song in the night," the woman interceded. "You've done it before, and You are more than able to do it again. It worked for Paul and Silas two millennia ago in a prison cell in Philippi. And, Lord, we know You are very much at work here in China."

Then, quietly, the woman began to sing one of the *Canaan Hymns*. To her great joy, it was not long before Han joined in.

Thinking about Singing through Difficulty

1. In 2 Chronicles we read a remarkable story of how God wins a battle for King Jehoshaphat and the country of Judah. Read 2 Chronicles 20:15–22. The Lord says in verse 15: "Do not be afraid or discouraged because of this vast army. For the battle is not yours, but God's." Then in verse 17 He says, "Do not be afraid; do not be discouraged. Go out to face them tomorrow, and the LORD will be with you." Then what happens in verses 18 and 19? What does Jehoshaphat do in verses 21 and 22?

2. Read Psalm 13. How did David end up responding to his circumstances?

3. Read the story of Paul and Silas in prison in Acts 16:19–34. How were they handling their difficult circumstances? Do you think you could do the same? How will you face your next battle?

4. What benefits did Mrs. Yang and Han find from singing praises to God? Can this work for you?

5. Read Romans 12:15; 1 Thessalonians 5:11; and 2 Peter 3:8. What role do friends play in helping us turn our eyes back to Jesus and sing through the storms of life? Can you be that kind of friend?

6. How will you now pray for your suffering sisters?

Stay Close to Jesus

As the Communist government has imposed restrictions on the church in Cuba, there is a song that Christians have sung over and over again during times of great persecution. They have put the words of Habakkuk 3:17–18 to music:

> Though the fig tree does not bud and there are no
>   grapes on the vines,
> though the olive crop fails and the fields produce no
>   food,
> though there are no sheep in the pen and no cattle
>   in the stalls,
> yet I will rejoice in the Lord, I will be joyful in God
>   my Savior.
>
> Aunque la higuera no florezca
> Ni en las vides haya frutos,

Aunque falte el producto del olivo
Y los campos no den alimento,
Aunque las ovejas sean quitadas de la majada
Y no haya vacas en los corrales,
    Con todo, yo me alegraré en El Señor,
    Me gozaré en Dios mi salvador.

Cuba: Alida

More than ten years ago, I met Alida, who was born in Cuba three years after Fidel Castro came to power. Alida was a "child of the revolution," and I will never forget what she told me.

After the Communist takeover on January 1, 1959, life became difficult for Cuba's Christian believers. When Fidel Castro seized the government, the church was cut off from the outside world, isolated, and repressed. Alida's father was a pastor, and his church suffered along with the others, but this did not deter Alida's parents from instilling in their young daughter a desire to serve the Lord. And as the years passed, the government gradually began to ease its tight rein on the church.

In her late teens, Alida went to Bible college. There she fell in love with "Pedro," and before long the two were married. After graduation Pedro became assistant pastor in his father's evangelical church, and the first four years of Alida and Pedro's marriage were very happy. The newlyweds were surrounded by Christians who supported them in their ministry.

In 1989 the Holy Spirit moved in a mighty way in Cuba. Many people came to the Lord, churches overflowed, and countless house churches were born all over the country. However, with the revival came more oppression. Government spies were sent to attend church meetings.

Alida and Pedro's church, like many others, was watched carefully, especially because Castro's secret agents happened to have their office right across the street. From there they watched the pastors' every move. Alida and Pedro were often followed when they left their house, and virtually every month Pedro was called in by the security police and interrogated.

Alida was really afraid for her husband's safety. When she was expecting their second child, Pedro was once again apprehended by the authorities. Though this had become almost routine, usually the interrogation sessions lasted only a few hours. This time Pedro did not come home when Alida expected him. The security police held him for a whole day. In her fear Alida cried out to God. He answered her through Isaiah 54:17: "No weapon formed against you shall prosper" (NKJV).

"Lord!" she cried. "I know you spoke those words to your people Israel, but please make them true for my husband today."

After hours of harassment and intimidation by the police, Pedro finally came home late that evening. Alida was overjoyed to see he was alive and well, but it was not his last interrogation. During the following years, the Lord often reminded Alida of the promise in Isaiah. At times he also warned her of imminent danger.

"We have always lived with fear," Alida told me, "but fear has not conquered our hearts."

Fear and high-risk circumstances were not Alida's only problems. After the revolution, Cuba became increasingly poor, and most families lacked the basic things they needed. Cuban women had no choice but to go to work, and they had to work for the government, since it was the only employer. It was a challenge to hold a full-time job while properly caring for their families. Household appliances, so common in the Western world, were largely unavailable. To make time for God in their busy days, it was crucial for women like Alida to keep themselves and their families on a strict schedule.

Meanwhile, Pedro became involved in the unofficial distribution of Bibles. For security reasons, Alida was one of the few people

45

he relied on to help him in this dangerous ministry. Her life was already hectic, and it was essential for her to depend on God for the provision of their family's daily needs. Sometimes she and Pedro entertained unexpected guests in their home, which meant providing food they often did not have. All she could do was turn to her Father in heaven and ask Him: "Give us this day our daily bread." When Alida described her challenges and how they were met, her face seemed to glow. "Many, many times I've seen God bless and multiply what little we had!"

Like all children in Cuba, Alida's three sons attended public school. The atheistic philosophy they were taught was far different from what the boys learned at home and in church. Sometimes Christian children were singled out in class and punished for something a whole group had done. All their parents could do was commit their children to God daily and ask Him to keep them.

"God heard our prayers for our children," Alida told me. "The Holy Spirit is moving in wonderful ways in our country. Many teachers have testified that the witness of Christian children in their classrooms has affected their lives. We praise the Lord for that."

As we said good-bye, Alida had one final thing to say to me. "You know," she said, "the years that my husband and I have served the Lord have not been easy. We have often faced danger, but it has been worth the risk. Without God's presence we could not exist. I pray daily that God will always be first in our lives and that He will not allow riches or poverty or anything else to come between us. It is good to have to depend on Him for everything. We have learned to live on our knees."

One of the most precious women's meetings I ever attended took place in a country I cannot mention by name. One by one the women filtered into the house, aware that meetings like this were prohibited by the authorities. They came

from different denominations; most of them were pastors' wives. Not used to special women's meetings, they looked at me suspiciously at first, so I explained to them why we were there together. I told them about my friend 'K Sup in Vietnam (you can read her complete story in Hidden Sorrow, Lasting Joy*), who had been so isolated after her husband was imprisoned that through a set of tragic circumstances, in desperation she had taken her own life.*

"I know things are difficult for Christians in your country," I told them. "If you ever find yourself in 'K Sup's situation, I want you to know that you are not alone! Christians around the world will be praying for you." Then we looked at the biblical story of Hannah, found in 1 Samuel 1 and 2. Because Hannah was unable to have a baby, she was deeply grieved. She felt that nobody understood her pain, and she had no one to turn to but God. She poured out her heart to Him, and as the Bible tells us, "the Lord remembered" Hannah (1:19).

After a time of conversation, these women and I prayed together for prisoners and their families in that restricted country. It was a beautiful scene. Some stood; others knelt down. A couple of young women swayed gracefully on their chairs. One woman quietly hummed a song, and a few whispered their prayers while others prayed more audibly.

A year later one of our colleagues met some of the women who had been present at that meeting. "Tell Anneke that I am Hannah!" one of them said. It turned out that three of the husbands were in prison.

Sometimes our sorrow is just too personal or painful to share with others, and God is the only person we can turn to. But He is always there. Like Hannah, we can go to Him, weeping and pleading for mercy. He sees, He hears, He understands, He is concerned, and He is able to help.

Gulja must have felt like Hannah many times. She grew up in the Communist Soviet Union. She is now suffering because of her Central Asian country's desire to find its new identity in Islam. She lives in a city and a country that I cannot reveal to you because of security issues. But thankfully, Gulja has learned that no matter how unjust the world can be, and no matter whether or not we have anyone to rely on, Jesus is there. He hears our prayers—every one of them. And He is ready, willing, and able to answer us.

A Central Asian Country: Gulja

Sarah was coming home!

Gulja couldn't wait to see her sister-in-law again. She and Sarah were more than in-laws. They had become dear friends, and Gulja had very much missed her friend. Many people had moved away from their local area—an agricultural center that had fallen on hard times. Sarah had gone to live in her country's capital city, a two days' drive away, because it had proved impossible to find work in their small hometown. On difficult days Gulja sometimes wondered if God had forgotten them and their remote part of the country. But today all the gloom had vanished. Sarah had been away too long, and Gulja couldn't wait to see her.

"I have news for you, Sarah," Gulja said shortly after their happy reunion. But it was a few hours before they found a moment for themselves, sitting together in a corner on the floor, sipping tea in Gulja's small, sparsely furnished living room.

"Do you like my new *showpakas*?" Gulja asked, stroking the colorful, thin mattress she was sitting on. "I found this fabric at the market." *Showpakas* played a major role in her home furnishings. In that country, thin mattresses serve as chairs during the day, and at night they become beds.

But Sarah wasn't all that interested in Gulja's *showpakas*. "Come on, what's your secret?" she prodded impatiently.

"I am going to have a baby!" Gulja smiled, adjusting her long yellow velvetlike dress and shyly tucking a strand of her black hair behind one ear. "I am so excited, Sarah! I haven't told anyone but Solomon. When I heard you were coming, I wanted you to be the first to know!"

Gulja's dark brown eyes sparkled with joy. Born and bred in Central Asia, she looked neither Asian nor Caucasian. Sarah had always envied her sister-in-law's beauty. She did not have the broad Mongolian features that Sarah and her brother Solomon—Gulja's husband—shared.

"Oh, Gulja! I'm so happy for you!" Sarah exclaimed. "This baby will bring us all so much joy!" This would be Sarah's first niece or nephew, and it was certainly good news to hear that she would at last become an aunt. As Gulja poured more steaming tea from her beautiful blue porcelain teapot, the two friends chattered and laughed. They had so much to catch up on.

However, Sarah kept her most important news until later that evening, when her brother was home. She wanted him to hear it too.

"I want to let you know what has happened to me," she began when they sat down for a dinner of bread, vegetable stew, and fruit. "A few months ago, one of my friends from work invited me to go to a Christian church meeting that she hosts in her home. I went just to please her. As I'm sure you know, religion has never really interested me."

"That's one subject we never talked about at home," Solomon nodded. "Our parents may have called themselves Muslims, but I never noticed any particular evidence of religious faith in their lives."

49

"You're so right. Anyway, while I was in this meeting, something just gripped me," Sarah went on. "I'd never experienced anything like it before. The wonderful singing at the beginning of the meeting, the faces of the people there, the stories they told of what happened after Jesus came into their lives—it really was completely overwhelming. Then one man stood up and began to talk. Later I found out that he's their pastor—kind of like their imam, I guess you could say. He opened the book of the Christians, the *Injil*. He read from a part called Romans and began to explain that none of us are good enough to face God, no matter how hard we try.

"Contrary to what Islam teaches, he explained that no matter how many times we pray, how many good deeds we do, we're never good enough to face God. At first the message sounded depressing, but then he began to talk about the solution. Their God has created an unbelievable solution to our problem. Out of love for us, God sent His own Son from heaven to earth. There He died on a cross to pay for our sins. No, not just sins—the bad deeds we do—but also the inbred inclination to do evil that we were born with."

Sarah looked at her brother and sister-in-law to see how they were reacting. They seemed to be listening, so she continued, "In our own strength, we can never please God. But the pastor said that when we acknowledge that we are sinners and confess our sins and really are sorry about them—Christians call that repentance—God will forgive us. Why? Because His Son Jesus Christ paid the price for us. Jesus not only died on the cross, but He came back to life again—He is still alive, even now. And He hears our prayers."

There was complete silence in the room. Sarah concluded, "I didn't believe it at first, but afterward I couldn't stop thinking about what I'd heard."

"That's quite different from what I've read in the Qur'an," Solomon said.

"I know. It's very different. My friend gave me an *Injil*," Sarah went on. "I read most of it and decided this was for me. So I repented, meaning I told God I was sorry for my sins, and I became a Christian. I couldn't wait to tell you; in fact, that's the main reason I came home. Do you want to believe in Jesus? Do you want to repent?"

Sarah had never been one to beat around the bush. Solomon was too taken by surprise to say much. Gulja didn't know what to think. But to please their sister, they just did what she asked of them. "Please pray after me," Sarah said. "Just repeat the words I say . . ."

In a daze, Solomon and Gulja repeated the words of something Sarah called a "sinner's prayer":

Heavenly Father,
  I come to You in prayer asking for the forgiveness of my sins. I confess with my mouth and believe with my heart that Jesus is Your Son and that He died on the cross so I could be forgiven and have eternal life in the kingdom of heaven. Father, I believe in my heart that Jesus rose from the dead and I ask You right now to come into my life and be my Lord and Savior. I repent of my sins and will worship You all the days of my life.
  In Jesus's name, Amen.

New Friends Come to Call

A few days later, when Solomon came home from work, he noticed an unfamiliar car parked in front of his house. A group of children was crowded around it, and as he got closer, some men got out of the car. "Are you Solomon?" they asked. "We're your brothers!" They must have noticed the surprised look on Solomon's face, but it didn't seem to put them off. "Sarah asked us to come and see you. We're from her church."

Politely Solomon welcomed them in. He couldn't help but notice their camera, which looked both new and expensive. "Can

51

we take a picture of you and your wife?" they asked after Gulja had served them tea and cookies.

"Sure, no problem," Solomon said, unable to keep his eyes off the camera. To him, a poor man in a poor country, it looked like the ultimate treasure. In spite of himself, and even though he knew he was wrong to even think about such a thing, he kept wondering if there might be some way he could steal it.

"We've never been to this part of the country before," one of the men said. "Can you show us around a little?"

Solomon suggested that they go and visit another of his sisters. "She lives about four miles away. I'll tell her you're Sarah's friends and see if she'll invite us for dinner. Sarah's staying over there now, so we'll have a chance to see her too."

So Gulja and Solomon went in the car with the visitors and drove across the countryside. Cotton fields that had once provided a beautiful crop each year were now withered and sparse. Over-cultivation had ruined the soil. So now there wasn't much to see in the town, or outside—no historic buildings, no bustling town center, just dirt roads and shriveled fields. Even the houses looked depressing. It was clear that this area had seen better days and that a prosperous future would be a long time in coming.

Men on a Mission for God

Sarah was excited to hear that her friends had arrived. Quickly she and her sister got to work organizing the evening meal. Even though hospitality is very much a part of their culture and guests are offered the best of everything, visitors mean hard work for women. Gulja joined the other two in the kitchen as soon as she arrived. Solomon's mother was helping too. She had rushed to the market to buy bread and sweets. Sarah cooked the soup with their traditional fried flour balls while her sister collected some fruit from the garden to fill in the gaps on their tablecloth, which was already spread out on the floor. The guests were shown into the dining area.

While the others busied themselves, Solomon sneaked out, pretending to go to the "bathroom," which was nothing more than a wooden shed atop a deep hole in the ground. In truth, relieving himself was not what was foremost on Solomon's mind. He had not seen the men take the camera into the house. Was it still in the car? Was there any way to get his hands on it?

To his dismay, the car was locked. And even if it had been open, it would have been difficult to steal the camera. Children were flocking around everywhere. Disappointed, Solomon went back into the house.

After the food was served and the small talk was over, Sarah's friends did not waste any time. It was clear from the start they were there on a mission. Pastor Sergey, their leader, had brought his New Testament. The Old Testament had not yet been translated into the local language, but occasionally he read from the Russian edition. Most people had learned Russian in school. In fact, it was not until 1991, just four years before, that their Central Asian country had gained independence from the Soviet Union.

Sergey read and explained passages that are well-known to Christians around the world. But for Solomon, Gulja, and their family members, the message was absolutely new. For years they had been taught that there is no God, and any kind of religious worship had been unlawful. And nowadays the only God they heard about was Allah.

Solomon and Gulja listened intently to Sergey. A few days ago Sarah's cascade of words had been too fast, excited, and over-whelming for them to grasp. This time they understood better. After Sergey finished speaking, Solomon was quiet for a while. Something had happened inside him. Could it be that God was speaking to him? There were about ten people in the room, and several family members were asking questions. A lot of questions flooded Solomon's mind too, but first he had to do something else. He had a confession to make.

"Before you started talking, Brother Sergey, I went outside," he admitted, "and although it may have looked innocent to everyone else, I really went out to try to find your camera and steal it. The only thing that stopped me was that the car was locked. Now that I've listened to you, I see that the reason I wanted to do that so much is because I am a sinner. If I understand you, you're saying that Jesus died for me, personally, because I am a liar and a thief. Is that true?"

Sergey was so surprised by Solomon's confession that he almost laughed out loud. Instead, he smiled and nodded his head. "That's right, Solomon. It is true for every one of us. We're all sinners."

"Well, I'm sorry. I prayed the 'sinner's prayer' when Sarah asked me to a few days ago, but I really didn't know what I was doing. I just did it for her. Now I want to accept Jesus into my heart because I really understand that I'm a sinner and I need forgiveness."

Solomon was not the only one in his family who repented that afternoon. Gulja, Solomon's sister, and his mother prayed for forgiveness and salvation too. Two other friends who had joined them during the meeting also became believers. Altogether, Sergey baptized six new Christian believers that day.

"I think God has put it on my heart that you should be His servant here," Pastor Sergey told Solomon before he left. He handed Solomon a copy of the New Testament. "You should read this. Then ask for God's wisdom and understanding. And start preaching!"

A New Way of Life Begins

The very next day, more than forty people gathered in Gulja and Solomon's house. When she saw them arriving on foot and by the carful, Gulja knew right then and there that her life would never be the same again. Solomon preached a simple message—clear and to the point due to his limited knowledge. He didn't know much of the Bible, but for all who were there, the power of God was present and evident. *If only Sarah could have stayed a little bit longer,* he thought. *It would have been so good to have her around. She knows so much more than I do.*

But Sarah had returned to the city. And, other than his wife's prayerful support, Solomon was on his own. Still, he was not alone. As the Holy Spirit moved among the forty-plus people gathered in His name, God met them that day. A number were born again and a few were even healed—some of them physically, others emotionally and spiritually—after they prayed to Him, in Jesus's name.

"You have special power as a healer," someone enthusiastically said to Solomon after the meeting.

Solomon shook his head emphatically. "No, I'm *not* a healer. I've been trying to explain to you some things I've just learned myself. Adam sinned, therefore we've all sinned. Believe me, I've never healed anyone."

Week after week, people kept coming to hear the gospel and read the New Testament together. They tried to sing together too. At first, they had only Russian songs to sing, since no Christian songs had as yet been translated into their local language. Maybe that's the reason their voices didn't sound especially harmonious or heavenly. Still, it must have been music to God's ears to hear these new believers wholeheartedly worshiping Him.

Several months later, a son was born to Gulja and Solomon— their first child. Solomon's mother moved in with them so she could watch the baby while the parents worked. Their lives were full, combining work, family, and ministry. But thankfulness for their new life in Christ far surpassed the weariness they often felt.

As the size of their group increased, Solomon began to see how much he needed further training in biblical studies and Christian beliefs. He consulted with Pastor Sergey. "More and more people are coming to our meetings, and they're asking me all kinds of questions. For some of them, I can find answers in the New Testament. But I'm still such a new believer myself. I wish I could study the Word of God more."

"I'll tell you what I'll do," Sergey answered. "I'll arrange for you to study at a Bible college in Kyrgyzstan for three months. They have a course that's especially designed for new believers like you. Do you think you could possibly leave your family for three months?"

Sergey offered to help Solomon and Gulja financially for the time Solomon would be away. When Solomon told his wife about the idea, Gulja saw immediately how much the prospect of studying the Bible excited her husband. How could she object? Her job as a computer trainer would keep her busy, and her mother-in-law could watch the baby while she was at work.

"You go!" she smiled at her husband. "Don't worry about me. I'll be all right."

The three-month course was not wasted on Solomon. He returned home far better equipped and with even more enthusiasm than before. He shared the gospel with everyone who wanted to hear. Their living room soon became too small to contain all the people who came to the meetings, even though the only furniture in the room was a cupboard against the wall.

Sergey came to their aid again. He helped them buy a bigger house, with a large room they could use for meetings. Soon the number of people attending Solomon's Bible study classes grew to about three hundred. Perhaps his success was the reason for the problems that followed.

As Good as Dead

Solomon and Gulja were part of a large, extended family known as a clan. In that part of the world, one's first responsibility is always to clan members.

One day about a year after Solomon had first believed in Christ, at a clan meeting, the elders of the family turned on Solomon. "You have shamed us!" the head of the clan declared. "You have embraced the Russian God. How dare you? Our people have finally freed themselves from the yoke of the Russians, and now you embrace their faith! The true religion of our people is Islam. You know that! So now we're giving you a choice: your family or this Jesus of yours. You make up your mind. If you continue in your foolish ways, we will consider you dead."

Solomon's face flushed, and he lowered his eyes in stunned silence. Finally he managed to mumble that he needed time to think. That night he and Gulja talked until the first light of morning. "What am I going to do?" Solomon asked again and again, without really expecting an answer. "I can't deny the Lord, but I don't want to lose my family, either."

"Why don't we pray together and ask the Lord to show us the way?" Gulja finally suggested. Pray they did, and not just that one night. Solomon prayed and fasted for a week. An intense spiritual battle was raging deep inside him. Then one night a voice in his mind woke Solomon from his sleep. "Open your Bible to Acts 13:47," he heard the voice say. Solomon had learned to listen when the Holy Spirit spoke to him, so he opened his Bible and read: "I have made you a light for the Gentiles, that you may bring salvation to the ends of the earth."

That settled it for Solomon. He knew what to do. The next morning the clan gathered to hear his answer to their ultimatum. For three hours Solomon spoke to them, uninterrupted. He explained the Christian gospel as well as he could. The clan's only response was silence and hateful looks.

Finally, Solomon's uncle spoke. "You are no longer part of our clan," the old man proclaimed. "To us, you are as good as dead. You can't count on our help and our support any longer." Solomon felt grieved, but somehow, at the same time, he was strangely relieved.

Problems with the Authorities

Difficulties over their newfound Christian faith didn't stop with Solomon's clan. As Solomon and Gulja's church grew and news of their Christian beliefs spread through their town, others also began to oppose them.

Gulja's boss called her into his office one morning. "As a civil servant, you cannot work for our government and at the same time embrace the faith of the Russians. You're fired!" Gulja realized that any kind of protest about unfair treatment would only make matters worse. Subdued and scared, she left the office and slowly made her way home.

How will we manage now? Gulja pondered the question as she walked the familiar streets that led to their house. Her dismissal meant a dramatic cut in family income. Recently Solomon had spent almost all of his time pastoring their house church. Her salary, small as it was, had been a lifeline for them, and now it was gone. She hugged her little boy as he came to greet her at the door. Then she turned to Solomon. "I have bad news for you," she told him tearfully.

"Thank you, Lord, for our food," Solomon prayed that evening as they sat down on the floor for their meal. "We trust You to provide for us. You know our every need."

Others in their congregation lost their jobs too. Children of believers were expelled from their schools. Pensioners were threatened by the loss of their pensions. It was a very difficult time for them all. And for some, the pressure proved too much. The numbers dwindled rapidly until there were only a few Christians left who still openly professed their faith.

Discouragement often knocked on Gulja and Solomon's door. Yet they clung to Jesus, crying out to Him when adversity seemed to overwhelm them.

"He warned us that following Him wouldn't be easy," Solomon reminded Gulja one night as they struggled to find enough food to feed their son. "We really shouldn't be surprised about what is happening. Persecution is part of following Jesus."

"I Will Be with You"

Three years passed during which Solomon had no contact with the clan. They seemed to have taken seriously the idea that he was dead—at least dead to them. As for Solomon, he didn't try to get in touch with them, either. Then one morning he heard the voice of the Lord speaking to his spirit once again. "You haven't lost as much as you think you have," He said.

Solomon had no idea what to make of the thought. "What are you trying to say to me, Lord?" he prayed. When he shared the enigmatic words with Gulja, she too could only guess about their meaning. But it wasn't long before they understood.

While they were eating their simple breakfast—bread and tea—there was a knock on the door. When she went to answer, Gulja saw Solomon's aunt standing outside. Her husband, the leader of their clan, had sent her. He wanted Solomon to come to his house that very morning.

Both uneasy and curious, Solomon set out with his aunt. When he arrived, the whole clan was gathered.

"Why don't you come and visit us anymore?" his uncle's gruff voice broke the awkward silence. "We haven't seen you for more than three years!"

Isn't the answer kind of obvious? Solomon thought to himself. But he managed to hold his tongue.

"I'm getting old," his uncle continued. "We've decided that from now on, you will be the leader of our clan."

Solomon took a deep breath. *Leader of our clan?* He couldn't believe his ears. Was he dreaming? What on earth had happened? Why had these men changed their minds?

Just then Solomon remembered the words God had spoken into his heart that morning, and realized that God had intervened.

59

Three years before, he had chosen God over his family, and the decision had been costly. He and Gulja had missed their family gatherings. Worse yet, without the support of their clan, they had struggled in their community. Now God had given back to Solomon what he had offered up to Him.

That evening God spoke to Solomon again: "Take one step at a time, and I will be with you." During the days and months that followed, Solomon often remembered those words.

"Pray for Me!"

By now it had been four years since Solomon had first believed in Christ. He was amazed by the family reconciliation, but not long afterward far more serious problems arose. Of the handful of believers who remained in their congregation, three men were arrested.

Then the local authorities came for Solomon.

One afternoon he and Gulja were hiding from the hot afternoon sun, enjoying a little siesta in their cool, yellow brick-and-plaster house. Suddenly they were awakened by the violent rattling of their galvanized iron gate. Half asleep, Solomon got up and went out to the gate to find out what was going on. When he returned to the house, three policemen accompanied him.

"Open that!" one of them demanded, pointing at the cupboard in their living room. When the policemen saw copies of the New Testament in their local language, as well as some Russian Bibles, they confiscated them angrily.

"And what are these?" one of the men growled, leafing through some sheets of paper with songs written on them.

"That's our songbook," Solomon offered, hoping they would at least leave those alone. He could see in his mind crippled Gulnera, a bedridden sister of their church, who had composed the songs, painstakingly writing out every one of them by hand.

"Lord, watch over your Word," he prayed quietly. But the men took all the books and papers. Then they turned to Solomon. One of them grabbed him roughly by the arm. "You're under arrest!" he announced. "You come with us."

Gulja watched all this in silence. She was afraid to breathe, much less to intervene.

"Don't you dare tell anyone what happened or we'll come for you too!" one of the policemen shouted at her.

There was no time for a proper good-bye. "Pray for me, Gulja!" Solomon called out to her as he was led away. It was all he had time to say. By then tears were pouring down their little boy's face, and the baby in Gulja's womb was urgently moving around. Mother and son stood in complete silence as Solomon was led away.

Gulja's worst ordeal had begun. She had been left without her husband, without a job, without money. To make matters worse, when the members of their fellowship found out what had happened, they were afraid to come and help her. All she could do was what she and Solomon had always done—cry out to God.

"Pray for me," had been Solomon's last words to her. And pray she did, morning, afternoon, and evening. She often woke up praying during the night as well. When that happened, it seemed like a sign to her that Solomon was in need of her prayers.

Four times Solomon was brought before different courts, but Gulja was not allowed to be present at any of the hearings. When they spoke to her at all, the authorities threatened that she would never see her husband again. Somehow Gulja was unable to believe them. From the moment they took him away, she had felt strongly that God had somehow promised her that He would not allow her husband to be killed. One day Solomon would return—of that she was sure.

When at last she was allowed to visit him, she found him sad and depressed. "Why doesn't anyone come to see me?" he asked. "I was told that the brothers who were taken from our church have since been freed. After what they've been through, I can understand they wouldn't want to come back to this prison. But

61

what about the others? And what about Pastor Sergey and the brothers from the church in _____? Why don't they come? I don't understand it! Certainly thirty miles is not too far to visit a fellow believer who is in prison. Why doesn't Sergey come? If ever I needed to talk to him, it's now."

Gulja had no answer. Both she and Solomon assumed that everybody they knew had heard about Solomon's imprisonment. Apparently the others had simply forgotten him.

Solomon said little about the conditions in prison, but Gulja could see that he was suffering. His long face looked hollow. His dark, almond-shaped brown eyes were sunken. His skin had weathered, and it was obvious that he couldn't bathe or clean himself in any way. His hair was filthy, and he smelled terrible.

Solomon's condition broke Gulja's heart, but she didn't dare try to talk to him about it. A guard stood nearby, clearly listening to every word they said. Only after his release did she learn that Solomon had been kept in solitary confinement in a cell of only one square meter. He'd had no mattress to sleep on. He'd been given only bread and water to eat and drink.

During that dark season, finances were very tight for Gulja. Their social security payments had stopped. Her clothes were wearing out, and her son was growing too large to fit into his trousers and shirts, yet she couldn't afford to buy anything new. Even though she was pregnant, whatever food she had, she saved for her son, allowing herself only one meal a day. Thankfully, it was summer and their small cottage garden provided vegetables and fruit, some of which she traded at the local market to buy other necessities. Still, hard as she tried to make ends meet, there were days that they had almost nothing to eat.

Then very slowly things began to change. "Hard as it was," Gulja later told her friends, "Jesus was there all the time."

As Gulja made her way to the market to sell some fruit one morning, a man suddenly approached her from behind, grabbing her heavy shopping bag out of her hand. Just as she was about to scream, she spun around and looked into the smiling face of her husband. God had been true to the promise He'd made to Gulja's spirit. Solomon was home, safe and sound. His black trousers looked dirty and worn, his T-shirt was faded, and two months of house arrest followed, but he was free!

"I still find it hard to understand why nobody visited me while I was in prison," Solomon complained to Gulja one day. "Why didn't they come?" He seemed almost obsessed by the question.

"Maybe no one knew where you were. The brothers were probably afraid to talk about you over the telephone," Gulja suggested, not for the first time. "You know you can never be sure who is listening. Remember, many of them had been arrested as well. They must have felt threatened."

One day a car pulled up to their house and three familiar faces appeared at the door. "Solomon! Brother, I am so glad to see you!" Pastor Sergey greeted Solomon with a warm embrace. The others seemed equally delighted. "Why didn't anybody tell us what had happened to you? We just heard this week that you had been in prison. You were only thirty miles away from us, but we had no idea. You must have been so disappointed we didn't come to see you!"

Finally Solomon was able to communicate all the pain and frustration he'd felt during the previous months. As he talked to these friends and others, he learned that no one had spoken of his plight on the phone for fear of making his imprisonment worse and endangering others. At last he understood.

More happy days followed. Shortly after he returned home, Gulja gave birth to their second child, and before the year was over, she was expecting again. Their small family was growing rapidly.

Continued Threats

Unfortunately, Solomon's release was not the end of the trouble for the young church. Opposition and threats were more the rule than the exception. Sometimes the persecution came from government authorities and sometimes from the family members of new believers. Threats, harassment, and abuse continued. Solomon and Gulja prayed and pleaded with God to intervene and protect them.

Often Solomon was summoned to the police station. "We want you to leave this town. There's no room for Christians here," the authorities threatened. "Why don't you move to _____ [the capital city]?"

"Because God has told me that my work here isn't finished!" Solomon responded.

The mayor of the town was particularly hostile to the young church. One day he came to Solomon and said, "You are a filthy dog! From this day on I declare war against you, and I won't stop until there is no church left here."

Another man threatened to burn down Solomon's house.

Even the Christian children were harassed. The headmaster called in Solomon's young niece one afternoon. "If you go near your uncle Solomon, you will be expelled from school," he threatened.

Yet in the midst of all this, Solomon and Gulja's house church began to grow again. More and more people were searching for the truth. New believers witnessed to friends and family members and invited them to the meetings. Eight years after the gospel was first preached, there were at least two hundred Christians in town, most of them in their late twenties. Since it was not safe to meet with such a large group in one house, small groups of forty met together in the thorny bushes outside town or in different homes. The government would not allow them to register their church, so their meetings were considered illegal. But legal or not, every night the men of the fellowship met together for prayer.

Gulja's Song

One summer evening in 2004 the situation escalated. It had been a long, hot day, and sometime in the afternoon a young man came

64

to the house to talk to Solomon. He was earnestly searching for the meaning of life, and full of questions, he had finally gathered up enough courage to find out more about the Christian faith. As Solomon explained the gospel to him, it was as if every word were a seed that fell into fertile soil. The Holy Spirit had perfectly prepared the young seeker's heart, and that very day he prayed that through Jesus, God would take away his guilt and give him a new birth in Him.

Unfortunately, however, the young man was too excited to keep the good news from his father. And to put it mildly, the father did not share the newfound joy his son was experiencing. Raving mad, the older man headed out to find some allies, and he had no trouble putting together an agitated gang of men who hated the "Christian dogs" that polluted their town by their very presence. By the time they all set out to take care of the local infidels, most of them were not only angry but also very drunk.

When Solomon heard the shouting and cursing outside his house, he knew there was going to be trouble. Quickly he called the leaders of his church. "Please, come over here," he pleaded into the phone. "I need help!"

Shivering in terror, Gulja hid in the bedroom with their children. Her youngest child was only six months old, and Gulja's sense of helplessness was acute. All she could do was pray. "Lord Jesus, please!" she cried out again and again. "Send your angels, and please protect us."

Minutes later their Christian friends arrived. Without betraying their identity, they found their way through the surging crowd until they were close to Solomon. With some fast talking and a few clever tactics, all the Christians were able to hide, even managing to place Solomon in a hidden spot, out of reach. Meanwhile, their persecutors, because they were so drunk, became confused and eventually vanished into the night.

"Don't think this is the end of it," one of them warned as he staggered off, the alcohol slurring his speech. "We'll be back. We'll burn your house down."

After this close call, Solomon thought long and hard about a conversation he'd had a few weeks before with a local police official. "I am warning you again," the policeman had told him. "If you don't stop your Christian activity, serious harm will be done to your family. And I'm talking about your wife and kids—not just you!"

It was time for a serious talk with Pastor Sergey. Solomon called and told him what had happened. "I'll be over there as soon as I can, and I'll bring Zakir and some of the other brothers with me." Sergey and the others arrived, and after discussing the mob scene that could have cost Solomon's family their lives, they decided it would be wise for Gulja and the children to get out of town—to live for a while in another part of the country. Solomon would stay there, at least temporarily, to continue to lead the church and to seek God's direction.

And so it was with a heavy heart that Gulja prepared to pack up her few belongings and her little ones and move away from her husband. She couldn't help but wonder, *Will we ever meet again?*

"Gulja, I love you all so much." Solomon's face was a study in grief and uncertainty as he kissed his wife good-bye. "How can I let you go by yourselves? It's my responsibility to take care of you and the children."

"But it's also your responsibility to take care of the believers here," Gulja countered, with as much courage as she could muster. "My dear Solomon, we both know that it's the price we have to pay for following Jesus. Let's just be thankful that we've been counted worthy to suffer for his name."

Tears poured down their faces as they looked into each other's eyes. "You're right, Gulja," Solomon said quietly. "We have been counted worthy. Whatever happens, let's promise each other that we'll stay close to Jesus."

Gulja did her best to smile. "I promise . . ."

Even as she and the children were driven away into an unknown future, Gulja remembered Solomon's words. In fact, they played through her head like a song:

> Whatever happens, stay close to Jesus.
> Never forget that He is with us always.

Gulja knew in her heart that Solomon's words were true, and in spite of everything, her spirits began to rise. The presence of Jesus had carried her through the dark months of Solomon's imprisonment. He had been there in both good times and bad. He was with her now. And she decided right then and there to never doubt that He would be with her in the future too. She would stay close to Him, no matter what lay ahead.

Thinking about Staying Close to Jesus

1. Daily Alida and Gulja relied on God's omnipotence, omniscience, and omnipresence in His loving care for them. According to the following Scriptures, in what different ways does God care for His children?
   Matthew 28:20
   Psalm 40:1
   Psalm 100:3
   Psalm 121:1–2 and Psalm 54:4
   Psalm 144:3
   Psalm 145:18 and Lamentations 3:57
2. How can you be praying for your suffering sisters in light of the above passages?
3. Like Peter walking on the water (see Matt. 14: 23–31), we learn it is to our benefit to keep our eyes on Jesus. As obe-

dient Christians, we have responsibility for keeping up our relationship with God so that we are aware and feel the nearness of God. What do the following Scriptures challenge us to be doing?

1 Chronicles 16:11–12

Psalm 66:16

Psalm 100:2

James 4:8

1 Thessalonians 5:16–18 (three vital actions)

Which of these things do you remember to do? Which do you need to work on?

4. How are you personally going to apply the lessons learned in this chapter?

5. How can you pray for our persecuted sisters as they struggle (as we do) to live obedient Christian lives?

3

Feed on God's Word

Under the Marxist Mengistu regime (1974–1991), the church in Ethiopia went through a severe period of persecution. In recent years members of evangelical churches have suffered violent attacks and persecution at the hand of the Ethiopian Orthodox Church. And in areas where Islam is strong, Christians are under increasing pressure, though the situation varies from region to region. Choirs and singing play a prominent part in the liturgy of many evangelical churches. Bible choruses are sung over and over again. This serves a dual purpose, as a means of waging spiritual warfare and as an opportunity for illiterate church members to memorize Scripture. The following, from Psalm 18:1, is such a song:

I love you Lord, my strength.
It is because of you:
I walk over mountains
And go through valleys.
I love you Lord, my strength.

Gulbete hoye Ewedehalew (Amharic)

Gulbete hoye ewedehalew ewedehalew
Bente terarawen wetechalew
Bente shelkowen werejalew
Gulbete hoye ewedehalew

Eritrea: Salam

After a thirty-year struggle for independence from Ethiopia, and following a two-and-a-half-year border war, the small African country of Eritrea attained peace in 2000. After Ethiopia's rule finally ended, religious fights were laid aside in an effort to rebuild the little nation. But the truce between religious groups didn't last long. For part of the population, the joy of their newfound national freedom was short lived.

In May 2002 all of Eritrea's independent Protestant denominations were shut down by a government order. These Christians were forbidden to worship together, even in their homes. In the ensuing months, government authorities began raiding the private homes of evangelical Christians, arresting and jailing entire families who were caught praying and reading the Bible together. At the time I write this (September 2006), it is estimated that more than eighteen hundred Christians are incarcerated in Eritrea. These prisoners include pastors, women, teenagers, children, the elderly, and dozens of soldiers. Some have been subjected to severe torture, while the rest survive in intolerable conditions.

In this small country on the horn of Africa, meeting with foreigners can be dangerous for Christians. But to make their plight known to the outside world, some Eritreans have been willing to take the risk. In a certain town (I cannot reveal its name) some visitors from abroad were told they would be welcome to attend a house-church meeting. But at the last minute the plans were changed. During the days prior to the visit, the leaders of the church realized they were under close surveillance. Instead of meeting in a house, the Eritrean Christians arranged a rendezvous with their visitors in a previously arranged public place.

After dark, five young men and two women crept, one by one, into the room. They quietly shook hands with their guests, introduced themselves, and sat down. The Eritrean pastor who brought the foreigners started the meeting with prayer. Then, as was his custom, he took a few moments to read and meditate on a passage from the Bible.

"Let us turn to the Word of God," he began and read aloud Luke 18:1–8, the parable of the persistent widow. "Like the widow in this story, we need to cry out to God, because justice is in His hands," the pastor said. He went on to explain how God has a purpose for each of our lives and for the church. "Even though we are undergoing persecution, God is with us," he explained, hoping to encourage the small group of believers. "Justice is in the hands of God, and we must not give up hope. We need to pray continuously that justice will be restored in our country."

Apart from the Orthodox, Lutherans, and Roman Catholics, all other churches in Eritrea have been denied registration, making them illegal. "But God can do anything," the pastor said. "He is able to reverse the government's decision at any time. We will continue to seek official recognition for our churches. And at the right time, the answer will come."

A tall, slim young lady with long, braided hair—we will call her Salam—listened quietly. Salam was dressed in Western clothes—a bright red skirt topped by a neatly ironed white blouse. After the men spoke, it was her turn to describe some of her recent experiences.

She talked about how the police had interrupted a meeting at her church. She and twenty other members of the congregation had been taken to a police station where they were held for seven days. While the group was incarcerated, they had no access to the Bible. On the fourth day, they'd become desperate and had almost lost hope. They needed so much to read God's Word for encouragement and direction.

To keep up their spirits, they sang hymns and choruses. Initially this greatly upset their guards. But the Christians ignored the guards' demands for quiet and not only sang but also prayed—something they did continuously. They also spoke to the other prisoners about their faith in Jesus. After a few days, the behavior of the Christians so touched the guards that some of them changed their attitude toward them and became quite friendly. After a week, to their great relief, the Christians were released. They were grateful, knowing very well that others had been imprisoned far longer for the same offense.

"Is there anything you learned from your ordeal?" one of the foreign guests asked after the young lady had finished her brief testimony.

"Yes," she answered instantly. "I learned that I need to take more time to memorize and study the Word of God." Salam knew that rearrest was, for her, a very real possibility. "I intend to take the Bible much more seriously than before. I want to have a deep knowledge of God's Word to prepare myself in case more trouble comes my way."

Salam understood that in times of hardship, the Bible is a tremendous source of strength. There are many ways in which God speaks to us, but nothing supersedes the Word of God. If our faith is not based on what is revealed to us in the Bible, it will not stand when everything around us falls.

Johan and I will never forget March 1975. While our family of four attended a regional church conference in Da Nang, Vietnam, the North Vietnamese army invaded South Vietnam. Because of the danger, I could not return to the city where we were missionaries. Only Johan was allowed to go back to try to make arrangements for us. We assumed that if we were to stay out of the area for about six months, the situation in the country would stabilize. It did not happen that way.

The political situation deteriorated so rapidly that Johan was not able to make it back to Da Nang. Refugees flooded the city, one of the northernmost cities in what was then South Vietnam. Everybody wanted to go to Saigon, the capital, and flee the country from there. Although our mission leaders advised me to fly to Saigon with the kids, no plane tickets were available.

Of course, in those days we had no faxes, emails, or mobile phones. Johan and I could not contact each other. Very occasionally telephone contact between the Christian and Missionary Alliance headquarters in Saigon and the Da Nang mission station was possible. During one sleepless night, I tossed and turned, wondering again and again when I would be able to get out of Da Nang and when I would see my husband again. For no particular reason, I picked up a small booklet that lay on my bedside table, opened it, and the first words I read were "I will provide." It was a poem on the subject of God's provision for Abraham at the most crucial moment of his life—the binding of his son Isaac to

*the altar on Mt. Moriah. That night "I will provide" was God's
special word for me. It didn't take me long to fall asleep after I
received it. And a few days later an overjoyed Johan met our
two small children and me at Tan son Nhut airport in Saigon.*

*It is wonderful when people give us encouraging Scripture
verses, but I have found that in times of need, nothing
compares to God speaking directly to my heart through His
Word. Some days I read the Bible out of discipline, simply
because I know it's good for me, but I seem to gain little from
it. Yet on many other occasions—particularly in times of
deep distress—the Word of God has encouraged and guided
me. And it has always proven itself to be true. I don't know
how I would live without it.*

*My friend Maryam's life also affirms that there is great
power in the Word of God—power to guide, power to sustain,
power to deliver, and power to comfort. The Bible truly is a
lamp to our feet and a light to our path (Ps. 119:105).*

Pakistan: Maryam

Maryam literally grew up in the church. Her father was a pastor and the parsonage was her home—a house that was con-
nected to a towering yellow-plastered church with stained-glass
windows. Maryam's father was a highly respected leader in his
denomination. He managed his church and family well, as was
expected of a man in his position, and Maryam was an obedient
and religious girl. She attended every church meeting, she read
her Bible, and she prayed her prayers. All these things gave her
a Christian identity. In Pakistan that made her exceptional, for
she was a minority in a country where more than 96 percent of
the population is Muslim.

Until she was seventeen, Maryam called herself a Christian. Then one evening the veil of inherited religion was torn away.

Rev. Uttar Singh, a Sikh convert, stayed with Maryam's family in the parsonage for a week. He had the gift of healing, and for five consecutive evenings, the church was packed with people. Every night after Rev. Singh preached the gospel, people found salvation in Christ and many were healed of illnesses. One evening Rev. Singh prayed with Maryam and her brother. During that time of prayer, Maryam dedicated her life to God's service.

"God wants to use you!" Rev. Singh admonished her. "Look at what Jesus commanded us to do. He said, 'Go into all the world and preach the good news to all creation. Whoever believes and is baptized will be saved, but whoever does not believe will be condemned. And these signs will accompany those who believe: In my name they will drive out demons; they will speak in new tongues; they will pick up snakes with their hands; and when they drink deadly poison, it will not hurt them at all; they will place their hands on sick people, and they will get well'"(Mark 16:15–18).

The next evening Rev. Singh asked Maryam to pray for the sick, for he believed strongly that Jesus had given this authority to all his disciples. She obliged him and went to the platform. She nervously laid her hand on an old man who was losing his hearing and quietly prayed for him.

Within minutes, the old man's voice could be heard all over the church. "I can hear! I am healed!" He wasn't the only one whose life was touched by Maryam's prayers that night.

"O Lord," she whispered in prayer, overcome by emotion. "I didn't know that Your name was so powerful!"

In the days that followed, Maryam began to reach out to others. Late every afternoon she gathered a group of children in the courtyard of the church. As the eager children sat on the floor around her, she told them Bible stories and taught them Christian songs. Most of them came from poor families and had different kinds of illnesses. Maryam asked Jesus to touch them with His healing hand, and her prayers were often answered. Meanwhile, after hearing about her gift, some of the adult members of her father's congregation asked her to visit their homes to pray for those who were sick. No one was more amazed than Maryam to see health restored to God's people through her prayers.

A Special Promise

As long as she could remember, Maryam had looked forward to a week of summer camp at Murree Hills. It was a yearly tradition for her family to enjoy a week of fellowship with Christians from all over Pakistan. The climate in the Himalaya foothills was cool and pleasant, nothing like the stifling heat on the Punjabi plains. Patches of exquisite flowers bloomed among the rocks, providing a welcome break from the dusty streets and concrete houses in the bustling city.

Because of the change of heart she had experienced the previous winter, Maryam packed her bags with a different mind-set when it was time for the family's summer trip. She was more interested in being equipped and refreshed for her new ministry than in simply enjoying a holiday with her friends.

The meetings were held in what had once been a missionary language school. Because the Pakistani government no longer issued missionary visas, the tin-roofed brick buildings had been converted into a conference center. There were separate meetings for adults, youth, and children each morning. And every evening gifted Bible teachers taught lessons from the Word of God to the entire group.

"It is so good to be here!" Maryam expressed everyone's feelings when the family arrived at the center. As always, she was enthralled by the beautiful scenery. For a whole week she delighted in the magnificent view of the mountains in the distance and the scent of the pine trees that covered the slopes. But her mind often returned to the new commitment she had made to the Lord and the ministry of healing He had given to her.

Twice during that week, Maryam had a close brush with death. She was somehow stopped short from tumbling into a ravine on one occasion. A couple of days later, she found herself only inches away from a deadly snake that had entwined itself in a tree.

One night Maryam and a group of her friends decided to have a time of prayer together. Maryam poured out her heart before the Lord, and as soon as she said, "Amen," another young woman received a word from God specifically for her. Putting her arm around Maryam's shoulder, she spoke the words that she had heard in her heart. "The Lord is saying, 'I will take you to distant lands and I will bless many people through you.' Just take your first step—the Lord is with you."

Maryam wrote the words on a scrap of paper and placed it in her Bible. As she lay on her camp cot that evening, Maryam read and reread it, pondering the promise she had received. In her heart she had always known that God had a special purpose for her life, even before she had come to personal faith in Christ. It wasn't hard for her to believe this new word about her future. She accepted it wholeheartedly, but now all she could do was wait and see how God was going to fulfill His word to her.

University and Marriage

When the summer camp week was over, a new phase in Maryam's life began. She registered in a local college and started to study for her bachelor's degree. Maryam was a good student and she enjoyed her classes. She had always loved to read, so she chose English literature as her major.

Tall and slim, with a round, friendly face and waist-length black hair, Maryam was an attractive girl. She dressed in the traditional *shalwar qamiz*, a long-sleeved, colorful dress worn atop loose-fitting pants, with a matching long scarf that wrapped around the shoulders or head.

She was refined, polite, and unobtrusive but always active in her church activities. And she came from a distinguished family. All these qualities made her a very desirable candidate for the families of young men on the lookout for a suitable wife for their sons. Even among most Christians, Pakistani marriages are still arranged by the parents.

Emman Masih, a businessman who worked in Saudi Arabia, met Maryam during a special interdenominational church meeting. Apparently he liked what he saw, because it wasn't long before his family made their appearance at the parsonage to ask for Maryam's hand in marriage. But the first answer they received was not positive.

"We know very little about this boy's family," Maryam's father told her later. "Let's take things slowly. We have to be careful, especially with young men who are living abroad." Years of ministry had made him cautious. He did not know Emman's family, and he had no idea about their reputation or their lifestyle.

But Emman did not give up easily. After he returned to his job in Saudi Arabia, he earnestly sought the Lord's guidance in the matter. He prayed and fasted for three days, and his attraction to Maryam remained. On special occasions he phoned her family to inquire about her parents' health. He even got in touch with them when he found out they were celebrating their twenty-fifth wedding anniversary. Eventually his thoughtfulness and kindness won them over. After a year, Maryam's father decided to look into Emman's credentials.

Soon afterward, Maryam and her mother were asked to come to her father's office. The three of them sat down for a serious talk. "I found that Emman is from a respectable family and he is a good Christian," Maryam's father informed her. "He has a well-paying job and is a few years older than you, and we believe he would be a good match." The kindhearted pastor looked relieved as he passed on the good news to his daughter.

Maryam could have refused the offer, but she did not. Usually children in Pakistan trust the wisdom of their parents in finding them the right marriage candidate. Maryam was no exception.

Ever since his family had expressed an interest in her, she had tried to picture Emman in her mind. She had seen him only once during the church meeting. She remembered that he was muscular, wore glasses, and had a thick mustache. His dark hair was combed to the side, and he was about her height or a little taller. It was too early to tell if she would fall in love with him, but she felt optimistic.

While Maryam continued her education, Emman carried on his business in Saudi Arabia. By now they had their parents' permission to talk on the phone and to write letters to one another. As time passed, their relationship deepened. And finally, when Maryam was twenty-two years old, at an elaborate church wedding with many guests, Maryam became Mrs. Emman Masih.

"I Will Give You Success"

Before he met his bride, Emman had built, as an investment, a large house in a newly developed area of Pakistan. The newlyweds were able to move in immediately. Emman gave up his job in Saudi Arabia but continued to work in business in Pakistan. Then he received an unexpected and interesting offer.

His cousin Abdul asked him to join him in his outreach ministry, working with the poor and marginalized Christian community in Pakistan. Together the cousins, who were about the same age, gave seminars to encourage isolated pastors, teaching them from the Word of God and equipping them to spread the gospel more effectively.

Illiteracy in Pakistan was high, and research had established that among Christians, the percentage was at least 9 percent higher than for the general population. Besides the limitations illiteracy placed on them socially and economically, how could believers grow in God's Word if they couldn't read it? With this in mind, the cousins set up literacy classes for disadvantaged Christians in several Pakistani provinces.

Emman found his new work both enjoyable and rewarding. He had business skills that complemented his cousin's theological background. His daily routine was very different from the life he had led in Saudi Arabia, and it was far less lucrative, but it made him happy to know he was having a lasting effect on people's lives.

Maryam supported her husband wholeheartedly in his ministry, but she was kept busy at home. A year after the wedding, she gave birth to a baby girl, whom she and her husband named Sara. Maryam was also continuing her studies, this time working for her master's degree, again in English literature.

By the time Sara was two years old, Maryam was longing for another child. She prayed for a son, and God answered her prayer. Although the delivery was frightening, and for a time the doctor feared the worst, Dawood came into the world safe and sound.

Now Maryam's life went from busy to hectic. Besides caring for her little ones, she was teaching twenty preschool children in her home, all of them from Muslim families. Most of the children arrived at school wearing amulets (usually intended to ward off evil spirits).

"It's not a good idea for you and your babies to have these children roaming around your house," Maryam's Christian maid warned her. "Those charms they're wearing are powerful. They could have a bad effect on your family." Maryam brushed the young servant's concerns aside. Since she believed in Jesus, she thought that no other spiritual force could harm her. She had much to learn about the occult.

As time passed, Maryam found it more and more difficult to cope with her busy life. And Emman's packed schedule didn't help. Every morning at six he was ready to go, often waking up his weary wife just before he left the house. A master organizer, he soon became the executive director of Abdul's fast-growing ministry. Often he was so engrossed in his work that Maryam felt he was living more like a single man than a married one. He seemed to be spending all his time with his co-workers and very little with his wife and children.

"I can't do this anymore, Lord!" Maryam cried out one day. "I need help!"

Over the years, she had learned to recognize the still small voice of the Lord speaking to her heart. Suddenly she remembered the story of David, a young shepherd boy, who killed Goliath. A thought came into her mind, and it seemed as if the Lord was speaking to her, "David was not skilled to fight a fully armed man, but I was with him. And in My name he killed the giant."

Just as Maryam realized the Lord was trying to tell her something imporant, He spoke one more phrase into her heart. "Go in My name, Maryam, and I will give you success."

And so He did. After Maryam had received her master's degree, she began to sense a change in her spirit about what she should do next. She stopped teaching the preschoolers and devoted the next two years to the study of God's Word and prayer. There was a growing desire in her heart to be involved in her husband's ministry, but she hadn't told Emman or his cousin about it. She believed in her heart that God would speak to Abdul about it when the time was right.

An Unexpected Attack

However, as time passed, Maryam—always the emotionally stable and sensible one—seemed to be losing her spiritual enthusiasm. Discouragement had set in. Joy had vanished. Hope for the future was eclipsed by depression and fear. In the past the beautiful flowers in her garden, particularly the fragrant and colorful roses,

81

had always captivated Maryam. Now she hardly noticed them. Instead, she found herself identifying with the weeping willow that drooped at a crossroads near their home.

"Lord, what is wrong with me?" Many times she cried out to the Lord for help, but like the songs of praise that had once played in her heart, heaven seemed to have fallen silent.

Before long, Maryam stopped trying to accomplish anything. Her chores were left untouched. She found herself in tears for hours, sometimes for days. She developed all kinds of physical ailments, and at times she feared that she was dying. Wondering what had happened to the lively young woman he had married, Emman arranged a thorough medical checkup for her. Doctors confirmed that she had tendonitis, which accounted for some of the aches and pains, but concluded that her other symptoms had to be caused by depression rather than any physical condition.

Maryam tried to pray. She tried to focus her mind on the Bible, but nothing seemed to help. She simply could not find her way back to peace, hope, and joy, no matter what she did.

One day she picked up a book that was gathering dust on a shelf in her husband's library. The title caught her eye: *Christ Supreme over Satan*. A well-known missionary, Vivienne Stacey, had written the book, and it explained that all Christians in Pakistan should be aware of Satan's subtle attacks. The author pointed out that the spiritual consequences of living in a Muslim community, with its occult practices of folk Islam and frequent use of magical powers, should not be underestimated.

Again and again Maryam read the words: "If we are not aware of Satan's secret plans, it can have an effect on Christians as well as Muslims. Satan will do everything in his power to prevent us from fulfilling the plan God has for us."

It dawned on Maryam that she had overlooked the true source of her struggles. She was experiencing spiritual oppression, not a physical or mental illness. Satan had attacked her mind and her body, attempting to immobilize her. He had used his favorite tactic of discouragement to sap her strength. She wanted to glorify God, but the Enemy had other plans. The book also reminded Maryam of the good news that was hers in Jesus Christ, the victory that he had won on the cross. He had, through his death and resurrection, disarmed Satan and his minions.

As she began to understand better the ways Satan manifests himself in the lives of Christians, she put down the book and closed her eyes. What could have influenced her, she wondered? Why had she grown so afraid of death? Why had she allowed all sorts of doubts, worries, anxieties, and fears to reign in her heart? What could have happened in the past that made her vulnerable to satanic influences?

Maryam knelt beside the sofa in their living room. She wept and she prayed. And she proceeded to take a stand against the evil powers trying to attack her. "Satan, my price has been paid by my Savior," she stated out loud. "His blood was shed for me. I want nothing to do with you, because I belong to Jesus. Because of Jesus, you are defeated and you have no right to torment me any longer."

Maryam had been crying for days, but now she stopped. Her weeping turned into worship. She felt as if a heavy stone had been lifted from her heart. She knew the battle was won, and a warm feeling enveloped her, as if Jesus Himself had enfolded her in His arms.

As she regained her physical strength and recovered emotionally, a new day dawned for Maryam. She realized the battle she had experienced had everything to do with the plan God had for her life. The devil had tried to block her progress, and in fact she now remembered the two brushes with death she'd had in the days following her first commitment to Christ. But what Satan meant for evil, God used for good. She had been unaware of the spiritual battle she and other Christians faced in her country. Now she had a better understanding, not only of the Enemy but also of the power of Almighty God, whom she served.

One night Maryam had a dream. She was standing on top of a high building, bending over to look down at the street below. She tripped and almost fell, but somebody caught hold of her. She heard a loud voice reciting Psalm 34:7: "The angel of the LORD encamps around those who fear him, and he delivers them." Then she woke up. Immediately Maryam began to pray for her family, claiming the blood of Jesus to protect them, although she had no idea what the dream meant. The very next morning Emman was involved in a terrible car accident, but the Lord miraculously spared his life.

Reaching Out to Others

"Maryam, we need you in the ministry," Abdul's words came as a long-awaited answer to her prayers. By this time Maryam felt more than ready to become involved in full-time ministry. Abdul's wife, Lydia, had developed an outreach among poor and uneducated Christian women. She and her team of co-workers taught them crafts, such as sewing, embroidery, and batik and tie-dye textile techniques, providing the women with skills they could use to earn a living. Not only did this ministry assist with the women's physical needs, but it also empowered them spiritually by teaching them the Word of God.

Maryam helped Lydia whenever she could, but her heart was set on the literacy project. As a qualified teacher, she knew she had a lot to offer. It had been more than ten years since Abdul and Emman's literacy classes had started up in different parts of the country, and several former students were now teachers. More and more female candidates were needed for teaching positions, and all of them had to be interviewed and instructed. This was where Emman asked Maryam to help him. Before long she was teaching English too.

Maryam enjoyed working with Emman. The longer she was married to him, the more she appreciated him. As time went on, they had worked through their differences and become good friends. Ministering together had made them realize that their gifts were complementary, and Maryam was thankful they could both use their talents for the same cause, strengthening the small Christian community in Pakistan.

At times Maryam thought of the promise she had been given years before at Murree Hills camp. God was using her, she knew. But were her present responsibilities the complete fulfillment of the promise? She was not sure. In any case, for now at least she had her hands full.

Christians and Muslims

Christians in an Islamic culture face unique struggles. All too often Maryam felt as if her whole family was living under an oppressive umbrella. Their Christianity was permitted in Pakistan, but Islam influenced every area of their lives. They were relentlessly bombarded with a worldview that was not their own. Islam was forced on them from the loudspeakers of the minarets; through television, newspapers, and magazines; by the textbooks in schools; and even aboard airplanes, where Muslim prayer was recited before takeoff.

The only way for a Pakistani Christian family to be free from Islam's pervasive control was to emigrate. Many of Maryam and Emman's family members had done so, and no one could blame them. But Emman felt called to stay and continue his ministry with Abdul. Maryam respected that, and she knew Lydia did too, but life was not easy. She was well aware that a battle was raging all around her.

For lack of a Christian alternative, Maryam and her husband enrolled Sara and Dawood in an Islamic primary school. During the day, they were taught Islamic doctrine. One day Dawood came out of his room carrying a small rug.

"What do you need that for?" Maryam asked him.

"We're going to pray, and the teacher says we have to pray kneeling down on our prayer rug, facing Mecca," he answered, getting on his knees.

Maryam gently but firmly explained to her son that praying to Mecca wasn't necessary—that their God would hear his prayers no matter when or where or in what direction he prayed. Often she and Emman found it necessary to spend extra time with their children in the evening trying to explain the difference between the Islamic teachings they received at school and the ways of Christ as revealed in the Bible.

Christian holidays were especially difficult. During Christmas and Easter, programs were broadcast on national television ridiculing Christian beliefs. "Jesus never died," a television host announced on Good Friday. "The Jews nailed a substitute Jesus on the cross, and then when Jesus reappeared after a few days, the Jews lied to the people and said he had been resurrected from the dead."

"Why do we have to put up with this nonsense?" Emman angrily clicked off the TV. "We respect their religion, so why do they have to make a mockery of ours?" he protested to Maryam. "It's infuriating!"

The Day the World Changed

September 11, 2001, shook the world, and it forever changed the lives of Christians in Muslim countries. In Pakistan, for many decades, Christians had long coexisted peacefully with their Muslim neighbors. Groups of Muslim extremists had always been a cause for worry, like dormant volcanoes that could erupt into violence without warning; and Christians were clearly discriminated against, but as a group they had not been threatened since the country's founding in 1947.

September 11 and the subsequent invasion of Afghanistan polarized the world. Christians in Pakistan felt they were paying the price for everything that had happened, even though they had nothing to do with either side of the conflict. During 2002, more than forty innocent Pakistani Christians were killed and more than one hundred wounded or disabled in terrorist attacks.

Militants representing Al-Qaeda and the Taliban believed that by killing Christians they were taking revenge on America and its Western allies, which included Pakistan's government. Muslim fanatics attacked several churches during Sunday services. A number of Christians lost loved ones, and some saw them brutally murdered before their eyes. Threats of further attacks on churches fanned the flames of fear throughout the country. Anti-Christian demonstrations thronged city streets. Muslim extremists issued statements warning that any Christian gathering, including Christmas festivities, would result in a bloodbath.

The situation took its toll on Abdul and Emman's ministry. They and their co-workers were officially warned to take extra precautions and increase security measures. Telephone and letter threats, usually addressed to Abdul, became more frequent.

Persecution of Christians was not a new phenomenon to Maryam. Her father was a convert to Christianity from Islam—sometimes called a Muslim-background believer. Even as a young girl she had been aware of repeated threats on his life by his relatives, who saw his conversion as dishonoring to their family.

It is common knowledge in Pakistan that any Muslim converting to Christianity is in for trouble—it is seen as a capital crime. Muslim Sharia law states that those who convert from Islam should be killed. Sometimes the harsh Islamic laws are overruled by the mercy and compassion of family members, but all too often zealots carry out the letter of Qur'anic law in "honor killings."

Even when they are not murdered, Muslims who become Christians are often ostracized by their families and threatened by their neighbors, especially after they are baptized. Blasphemy laws endanger believers. Maryam knew of people who were in prison because they had been falsely accused of blaspheming the name of Muhammad or the Qur'an. These laws, under which anyone can be accused of defiling or blaspheming the Prophet or the Islamic holy book, endanger Muslims and Christians alike.

In the difficult days following 9/11, whenever fear tried to take hold of her heart, Maryam turned to the Word of God for comfort. Time and again God showed her that He was stronger than Satan. More than once she turned to 1 Samuel 17, the story of David's victory over Goliath. The church in Pakistan was small and weak, like David, but in God's strength they could be victorious as well.

She came to see that their battle was not against a physical foe, like Goliath. Her Muslim neighbors were not really her enemies. Spiritual forces of evil in the heavenly places were the ones waging war, and they could be fought only with spiritual weapons—especially faith and prayer. Maryam chose to believe that God is stronger than Satan, and that the "prince of this world," as he is sometimes called (see John 12:31), is already a defeated foe.

Maryam and the Christians around her did not need the metallic voice of the muezzin, crying out from a mosque's minaret five times a day, reminding them to pray. They chose to pray voluntarily, not out of a sense of duty or to add points to their spiritual scorecard. Christians prayed because they wanted to pray. They prayed because they believed in prayer. They prayed alone and they prayed with their families and in their churches. Pakistan's Christians believe that the victory over Satan and his spiritual minions was won two thousand years ago at the cross of Calvary, but they also know very well that in daily reality, battles are still being fought.

Nothing could have hurt Maryam more than seeing her children suffer. She and Emman could not hide from them the fact that Christians were targeted, and by that time they were old enough to understand the sandbag barricades and the armed soldiers that now guarded their church. They overheard their parents' anxious voices as they discussed the latest developments.

When Murree Christian School, a school for missionary children, was attacked, the whole Christian community was shaken. Miraculously none of the students lost their lives, but six of the Pakistani support staff were killed. In a terrorist attack on Taxila Christian Hospital, three nurses were killed and several others wounded. During a Christmas meeting in a Christian village, a church was attacked and three children died while thirteen children and their parents were wounded. Every time something like that happened, shock waves rippled through the Christian community.

"Mommy, are we going to be killed today?" Dawood asked one Sunday morning. "What is heaven like? We are probably going to be in heaven today!"

The words pierced Maryam's heart like a sword. Along with most of the other Christians they knew, their family kept going to church, despite the danger. They could not and would not give in to the terrorists' threats. But hearing her son expressing his fears troubled her deeply.

In as calm a voice as she could muster, she answered, "Remember the Scripture verses we memorized, Dawood? The ones from Psalm 91? 'If you make the Most High your dwelling—even the LORD, who is my refuge—then no harm will befall you, no disaster will come near your tent' [vv. 9–10]. Let's say it out loud together."

As they recited the passage, Maryam watched Sara's face. She could almost read her daughter's mind before she spoke. "But, Mommy, the families of the children who were killed must have known and believed that Scripture verse. So what about them?"

Ever since the incident, the same question had haunted Maryam. She was glad her husband came to her aid. Emman was never quick to voice his opinion, but this time he spoke up without hesitation. "We always have to remember that terrorists can't do anything to us that God doesn't allow. Neither the devil nor evil men have the final say over our lives. Our times are in God's hands!"

"True," Maryam added, putting on her glasses and running her fingers through her hair. "The worst they can do to us is kill our bodies. Our souls will go straight to Jesus when we die. Come on, let's go to church."

With that, all four of them took their Bibles and hymnbooks and headed for the car. Hours later they returned home, safe and sound.

More Tension, More Trouble

In 2003, when the war in Iraq started, security measures increased even more in Pakistan. All buildings that could be targets for terrorist attacks, particularly Christian ones, had to be guarded. Maryam saw added concern on the face of her efficient husband. He felt responsible for the different teams he coordinated. Many of his workers were on the road a lot of their time, traveling from one teaching point to another. Along the way they often encountered roadblocks, which could be deadly, depending on who had put them in place.

Sometimes team members brought back sad news about Christians in slums or in poor squatters' areas who had been harassed or tortured. Muslim extremists declared that the world's Christians were on an anti-Islam crusade, and in response, they would target Christians everywhere. Maryam's father and his congregation had to vacate their church one Sunday, due to a bomb scare. Sara's Christian high school was evacuated for the same reason. Nothing happened in either case, but the aim was clear—shake up the Christians, intimidate them, make them fearful, so that they will close down their churches, schools, hospitals, and other institutions.

Ever since her marriage, Maryam had loved their villa in its gated and guarded suburb of their city. They were on good terms with their friendly Muslim neighbors, and she felt safe. But to her dismay, after 9/11 she noticed more and more boys with green skullcaps playing in the street—a sign that they were being trained in militant Qur'anic schools, called *madrassas*. This worried her. Radical Islam was threatening the good relations between Pakistan's different faiths.

When it was rumored that people in the neighborhood were banding together to erect a mosque on a vacant lot adjacent to their house, Maryam was even more concerned. Mosques in the Muslim world are social beehives with people walking around in the courtyard at all hours of the day. It frightened her to think that radical Muslims might find out about their family's Christian activities and decide to break into their house through an open window, since in the hot summer months they often left their windows open.

There was nothing they could do to prevent a mosque being built. Protesting would not help; in fact, with the blasphemy laws on the books, it might even be dangerous. Their words could be twisted or misinterpreted, and in the worst case, one of them could end up in jail or dead.

During that summer, Maryam and her family went for a short holiday to visit their family members in the United States. When they returned, they were shocked to see that construction of the mosque was well under way. From then on they kept their windows closed and locked and their curtains drawn. Parties in the garden were no longer possible. They had to be very careful not to offend their neighbors.

One Sunday evening Maryam and her live-in maid went on their customary stroll through the neighborhood. Maryam found walking after a busy day relaxing. "What did you learn from the lesson we studied in Sunday school this morning?" Maryam asked her companion, not paying attention to the neighbors they passed as they walked. An interesting discussion developed about that day's church meeting. Oblivious to their surroundings, they shared openly what God was doing in their personal lives.

They should have been more careful.

The next evening Sara joined them on their walk. Sara was busy with her studies and Maryam's days were full, so they cherished this opportunity to talk. Deep in conversation, Maryam noticed a boy behind a tree. Suddenly he threw a stone that almost hit them. Sara jumped back.

"Don't worry," said Maryam. "He must have been aiming at a bird or a cat."

She was wrong. Before any of them realized what had happened, a brick hit her shoulder. She stumbled and almost fell to the ground.

"Mommy!" Sara screamed, grabbing her mother's arm.

"He aimed for my head!" Maryam murmured, shocked by the sudden blow. Her body was shaking. The piercing pain in her left shoulder was agonizing. Her jaw hurt too. The brick had brushed against it, scraping the skin.

Totally shaken, the women ran to the safety of Abdul and Lydia's nearby home. The attack marked Maryam's last walk outside her home. Emman bought her a treadmill for exercise, and from then on she left the house only by car, never again setting foot beyond her porch. Sara's and Dawood's lives also became more restricted following the incident. It wasn't long before the whole family was engaged in serious discussions about moving to a different house.

Back to the Promise

The Monday after another devastating attack on a Christian church, Maryam led the women she taught in a study on Romans 8. Despite all the turmoil, faith and peace returned when they read the comforting words of the apostle Paul in verses 35–37: "Who shall separate us from the love of Christ? Shall trouble or hardship or persecution or famine or nakedness or danger or sword?" The whole class read aloud the beloved Scripture: "No, in all these things we are more than conquerors through him who loved us."

After the children went to bed that evening, Maryam and Emman had a cup of tea together and talked about the events of the day. As she looked at her husband's familiar, friendly face, once more Maryam realized that their marriage had worked out very well. Emman was much more than a good friend to her. She had grown to love him.

As she shared the events of her day and about the encouraging time she'd enjoyed with the women in her class, she suddenly asked, "Emman, do you remember when I told you about the promise I received from God at Murree Camp before we were married?"

"Yes, I do remember," he replied. "But why do you ask?"

"I was just wondering. God promised He would bless many people through me. Do you think the work I'm doing now with the women is the fulfillment of that promise?"

Always thoughtful before he spoke, Emman took a moment to reflect. "It could very well be so, Maryam. During the last few years, I've seen God use you in tremendous ways to bless others. Not only are you a good Bible teacher, but you really love the women you teach, and they know it. Yes, I think that promise is being fulfilled."

"But how about the distant lands?" Maryam wondered, flipping through her Bible to find the note on which she had written the exact words of the promise—words that had become so precious to her over the years. When she found it, she handed it to him.

Emman read the words on the ragged and stained piece of paper: "The Lord is saying, 'I will take you to distant lands and I will bless many people through you.' Just take your first step—the Lord is with you." Once again he thought carefully about his wife's question, weighing his words. "I wonder if the secret is in the part that says, 'Just take your first step.' You've done that, Maryam. And if you keep following Jesus, who knows what will happen?"

Maryam pondered the promise. *Will God ever take me to distant lands?* she asked herself. Just then she remembered the words she and Emman often quoted to each other when things got tough. It had almost become their motto: "Not by might nor by power, but by my Spirit, says the LORD Almighty" (Zech. 4:6).

Maryam knew that she could not and should not try to make any promise from God come true. He was more than able to bring His word to pass without her help. God would bring His word to pass by the power of His Holy Spirit.

Thinking about Feeding on God's Word

1. The first story in this chapter is about Salam who spent a week in jail. She said, "I learned that I need to take more time to memorize and study the Word of God. I intend to take the Bible much more seriously than before." Why do you think she said that?

2. How can Bible study and memorization benefit not only someone in Salam's circumstances but every Christian? Read Psalm 119 (a wonderful Psalm to pray through when praying for the persecuted church), especially verses 9–16 and 97–104, for some ideas.

3. After 9/11 what was the story in 1 Samuel 17 that comforted Maryam? Would you find it comforting as well? Can you think of other Bible stories that would encourage someone facing hard times?

4. Read Romans 8:35–39. Why would Maryam find this passage reassuring? Do you?

5. How did Maryam use the Psalms to encourage her son when he was afraid?

6. How will you apply the lessons learned from this chapter and the verses you looked at above?

7. With the lessons learned in this chapter in mind, how will you pray for our sisters living with the daily stress of persecution?

Build on the Rock

Throughout the ages, the church of Jesus Christ has been persecuted, and often true believers who take God's Word seriously suffer the most. This is one of the reasons that during the Protestant Reformation one of that movement's great leaders, Martin Luther, faced many years of persecution. He was excommunicated from the Roman Catholic Church, he faced continued threats to his life and freedom, and he experienced times of intense spiritual battle. Many who have suffered for their faith have found comfort in the words of Luther's great hymn "A Mighty Fortress," based on Psalm 46.

> A mighty fortress is our God, a bulwark never
> failing;
> Our helper He amid the flood of mortal ills
> prevailing.

For still our ancient foe doth seek to work us woe;
His craft and power are great, and, armed with
    cruel hate,
On earth is not his equal.

Did we in our own strength confide, our striving
    would be losing,
Were not the right Man on our side, the Man of
    God's own choosing.
Dost ask who that may be? Christ Jesus, it is He;
Lord Sabaoth His name, from age to age the same,
And He must win the battle.

And though this world, with devils filled, should
    threaten to undo us,
We will not fear, for God hath willed His truth to
    triumph through us.
The prince of darkness grim—we tremble not for
    him—
His rage we can endure, for lo! his doom is sure,
One little word shall fell him.

That word above all earthly powers, no thanks to
    them—abideth;
The Spirit and the gifts are ours through Him who
    with us sideth.
Let goods and kindred go, this mortal life also;
The body they may kill; God's truth abideth still;
His kingdom is forever.

Martin Luther (1483–1546)

Indonesia: Three Mothers

Indonesia is a troubled land—a constellation of picturesque islands, turquoise-blue harbors, and festering religious anger. Easily the world's largest Islamic nation, its huge Muslim population

98

has had a history of peaceful coexistence with religious minorities, which include a substantial Christian community. However, in recent years the influence of radicalized Islam has gained a dangerous foothold, and incidents of violence and bloodshed have increased. In some areas, Islamist authorities are making life very difficult for Christian believers.

In June 2003 legislation known as the National Education System Bill became law in Indonesia, requiring all public schools to provide religious education for children of religious minorities attending their schools. As a result, a public elementary school in Babakan Jati, West Java, approached the church staff of nearby Gereja Kristen Kemah Daud (GKKD) to establish a Christian education program for the school.

The women of the GKKD church set up a "Happy Sunday" program, with Christian songs, games, and Bible study for children. The program was run by Ratna Bangun and Eti Pangesti, under the direction of their pastor, Dr. Rebekka Zakaria. After being in operation for about eighteen months, the number of children attending the program grew to forty—only ten of whom were from Christian homes. The rest were Muslim children, who were attending the popular program with the full consent of their parents.

Some of the boys and girls began to sing Christian songs at school and at home. It wasn't long before Islamic leaders in the 99 percent Muslim community were alarmed and began to take action against the Christians involved.

A ministerial decree requires all Indonesian churches to apply for a permit to operate. In practice, however, most local councils refuse to grant these permits on the grounds that the applicant church is in a majority-Muslim neighborhood. So Christian house churches often start with a handful of believers, grow larger and larger, and eventually get shut down by the authorities. In 2005 Muslim extremists forced at least sixty house churches in West Java to close.

One of these house churches, which met in Dr. Rebekka Zakaria's home, was forced to close down in December 2004. Nonetheless, she and the other two women continued to run the Happy Sunday program, which they did from Eti Pangesti's home. On May 1 that same year, a local Islamic leader interviewed four of the Muslim children who had attended the Happy Sunday program, asking whether the women had ever offered them money (there is a widespread rumor in some countries that Christians pay Muslims to convert). The children said no, although they had received a few small presents. Then one of them volunteered, "But when I asked for a Bible, they gave me one."

This was enough evidence to incite the Muslim authorities to take action. A case was filed against the three teachers for breaching the Child Protection Law of 2002, accusing them of "Christianizing" the children. On the evening of May 13, 2005, Ratna, Eti, and Rebekka were arrested and taken to the local police station for questioning. They were refused bail. This was a severe measure indeed, because it prevented them from remaining in their homes under house arrest, where they would have been able to care for their own children.

On June 1 the women were transferred to Indramayu State Prison. During the seven hearings that followed, truckloads of Muslim youth were brought in to demonstrate both inside and outside the courtroom. Many of them carried banners demanding a guilty verdict against the three teachers. As Islamist leaders railed against the three women through megaphones, the crowd responded, "Kill them! Shoot them! *Allahu Akbar*!"

On September 1, 2005, the day of the verdict, the court in Indramayu was filled with angry demonstrators. The extremists who crowded the courtroom shouted accusations and carried banners: "Close down Christian meetings!" "Imprison and destroy proselytizers!"

Some Muslim parents had attended Happy Sunday sessions and had even had their photos taken with their children there. When the trial began, however, these parents were intimidated by the furor that had been generated by local radicals, and they refused to testify in support of the Christians. Ultimately, proclaiming "deceitful conduct, a series of lies and enticements to seduce children to change their religion against their wills," the local court of Indramayu, West Java, sentenced Rebekka Zakaria, Eti Pangesti, and Ratna Bangun to three years in prison.

Prior to the trial, a co-worker from Open Doors was able to visit Eti, Ratna, and Rebekka in prison. This is what she reported about their conversation: "I'd heard lots of stories that these ladies are very strong and always joyful, even though they are facing a hard time right now. I really wanted to meet and talk to them in person. I had seen pictures of them, and it was such a privilege to recognize their familiar faces when I met them in the jail. They looked so calm, and all three of them had smiles on their faces. I introduced myself and shook their hands. They welcomed me with excitement and great optimism. Amazing! I was so touched to see their strength. I came close to Rebekka and I asked, 'Are you ready to face the judge's verdict?' Rebekka, without a doubt answered, 'I'm ready. Whatever the verdict may be, I'm ready. God talked to me that He could easily set me free from this place, from the crowd. It's just a matter of time. We wait for His time.'

"After hearing their story, I also became deeply concerned about the three women. Thankfully, I was also able to visit them in their prison and I saw with my own eyes their radiant joy, so evident in their faces and smiles. Clearly that joy was genuine, not a pretence. When I asked them how ready they were to face the verdict, which might turn out to be unfavorable to them, Ratna said, 'My hope is, of course, for the judge to set me free.'

"Eti added, 'But if this verdict is different, like Shadrach, Meshach, and Abednego [Dan. 3:8–27], I will continue to love God

101

more than anything. He will give me the best because He is in control. Of course I hope that the verdict will give us back our freedom. But if not, then praise the Lord anyway. He is the One who directs the course of events in our lives.'

"Survival in an Indonesian prison is anything but pleasant or easy. The guards are often drunk and sometimes abuse the inmates. And besides any mistreatment they may have experienced, for those three women, being separated from their husbands and children alone was heartbreaking.

"After the arrests, Open Doors launched a letter-writing campaign to encourage the women. When I met them, I was able to deliver to them some letters written by supporters in Jakarta. I could see the joy shining in Dr. Rebekka's eyes as she read them. It was so encouraging for her to know that other Christians hadn't forgotten them. I can imagine that, whenever they receive letters from the United States, from European countries, and from Australia and Africa, their hearts must overflow with gratitude and hope."

Within a week of their conviction, Rebekka, Ratna, and Eti filed an appeal at the High Court in Bandung. On February 7, 2006, the Supreme Court in Jakarta turned down the second and last appeal. The three mothers had a hard time digesting the decision of the Supreme Court, but they regained strength from the Lord.

No prison bars will ever keep their faith from shining through. They know in whom they have believed. They have built their faith on the Rock—the mighty fortress who is our God. For all Christian believers, no matter where we live, in these perilous times of international turmoil and terrorism, there can be no other foundation for our faith.

On the afternoon of September 11, 2001, while I was driving home from an uncle's funeral, I absently tuned in the car radio. Suddenly the broadcast had my full attention as I

heard the terrible news about terrorist attacks in the United States. As soon as I got home, I rushed inside and turned on the TV. I got there just in time to see the first World Trade Center tower collapse into rubble.

The phone rang. It was Johan calling me from his office. "Have you heard?"

Minutes later, our daughter Marjan phoned from England. "Mom, have you seen the news?"

Within an hour, both of our sons had telephoned too.

When we experience intense upheaval, when the ground beneath our feet quakes and everything seems uncertain, only the essentials in life really seem to matter—faith, family, and friends. And on that unforgettable day, how we prayed, how we wept, how we were tempted to fear the future!

In the course of the afternoon, I thought of the women around the world who are persecuted for their faith, many of whom face uncertainty every hour of every day. Like them, on that September day, I experienced the strength and comfort that can be found only through faith in Jesus Christ. Literally I felt as if my feet were firmly planted on the Rock. Whatever happens—and the Bible warns us of far worse things to come—if our house is built on Him, it will stand, no matter what may come our way. I know this is true because I've experienced His faithfulness in my life, and so have millions of other women. One of them is "Linda," a Vietnamese Christian whose life has been shadowed by threats, dangers, and uncertainties.

Vietnam: Linda

Panic filled the small, whitewashed, single-story house in Dalat, Vietnam, where Linda and her siblings had been left alone by their parents. The children were terrified. Little Khanh was critically ill, with diarrhea and fever wracking her malnourished body. Le, the oldest in the house, had been left in charge of the family. Medical care in their town had broken down and doctors were scarce, so as soon as Le realized something was seriously wrong with Khanh, she sent word to her mother, asking her to come home immediately. Linda, who was a teenager at the time, watched in silence as Le and their brother desperately tried to do what they could to ease their little sister's agony.

"O Lord, please get Mother here soon, and please help Khanh get better!" Linda cried out, unable to do anything but pray. Sadly, her prayers were not answered in the way she had hoped. It was a tense and heartrending day in which the siblings watched helplessly as their little sister grew weaker and weaker. Finally Khanh slipped away from them and died.

The children's mother, Mrs. Nguyen, lived and worked at her parents' farm a ways outside of town. As soon as she got the news, she hurried home. In her absence, neighbors guided her children in what needed to be done. She arrived at the very moment when the lifeless body of her daughter was being laid in a coffin. Their hearts aching with sorrow, she and her children waited for their father's arrival from Ho Chi Minh City. They had tried to postpone the funeral, but because Khanh had probably died of bubonic plague, she had to be buried immediately. The next day Linda watched her disconsolate father cry uncontrollably beside the freshly dug grave where the body of his youngest daughter had been laid to rest.

A Christian Heritage

Linda's sadness during that time contrasted sharply with her joyful and harmonious childhood. She had grown up in a closely knit Christian family where faith was central to everyone, including her parents and grandparents. Often Linda's paternal grandparents talked with their grandchildren about what a difference the gospel had made in their lives. Because missionaries had obeyed the call of God to go to Indochina to preach the gospel, the Nguyen family had found release from the depressing and binding fears of their Buddhist/animistic faith.

Like her grandparents, Linda's parents were committed Christians, and they were more than willing to share the gospel with anyone who wanted to hear. The familiar yellow-plastered church in their Central Highlands town was the center of their lives, both spiritually and socially.

The Nguyens' small family home seemed to have elastic walls. When Linda was a child, the house was always crowded. Apart from her own large family of eight girls and two boys, her father's parents and two servants lived there too. Now and then other relatives sent their children to stay with them for a while, in hopes that they would benefit from studying with their cousins. More often than not, around twenty people were living in the house at the same time. And even though the family was far from rich, there was always a warm welcome and enough to eat.

Dramatic Changes

In April 1975, when Linda was fifteen years old, her carefree life ended abruptly. She was a student at Dalat's most prestigious high school for girls when Communist North Vietnam took possession of the southern part of the country. Vietnam was in upheaval, but worst of all for them, the Nguyen family was torn apart.

Food grew scarce, and under the Communist system, farming became the most celebrated profession. Desperate to feed her children, Linda's mother, who had grown up in an agricultural family, moved to her parents' farm, about one hundred kilometers from Dalat. Although this was a wise move from an economic point of view, she was able to see her children only once a month.

Meanwhile, Linda's father, who had worked for the South Vietnamese government, witnessed the arrest of many of his former colleagues. At high risk of imprisonment himself, he fled to the home of one of his married daughters in Ho Chi Minh City—the new Communist name for Saigon, the former capital of South Vietnam. It was much easier for him to live in anonymity in that large metropolitan area.

And so it was that Linda and her siblings suddenly found themselves on their own. Before long the grandparents had passed away, the family could no longer afford servants, and their cousins and other guests no longer came to visit. Without enough food to eat or clothes to wear, the family faced a constant struggle for survival.

The entire country was in a state of chaos and fear. Without money, and disheartened by their doubts about the future, many students quit school and tried to find work. Most parents agreed that this was the best thing to do, but not Linda's father. Even from a distance, he tried to stay in touch with his children and provide guidance to them. He told them to continue their education, even though at the time it seemed like a frivolous idea considering their fragile financial situation. But he was determined. "And make sure you learn English!" he insisted again and again. "You'll need it some day."

Although Linda could see no point in continuing her studies, like her sisters and brothers, she obeyed her father.

Khanh's sudden death added more sadness to the trying times, and in the weeks and months that followed, Linda struggled with depression. During the dark days of the late 1970s, even the beautiful blossoms on the Japanese cherry trees that bordered her city's streets were wasted on her—nothing could reach her or lift her sagging spirits. The only glimmer of light that penetrated her darkness came when, after two years, her mother decided to move back home to be with her children.

By then the family's love for one another and their strong faith in Jesus was all they had left. Things they had valued before, such as work, possessions, position, and education, had become meaningless. Their mother tried to be encouraging and reminded them, "Nobody will ever be able to take Jesus away from you!" She assured them that He would hear their cries and see them through.

For her mother's sake, Linda tried to put on a brave face. But alone on her bed at night, she often cried herself to sleep. If things had turned out differently in Vietnam, she would have been at just the right age to have high hopes for her future, but now there wasn't much left to dream about. One night she slipped out of her bed and knelt down on the cold cement floor. "Lord Jesus, please do something!" she pleaded. "I want so much to marry a loving man, someone who is serving You, but I don't know how that can ever happen. Please help me!"

Although by now their pastor had been imprisoned, on Sundays the Nguyens still walked up the hill to their church where the elders divided up their absent pastor's responsibilities among themselves. State policemen showed up each Sunday, monitoring every word that was said, and more often than not the elders were interrogated afterward. During those difficult days, the enormous physical and emotional pressure on the church's individual members weighed heavily on their spirits. Yet there was a silver lining—all the heartaches they faced together had brought about a renewed sense of unity and love among the believers. It was almost—but not quite—enough to overcome the sense of sadness and hopelessness that prevailed in the community's life.

Life in Ho Chi Minh City

By the time she had finished high school, Linda had made up her mind to go to college. This meant leaving her hometown and moving to Ho Chi Minh City to attend a government school where

107

she was required to study the prevailing Communist ideology. Although the college was an intimidating and unfamiliar environment for Linda, she rose to the challenge, savoring every new learning opportunity.

The church Linda attended in Ho Chi Minh City was much larger than the one she had attended during her childhood years. In happier times it had been called the International Church of Saigon, and even now it was still a spiritual dynamo. After a decrease in attendance during the terrible months immediately following the new regime's takeover, once again God began to visit his people, beginning with Pastor Ha and the elders of the church. Many Christians' lives were renewed, hundreds were filled with the Holy Spirit, and thousands came to Christ. Linda and several members of her family were at the heart of this amazing revival.

Inspired and encouraged, Linda rededicated her life to God and was immediately blessed with a new desire to read the Word, to pray, and to please God. No longer hiding the fact that she was a Christian, she read her Bible openly and prayed in the college dormitory. She attended early-morning prayer meetings at the church and invited fellow students to join her, seizing every chance she could find to share Christ with others.

One day the director of the school called her in. "A girl in a Communist Party school cannot go to church," he warned her sternly. "Stop talking about your faith or you will be expelled!"

Without knowing how to answer, Linda left his office in turmoil. What was she supposed to do? There was no way she would quit going to church. She needed the fellowship, the teaching, and the prayers to help her keep in perspective the things she was being taught in college. Without proper teaching, how could she distinguish between God's truth and atheistic propaganda? Still, at the same time, she was resolute in her intention to finish her college education.

"Please pray for me," she asked her Christian friends. "Please pray that I'll be a faithful witness for Jesus and that I won't deny Him, but that I'll be wise at the same time."

Linda did her best to be more careful, even becoming covert about some things. Nothing stopped the threats from college staff members and the harassment of some of her fellow students, but she stood her ground. And just as she neared the end of her studies, Linda became increasingly aware of a specific idea about her future. As a teenager she had often told God that she would love to be a pastor's wife. Now, unexpectedly, that desire had been rekindled.

One of Linda's married sisters owned a small jewelry store in Ho Chi Minh City. Her sister's husband was in prison, serving a six-year term for fighting alongside the Americans against the Viet Cong, so in his absence, she asked Linda to come and help out at the shop. To Linda it seemed like another wonderful new opportunity.

Meanwhile, the revival at Pastor Ha's church continued. "When you face difficulties, pray!" he reminded his congregation again and again. "And when you face more difficulties, pray more!" And pray they did, because the Christian community's problems increased with every passing week.

It was not long before Pastor Ha was arrested. He was kept behind bars for more than six years. But his example and teaching had made an indelible impression on the hearts of many of the young people who had attended his church. If the government had hoped to terrorize the church's members and stop the revival, their plans had been thwarted. The church building was closed, but the revival continued, spreading all over the city.

A Man Called Minh

Linda and her sisters rented a room in a Christian family's house. The lady of the house wanted her children to be grounded in the Word of God, so she invited a local church worker to lead them in a weekly Bible study. To make the most of the teacher's time, she invited all her lodgers to hear him as well. She could never have imagined how this invitation would change Linda's life.

Short and slender, with a crop of dark hair, Minh was not that different from most Vietnamese men his age. But it didn't take long before Linda began to see that he was quite different from the others. It wasn't his outward appearance that attracted her. What got her attention was his heart for the Lord, his quiet strength, and his compassion for people. The more she saw Minh and heard his words, the more she began to wonder if this might be the man she had been praying for all along.

Linda didn't notice that the young teacher was attracted to her too. She wouldn't have believed that every day for a month he had been fervently praying, "Is this the woman you want me to marry?"

Linda was unwilling to get infatuated with someone who was not part of God's plan for her life, so she also prayed for God's will. Finally, after several weeks, Minh asked Linda if he could talk to her. "I want to tell you about my life before I moved to Ho Chi Minh City," he explained.

Linda couldn't have been more pleased. She wanted to know this man better, and that meant learning about his past. As Minh began to relate his personal journey, Linda listened intently. And the more she heard, the better she liked him.

"I grew up in Ban Me Thuot," Minh began. Linda knew the town—like her hometown, it was located in the Central Highlands, a market center for thousands of tribal people. "Even though my father was an evangelical pastor," Minh explained, "during all of my childhood years, 'God' and 'Jesus' were just distant deities I heard about at church. I had never experienced Jesus's love for me personally, and I was totally unaware that God had a plan for my life."

110

Minh went on to describe how, two years after the Communists took control over Ban Me Thuot, his father had been arrested. His mother was forced to move the family to a remote region, miles outside of the city, but Minh had stayed in Ban Me Thuot so he could finish high school. After the family moved away, Minh's mother gave birth to her eighth baby, a little girl. Eventually living conditions forced the family to move again. In Ban Me Thuot Christians were afraid to take Minh in because of his father's arrest, so Minh boarded with a stranger—a man who seemed intent on abusing him.

"Doubt and fear filled my heart," Minh went on. "Growing up in a war-torn city, seeing the suffering of Christians and non-Christians alike, I had a hard time believing in a loving God. Many times I overheard my parents' prayers for me. I was the oldest of their seven children, and they begged God to touch me so I would follow in my father's footsteps and become a pastor. But their prayers remained unanswered. Instead, I became depressed and rebellious. And after my father's arrest, I was raging.

"How could this so-called loving and all-powerful God allow my parents to endure such hardship? At times I felt like I would suffocate in my anger and grief. I tried to ease my pain with alcohol and nicotine, but nothing really helped. My life was meaningless, and too many of my questions remained unanswered. Why should I put my trust in a God who wasn't able to protect His people? Several times I came close to taking my own life."

Linda shook her head in amazement. She had been through her own times of darkness and depression, but it had been nothing like this. Suicide had never crossed her mind.

"To make matters worse," Minh continued, "because I was the son of a prisoner, I was stigmatized. After high school graduation I wasn't able to continue my studies. I couldn't find a job anywhere. I wrote a letter to the provincial authorities, pleading for my father's release. If you can believe it, because I questioned their judgment, they threw me in prison too, for a whole year! But it turned out to be a blessing because during that year I began to think about spiritual things again. I really missed my father. I kept thinking that if only I could talk to him, I could make sense of my life."

After his release from prison, some Roman Catholic friends invited Minh to stay in their home, and their priest taught him how to repair watches. In the Roman Catholic Church he found answers to some of his questions, but it still wasn't enough. Minh was addicted to smoking and drinking. He longed to be set free but didn't know how.

"Then I remembered a Scripture verse I'd learned as a child," Minh told Linda. "First John 1:9 says that if we confess our sins, Jesus is faithful and just to forgive us and to cleanse us from all our unrighteousness. I decided to do what the verse said, and I confessed my sins. I knew immediately that Jesus had forgiven me, because, for the first time in years, I felt warm and happy inside. Now I was determined to find out God's will for my life. Every day I prayed and read my Bible. Finally I knew what to do. I was hungry for more of God, so I moved to Ho Chi Minh City and started attending Pastor Ha's church."

"But I was there too!" Linda interrupted. "I'm surprised we never noticed each other."

"Maybe it wasn't the right time, with so much going on all around us. I was there when they arrested Pastor Ha." Minh was silent for a moment, then he looked directly into Linda's eyes. "So that's my story. What do you think? Do you want to be my girlfriend, now that you know all this?"

Minh wasn't about to waste any more time. He had prayed and was convinced Linda was the woman God had prepared for him. In the meantime, she was still trying to process what she had just heard. She knew Minh had suffered hardships in the past, but until now she had never imagined how difficult his life had been. She quietly studied his face for a few minutes. Finally she spoke.

"I am so glad you came to Saigon and we met."

"So . . . is that a yes?"

Linda smiled. She was feeling a little shy, because in that moment she was completely convinced that the answer to her prayers was sitting right in front of her.

"Why don't we get married?" Minh suggested not many days later. "We're both sure God brought us together, so why wait?"

There was nothing Linda wanted more, but she still wasn't quite ready. "What will our families say?" she hesitated. "We've known each other for such a short time."

Minh was convinced and confident. "If we believe this is from God, then I think we can trust Him to deal with our families."

Indeed, their families and their friends were surprised when they heard about Minh and Linda's wedding plans. Linda received a concerned letter from her older brother. As for her mother, the quality of the man Linda wanted to marry was of more concern than the timing of the marriage.

"Who is he?" her mother asked when Linda told her she had fallen in love.

"He's very poor . . . ," Linda began.

"I don't care about that," her mother pressed further. "I want to know if he's a serious Christian. Is he serving the Lord?"

When Linda told her mother about Minh's background and how she had gotten to know him, she was satisfied. She gave her blessing to the union, and so did her husband.

Minh and Linda were sure they were making the right decision. And by the time the big day arrived, so was everyone else. Both families rejoiced. And adding to their joy, shortly before the wedding, Minh's father was released from prison. The bride and groom didn't have much money, and the celebration was limited to snacks and soft drinks, but they were overjoyed.

In her light blue *ao dai*, embroidered with silk flowers, Linda looked gorgeous. Minh wore a suit he had borrowed from a friend. Like any couple on their wedding day, they had no idea what life held in store for them, but they knew that God had brought them together, and wherever He led them, they intended to follow. They would share the good days and the bad days, the joys and the sorrows.

Small Beginnings

Their first apartment was nothing more than a small rented room in a back alley. It was all they could afford, because Linda no longer had a job. Thanks to low profits and high taxes, her sister's jewelry shop had closed. Minh worked part-time as a watch repairman and part-time for the church. It was not long before Linda realized she was pregnant with their first child. The prospect of having a baby was exhilarating, but she couldn't help but worry a little—they really couldn't afford to have a baby.

"Linda, we need to talk," Minh said one evening. Tired, hot, and still feeling the queasiness of early pregnancy, she was lying down, trying to adjust the fan so it would cool her perspiring body.

"I think maybe this is the right time for me to quit my job," Minh announced.

Linda knew Minh had been praying for an opportunity to work full-time at the church, but his idea still seemed premature. "How will we live?" she asked him. "We can barely make ends meet as it is."

"The church will give me some extra money, though it won't be much," Minh thought aloud. "Still, if we believe this is the Lord's will for us, we should go ahead and trust Him to take care of us." Poor as they were, the young couple had been persistent about tithing the first 10 percent of their income. They were committed to financial faithfulness and believed that God would always provide for them.

"Let's pray about our situation," Minh said as he knelt down beside his wife. Prayer was always his first resort whenever he faced a problem. "But don't be surprised if you get a preacher for a husband after all!"

By the time they had finished praying, they both agreed that it was time for Minh to devote all his time to serving the Lord. He smiled as he turned off the light. "I'll talk to my boss tomorrow."

Even though they believed that their decision to serve God full-time was the right one, their financial problems continued. Money matters were a regular cause for quarreling. "We need to sit down and agree on a budget," Linda suggested. "I don't want to keep fighting over money." Minh agreed, but he also insisted—as he always did—that they take their need before the Lord.

Despite the financial challenges, Minh couldn't have been happier, teaching and discipling the many new believers. Tirelessly he rode his bicycle across the sprawling city, visiting people, conducting Bible studies and prayer meetings, and holding small-scale evangelistic gatherings.

During the years he had been in Ho Chi Minh City, Minh's faith had matured rapidly. He had seen so many answers to prayer that he dared to trust God for more and more as time went by. Those days he often prayed for a bigger place to live. "One day, we'll have a home of our own," he promised Linda.

After their first baby was born—a beautiful little girl—their need for a larger house became more and more pressing. God's answer to their prayers was incremental—the young family lived in rented apartments, gaining more space every time they moved. Four years after the birth of their daughter, Grace, their son, David, was born.

By that time, Linda no longer questioned her husband when he dreamed big dreams. She had come to admire his extraordinary faith, and now whenever she heard him pray for "a large house on a street where cars can park in front, house a big enough for meetings and lots of guests," she never doubted his wisdom. *I'll just wait and see what God does*, she told herself.

Times of Testing

The more people gave their lives to Jesus in Vietnam, the more the government cracked down. And the more the government cracked down, the more house churches sprang up all over the country.

Increasing government pressure had caused division in the leadership of the Protestant Tin Lanh church of Vietnam. Some of the denomination's leaders believed that the church should obey the government, even when seemingly unnecessary restrictions were placed on the church's operations. For example, no evangelizing was allowed outside the four walls of church buildings, reaching out to children under eighteen was forbidden, and theological training and ordination of pastors were prohibited.

At the same time, others, like Minh, who had experienced spiritual renewal and a powerful touch of the Holy Spirit, were convinced they needed to obey God and not the government. "The Bible teaches us to share the gospel with everybody at all times, not just when and where the government tells us it's all right," Minh argued.

This difference of opinion ran right through Linda and Minh's families. Minh's father had spent seven years in prison. His church in Ban Me Thuot remained closed, so he moved his whole family to Ho Chi Minh City, taking up an itinerant ministry there. He didn't share his son's views about defying the government's edicts through the house-church movement.

Several of Linda's family members were active in the Tin Lanh church, some living abroad, others in Vietnam. So when the congregation split, and Minh and other leaders and pastors were forced to leave the church where they had their roots, it was hurtful. A new denomination was formed, meeting in homes all over the city. Painful as it was, during the following years, God used the house-church movement to reach many Vietnamese and tribal people with the good news of Jesus Christ.

The rapid growth of the new movement brought with it even greater pressure from the government. Several times Linda and Minh's home was raided. The security police suspected them of hiding and distributing Bibles and Christian literature. Officers pounded on the door at all hours, even at midnight.

One night, as they searched the apartment, they found a large stack of books, which they immediately confiscated. The next day, Minh was summoned to the police station. "Who do these books belong to?" an officer demanded.

"They belong to my people; they're not mine," he answered truthfully. He had been given the material to pass on to new believers.

Minh was often called in for questioning, and it became tedious, but most of the time he got away with a fine and a threat to stop proclaiming the gospel.

The government refused to recognize the legitimacy of house churches. Officially, all house-church meetings were illegal. The authorities knew Minh was one of the leaders, but surprisingly they arrested him just once, and even then they held him for only a few days. They did no more than take away his ID card, knowing he would not be able to travel without official identification.

Linda learned to live with the threats and unpredictability of the police. Some officers treated the Christians with favor, while others misused their authority and tried to make their lives miserable. Most of the time the young couple simply persevered, doing the best they could, without allowing themselves to be distracted by fear.

Financial Temptations

"I think I've figured out a way for us to buy our own place," Minh announced one day. "We should start out by purchasing

117

a piece of land. Then the church won't have to pay me a salary anymore."

Linda knew that investment in land was the best way to quickly make money. At that time, Vietnam's economy was on the upswing, and land was appreciating at a rapid rate. Some of their Christian friends had bought and sold property with great success. As always, Linda trusted her husband's wisdom, and lured by the prospect of independence from the church, not to mention the possibility of having her own home, she agreed.

They bought a parcel of land, and sure enough, they were not disappointed. In a reasonably short time they were able to sell it, making a large profit. Instead of immediately buying a house, they decided to use the money to buy more land. Blinded by success, they forgot their habit of committing their ways and finances to the Lord, asking for His guidance in the matter. They went ahead, acting according to their own insight.

They bought and sold, but shortly after they had purchased several new plots of land, the market changed, and suddenly prices began to plummet. Their property value diminished to far less than the buying price. They couldn't sell the land, no matter how they tried. Soon they found themselves deeply in debt.

Desperate and despairing, the two of them turned to God. It wasn't long before they realized where they had gone wrong. Greed had been their downfall. They had allowed money to become the foundation of their lives, instead of trusting in God's provision. Deeply sorry, they repented. The young pastor and his wife publicly confessed what they firmly believed to be sin in their lives, and they asked the Lord to forgive them. As leaders in the church, they knew they had set a bad example. "Lord, we don't want to shame Your name," they prayed together. "Please help us pay back everything we owe."

Once they had poured out their problems to God, Linda never said a word about their money problems again. She believed God had spoken to her through His Word, when she read, "Through Jesus, therefore, let us continually offer to God a sacrifice of praise—the fruit of lips that confess his name" (Heb. 13:15). She quietly made up her mind to continually offer praise to the Lord no matter what happened.

In time, land prices went up again, and Minh and Linda were able to sell their land. Their financial ordeal had lasted eight years, but in the process they learned to trust the Lord more than ever before, to listen carefully to His voice, and to obey what He said. God was merciful to them, restoring and blessing them. Better still, He continued to enlarge their area of service.

Growth and Grace

By this time, Westerners were investing millions of dollars in Vietnam's economy, and tourism was becoming one of the country's most successful businesses. Linda's father's insistence that his daughters learn to speak English fluently was beginning to pay off. Linda found work as a teacher in an English language center.

In the meantime, Minh's prayer for a home large enough for house-church meetings was finally answered. At long last they were able to buy their own home, which turned out to be bigger and more attractive than anything Linda ever could have imagined.

The new three-story structure was quickly transformed into a multipurpose facility. One floor was for the family, the two other floors were used for offices, church meetings, and a dormitory. All kinds of people came and went, seeking advice, comfort, encouragement, prayer, and a brief respite from their work. Linda served countless cups of tea, and she always cooked far more rice than her small family needed, because guests invariably arrived to share their meals. She often thought of her childhood years. Her big, hospitable family had prepared her well for the life she was now living.

New house churches continued to spring up all over the city. By now Minh was a key leader in a network of these churches, and his many responsibilities weighed heavily on him. The ministry was spreading beyond the city limits to different parts of the country, but not without a price. Often Minh and Linda received reports that their co-workers had been arrested, and some of them had been sentenced to several years in prison. Though the churches tried to help the families of prisoners whenever they could, the assistance they could offer never seemed to be quite enough.

Linda worked hard to support her pastor-husband in his many responsibilities. Better than anyone else, she knew the burdens he carried. The authorities continually pressured him. Personality differences among the leaders of his network caused relational problems. Criticism from church members as well as management demands took their toll. Minh was forever counseling and comforting people, supporting the persecuted and the suffering, and studying the Word of God so he would have spiritual food to offer.

During the first few years of their marriage, Minh had been the strong one spiritually. Linda had admired her husband's vision and faith, and even though she had privately doubted that his dreams would ever come true, she'd followed him anyway. But as time went on, Linda's own relationship with Jesus had deepened. Through the Holy Spirit's work in her life, little remained of the insecure young girl she had once been.

The grave needs around her forced Linda to take action herself. After she quit her teaching job, she began to reach out to the women in their house-church network, teaching at special women's meetings, training women who could, in turn, train others. More and more house churches were formed around the city. One day, when a new group was formed, Minh could not find a man to lead it, so he asked his wife to become the pastor.

Sometimes the police disrupted the meetings she led, writing down the names of those present, then hauling everybody off to the police station. This frightened away some of the new Christians, and Linda made a point of visiting them in their homes, encouraging them to attend the fellowship meetings once again. As time went by, most of her congregation learned to take the police raids in stride. When they were required to write out their "confessions" for the authorities, they simply wrote out their personal testimonies about how they had come to know Jesus and why He meant so much to them. Eventually Linda's church got so big that it had to be divided, and about a third of them started worshiping at her house.

Building on the Rock

Linda has never forgotten the way the Lord has guided her steps throughout her life. She loves sharing with others the lessons she has learned about building her life on the Rock—Jesus Christ, the Rock of Ages.

During one particular women's conference, she looked across the room at the beautiful ladies in front of her, seated in their white plastic chairs, reading their Bibles. Tears came to her eyes. Suddenly her mind flashed back to the time she knelt beside her bed as a teenager. Not in her wildest dreams could she have imagined, when she asked God to let her be a preacher's wife, that He would make her a preacher too.

But that's exactly what had happened. Now Linda and Minh were partners in ministry. She delighted in passing on the lessons she had learned over the years—there were so many of them. Even in the structure of the house God had given them she saw a lesson. The secret of the three-story building lay in its firm foundation. Without that foundation, the house would not survive a tropical windstorm or a torrential rainfall.

Linda's life was also built on a firm foundation. Storms had come, and sometimes she had nearly collapsed. Unbelief and

121

disobedience had made her feel unstable, but her relationship with the Lord and her obedience to Him had undergirded her, keeping her firmly fixed on solid ground. With Jesus in her life, she had learned not to fear life's tests and troubles and not to break under the weight of sorrow or suffering. Just as He had supported her, she knew He would do the same for the women who sat in front of her.

"Find time to be alone with God," she encouraged them. "And don't just do it today and tomorrow. Make it your habit to spend time with Him every day of your life." Linda went on to teach the women about the importance of their walk with Jesus. She tried to help them see that if they weren't taking time for that—reading God's Word and praying on a daily basis—everything else would eventually fall apart.

After she finished her short devotional talk, she sat down, took a deep breath, and closed her eyes. Unexpectedly, she heard quiet sobbing from different corners of the room. Some of the women had begun to cry. Her words had touched them, helping them realize that they had tried to teach others about their faith without taking sufficient time to learn themselves. Not wanting to interfere, Linda sat still, praying and allowing the Holy Spirit to do His cleansing and healing work.

At the end of the week, before the ladies left the conference, Linda prayed for them. She began with a Scripture: "Therefore everyone who hears these words of mine and puts them into practice is like a wise man who built his house on the rock. The rain came down, the streams rose, and the winds blew and beat against that house; yet it did not fall, because it had its foundation on the rock" (Matt. 7:24–25).

"Lord," she continued, as they stood in a circle and held hands, "You have taught us through experience that nothing in this life is lasting. Positions, houses, money—all of these things can be taken from us. Even our husbands run the risk of being imprisoned and our children can get sick and die. But our relationship with You stands firm forever. Nobody will ever be able to take You away from us. *You* are our firm foundation. In everything we do, help us to build on that foundation. Help us to obey You. And please, Lord, continue to use us to teach others, so that Your kingdom will expand in our country and throughout all the world."

Thinking about Building on the Rock

1. Ratna, Eti, and Rebekka are in an Indonesian prison for teaching about Christ. What gives them joy, hope, and encouragement?
2. Contrast what happened in the lives of Linda and Minh when they took their cares and decisions to God in prayer and when they did not.
3. Read Matthew 6:19–21 and 7:24–27. On what unreliable foundations do we often rely instead of God? What is the folly in this?
4. When a "rock" is mentioned in the Old Testament, it is actually referring to a rock the size of a mountain that had an impenetrable fortress o n top of it. Of course our God is bigger and stronger than that, but that was the biggest and strongest word picture available at the time! As you read the following Scripture passages, meditate on what it means to you that God is your Rock.
   Psalm 18:1–3
   Psalm 31:1–5
   Psalm 71:1–4
   Isaiah 26:4 and 44:6–8
5. How will you pray more specifically for your suffering sisters?
6. How will you apply the lessons learned in this chapter to your personal walk with God?

Confess and Be Free

For more than seventy years, persecuted believers in the Soviet Union cried out to God for help and deliverance. Many died in Siberian prison camps. Fathers were torn away from their families, while mothers raised their children alone. Sons and daughters were harassed in schools; Sunday school workers were arrested and imprisoned. The list of atrocities committed against Christians could go on and on. Yet the underground church kept singing despite their suffering. Following is a song in which they expressed their feelings to their heavenly Father, crying out for His help.

> Stormy and black, the sea of life is raging
> Waves rock my boat and fill my heart with fear
> Lord strong and mighty, hear my call for mercy
> Seas do Thy bidding, O come, be Thou near

Merciful Father, pardon now I pray Thee
All of my sins, the flesh indeed is weak
Weary and faint, no longer can I struggle
Let me draw nearer Thy mercy to seek

Pilot and guide, into Thy peaceful harbor
Lead now my ship where storms and trials cease
Take Thou the helm and steer me from the
    current
Into Thy harbor where all shall be peace

The sea of worry and anxiety is getting strong
Huge waves are about to overthrow my boat
In a deadly despair God! My God!—I'm calling to
    You
Please, have mercy on me, and save me . . .

I'm struggling since the day I was born.
And I have no more strength to go on
My God, My God!—I am praying to You
Please lead my way to your quiet harbor
Rescue me from the dangerous pit
And help me get to your peaceful shores

India: Surinder

Two Indian high school students, Surinder and her older sister Anu, lived in a hostel away from home. Their father served in the Indian Army and their family was Sikh, a prevalent and well-respected religion in India. A senior girl in their school, Anita, was a devout Christian, and she shared the gospel with the sisters. Anu received the Christian message eagerly and asked Christ to forgive her sins and come into her life. But even after her sister became a believer, Surinder opposed the Christian message. She resisted until she was sixteen and in the twelfth grade. That year, 1991, Surinder joined her sister in her new faith. She gave her heart to Jesus Christ, even though she knew very well that her decision to follow Him would be costly.

When their parents bought a house in the town where the girls were studying, Surinder and Anu moved back home. This move meant that the girls could no longer spend quality time with their Christian friend Anita. But by then Surinder had learned enough to pay attention to what the Bible taught her and to obey what the Holy Spirit revealed to her.

One morning during a time of worship and prayer, the message to her heart was very clear: *Forgive all those who have hurt you.* It was a difficult thing to do, for some hurts from her past ran deep. Nonetheless, remembering what Jesus had done for her—how He had forgiven her and drawn her to Himself—Surinder obeyed.

The next step was more difficult to take: *Now go and ask forgiveness from all those whom you have hurt, and return all the things that you have in your possession that do not belong to you.*

Surinder was deeply troubled by this new instruction. She had never told anyone just how heavily the burden of past sins weighed on her. Alone in her room, she wept and protested. "Lord, you're asking too much from me!" Confessing her wrong actions and her wrong thoughts to God was one thing, but she couldn't bring herself to face humiliation by confessing her sins to other people.

Still, the more she struggled to find a way around God's Word to her heart, the more she was convinced about what He had asked her to do. If she wanted to follow Jesus, she had to be obedient. She had to deny herself, take up her cross, and follow Him. *I've got to obey Him,* she told herself, *and stop worrying about the outcome. That's His business not mine.*

Surinder obeyed. She asked for forgiveness from those she had hurt, and she returned the possessions that weren't hers. To her amazement, the consequences of her actions were not as bad as she had feared. Her confession to God and others resulted in deep peace, joy, and an increased awareness of the Lord's presence.

After some time, Surinder's father was transferred to the central part of India, and their whole family moved to this new location. The two sisters said a tearful good-bye to their friend Anita, realizing that now, as new believers, they were completely on their own. Between them, they had only one copy of the Bible, and they knew a few choruses and hymns that Anita had taught them.

Since they had become believers, the sisters had seen God's hand at work in their lives. The presence of Jesus was very real to them, and they were increasingly excited about their faith. As they settled into their new home, they began to share the Christian gospel with their family members. To put it mildly, their enthusiastic efforts at evangelism were not well received.

"Give up your stupid beliefs!" the girls' elder brother shouted as he forcefully lashed out at Surinder. In his rage he struck her repeatedly. The beating was physically painful, but with every blow Surinder focused her mind on Jesus. She knew she could not recant her faith, no matter what it cost her. In her mind were words she had read in the Gospel of Luke: "No one who puts his hand to the plow and looks back is fit for service in the kingdom of God" (9:62).

The upheaval in the family wasn't over. One day Surinder's father became enraged by something she said about Jesus. He grabbed her hair and dragged her into her bedroom, then threw her on her bed. Surinder was shattered by this unexpected abuse. Her father had always been such a loving man. Why was he suddenly so violent and dangerous?

That night her dad slipped into her room. Sitting on the edge of her bed, he wept. "I will be guilty of beating you for the rest of my life," he admitted. "Please, Surinder, give up your Christian faith. We are Sikhs, and we always will be Sikhs. Don't shame your mother and me."

As painful as it was to see her father weeping, once again a passage of Scripture came into Surinder's mind. "And everyone who has left houses or brothers or sisters or father or mother or children or fields for my sake will receive a hundred times as much and will inherit eternal life" (Matt. 19:29).

As the sisters continued to bear witness to their Christian faith in their home, the family did not give up their efforts to reconvert the girls. Anu and Surinder were sent to psychiatrists to test their sanity. Sikh evangelists were called in to try to convince them of their folly. Even Roman Catholic priests were summoned to the house in the family's effort to change their minds. All these experts were introduced for just one reason—to prove to the girls that their family's Sikh faith was the best path for them. None of these efforts succeeded, because, as Surinder says, "The Lord held our hand steadfastly and guided us at every point."

Since they had only one Bible between them, the girls divided it into two parts, exchanging them with each other when they needed to. The short time they had spent with Anita had prepared them to face the difficulties that now surrounded them. When they were discouraged, they sang the few hymns and choruses they knew. The girls had no church to go to, no fellowship with other believers, so they were entirely dependent on teaching from the Word of God and the guidance of the Holy Spirit.

Anu and Surinder were not permitted to pray openly in their home, so because of their lack of privacy, the girls resorted to spending hours alone with the Bible, locked away in the bathroom. It was during those quiet hours that the Lord led Surinder even more deeply into confession. "The Lord took me back in my life," she explained to me, "one phase at a time, leading me as far as my childhood days. He reminded me of all the sins I had committed. And He led me through a process of confession."

Because God was with her and spoke to her as a friend, Surinder says she never felt alone or afraid during those dark days. "The Lord guided me and taught me the deeper meaning of His Word." She smiled as we talked together. "My life became meaningful during this process because I knew I was important to the Lord. He did so many miracles for me that I can't begin to describe them all."

Thinking that separation from her sister Anu would weaken her faith, the family sent Surinder away to her father's relatives in his native state of Punjab. They hoped the Sikh environment around her would break down her faith and bring her to her senses. Instead, God began to use her in a powerful way. When she prayed for the sick, He worked miracles of healing. Not only was her faith strengthened, but it wasn't long before the whole village knew about her God.

Once again the family moved, this time to Punjab, and Surinder and Anu were joyfully reunited. But in spite of their ability to share their faith with one another, many other activities by now had been introduced into Surinder's life. Little by little she began to slip away from the enthusiastic faith she had once had. She never returned to worshiping idols or pursuing the Sikh beliefs of her family, but her first love—her zeal for Jesus—diminished in the hustle and bustle of her daily schedule.

Surinder drifted away from the Lord, but He never left her. He kept His hand on His child, and eventually she returned to Him, which brought her once again to a place of more confession and forgiveness. Finally, seven years after her conversion, Surinder was introduced to a church, which she attended secretly until the sudden and tragic death of her father in an automobile accident.

After her husband's death, the girls' mother started the process of seeking husbands for Anu and Surinder. At first, she tried to match Surinder with Sikh men from good families, but Surinder refused all of them, stating plainly that she would only marry a Christian. One day her mother accompanied her daughters to church and asked the pastor to help her find good Christian husbands for them. Gradually the girls' mother and other family members began to soften. Before long they not only understood but also supported the girls' Christian faith. At last Anu and Surinder were allowed to attend church openly.

Some years later, through a Christian Internet site, Surinder met the Christian husband she had desired. With the approval of both families, she married Vijayesh on January 27, 2002. Their marriage took place in Surinder's church, with her family by her side. In her view, this reconciliation with her mother and siblings was just one more of the many miracles God has performed in her life.

Hardship and persecution were not able to separate Surinder from the love of Christ. Confession and repentance led her to new freedom as He worked in her life to strengthen her in her areas of weakness. And today, because she understands what it is like to suffer for her faith, Surinder and her husband have chosen to reach out to the many Christians in their country who also suffer for their faith.

Like Surinder, I have heard the gentle voice of the Lord calling me to confess my sins and promising to set me free. Not long ago I attended a women's retreat organized by our church. One morning our speaker placed a large wooden cross in the front of our meeting room. She did a short study on the importance and meaning of the cross. She handed all of us a white slip of paper. Then she read the "works of the flesh," based on the list in Galatians 5:19–21. She read the list slowly, so we could write down anything we felt applied to our own lives.

"Adultery, fornication, uncleanness, lewdness . . ." My paper was pristinely white.

"Idolatry, sorcery, hatred, contentions, jealousies, outbursts of wrath, selfish ambitions, dissensions, heresies . . ." As she read on, my pencil was idle in my hand.

"Envy, murders, drunkenness, revelries, and the like," *she concluded.*

Quietly the Holy Spirit began to speak to my heart. As I sat there, pondering those last three words, "and the like," *I began to write, and the list on my sheet of paper became longer and longer. Most of the sins that surfaced that morning fell into that category. As the Lord spoke to me, I wrote down the things He brought to mind. Maybe others had noticed them, but until that morning I had not.*

I had always been quite a good girl. After becoming a Christian in my early teens, I had never lived the life of a rebel. Occasionally I had hurt people with my words or actions, but when it happened, I asked forgiveness from whomever I had wounded—my husband, my children, or my friends. That morning, however, the Lord reminded me of several things that had interfered with my relationship with Him and others. Immediately I knew that I needed to confess them.

Sin is a spoiler—it spoils relationships with both God and other people. It can spoil the future too, causing us to miss our life's goal. And sin dirties what is meant to be clean. I didn't want anything spoiling my relationship with Jesus, and I wanted to be clean. So literally I took my list of sins to the cross that morning. With a pin, I "nailed" my slip of paper on one of the crossbars. Then I knelt down and wept, because I realized afresh that it should have been me hanging on that cross. I was the sinner, not Jesus. But He died on the cross for me anyway.

Jesus was bruised and beaten. He suffered unimaginable agony to reconcile all of us who believe to His holy Father. Only He, the sinless, spotless One, was good enough to pay the price for me—for all of us. On the cross He did just that.

No other sacrifice could have bridged the gap between God and man, but Jesus's atoning death did. He died, and we were set free. That morning, I was reintroduced to the basic, wonderful truth of the gospel.

I was also reminded that we need to confess our sins daily, not just at special meetings or retreats. We need continual cleansing. The sinful environment we live in contaminates us, often more than we realize. We need the Word of God to show us where we have gone wrong and where we have allowed bad thoughts and actions to enter our lives. Otherwise the work of the Holy Spirit is hindered. "Surely you desire truth in the inner parts," the psalmist wrote; "you teach me wisdom in the inmost place" (Ps. 51:6).

China: Anna

Anna is one of God's special servants in China. And like Surinder and me, she has come to understand the power of confession. In fact, she has made it a foundation of her ministry. And God honors her faithfulness by doing great and mighty things in Anna's life—things she could only dream about when she started her work almost two decades ago.

It all began with what might have seemed a presumptuous, almost ridiculous prayer: "Lord, please give me all the children of China." Strange as it sounded, Anna meant every word of it. When she prayed that prayer, she knew she was asking a lot. It is estimated that one-fourth of China's population of 1.3 billion consists of minors. That was more children than either of them could picture in their minds. On top of that, it is still forbidden by law in China to tell children the good news of Jesus Christ. Of course that would make all efforts to reach them both difficult and dangerous.

None of this deterred Anna. God had given her a burden for China's children, and so she began to pray. And about twenty years ago, she began to take concrete steps to act on the vision God had given her. From day one, it took a lot of hard work and sacrificial living to make the dream come true, but Anna went for it anyway. Today, two decades later, millions of children have heard the gospel in China. These boys and girls know about Jesus because Anna obeyed.

"Give Your All to Jesus"

Anna knew her Bible, so she felt she should start the way her Savior did. She took note of the fact that twelve disciples, hand-picked and trained by Jesus, turned the world upside down. So Anna selected twelve dedicated young Chinese Christians, and she began to teach them the basic principles of child evangelism.

Because of the ever-present security police, Anna chose an inconspicuous place in the countryside to hold her opening seminar. She was the first to arrive, dressed in shabby clothes to mix in with the locals, her long hair tied back in a ponytail. One by one the students appeared at the door. For eight days, they locked themselves up in what, from the outside, looked like a barn.

"We have to be very careful," Anna warned everyone at the start of the first session. "You all know that if the police find out what we're doing, we could all be arrested. We're going to have to stay inside during the full length of our training period. Even after dark you can't be sure who is watching, so please—don't even go out for a breath of fresh air, as much as you may want to." Anna's strong personality commanded respect. Her students soon realized that she was firm and strict, but the rules she laid down were fair and sensible. With her sparkling, dark eyes, her infectious smile, and her passionate personality, she quickly endeared herself to them.

The daily schedule did not leave room for free time. At six in the morning, Anna and her students started with a two-hour period of worshiping the Lord. They took time to search their hearts and confess their sins. Anna continuously stressed the importance of confession in maintaining a healthy relationship with God, quoting 1 John 1:9–10: "If we confess our sins, he is faithful and just and will forgive us our sins and purify us from all unrighteousness. If we claim we have not sinned, we make him out to be a liar, and his word has no place in our lives."

"It's so important that nothing stand between us and the Lord," Anna urged. "Sin entangles and weakens us. It makes us fail and despair in times of testing. We need to be clean vessels if we want God to use us. What we are doing is dangerous work. It can have serious consequences."

Without stopping for breakfast, morning worship was followed by three teaching sessions. Anna lectured on practical matters, like setting up a Sunday school class. She shared what she had learned about effective teaching methods and how to tell a story. A curriculum that could be used in Sunday school classes was handed out. But throughout all the lessons, Anna emphasized the importance of maintaining a close personal walk with the Lord. "If you are wishy-washy, you won't be any good," she warned. "Give your all to Jesus so He can really use you!"

After the morning training sessions, Anna and her students ate a simple lunch together, and this was followed by three more teaching sessions. Following dinner, the students could either do their homework or receive more training. By the time they were finished in the evening, everyone rolled into bed exhausted but spiritually invigorated.

A long time has passed since Anna conducted that first seminar. After they completed their training in the countryside, those first twelve students diligently went to work, reaching out to children. In due time, after receiving more training themselves, they taught others, who in turn taught others. "Now I have more than four hundred trainers who are better at it than I am," Anna boasts with a radiant smile.

Since the beginning, Anna has not changed her program or her strict regimen. After twenty years, she and her co-workers still start every training day with a time of worship and confession, asking the Lord to cleanse them of their sins. Those early morning times of renewal are vital to her workers because they allow the Holy Spirit to have His way in their midst. Anna believes in what she is doing because she has seen it work.

The Need for Discernment

Like most other Christians in China, Anna knows that spies can infiltrate house-church groups, posing as sincere seekers. She has heard many "Judas" stories and knows that treachery can never be ruled out completely. Often the spies pretend to become Christians, then later betray their leaders and give the location of the meeting place to the security police. Every time she sets out to hold a seminar, Anna realizes the risk she and her co-workers are taking, but she goes ahead anyway. The children of China are worth the extra trouble.

To reach all the children of China, Anna understood from the beginning that her goal should be nothing less than establishing a Sunday school or a children's meeting in every village. To accomplish this, she traveled all over China to give her training seminars. On one occasion, she and some of her co-workers headed out to the far northwestern corner of the country.

It was a very long and tedious trip, and the team spent hours on trains and buses to reach their destination. When they finally got there, they had no time to rest. The eager students had already gathered, ready to begin. Well aware of the dangers they faced, as usual Anna had warned the organizers to take all necessary precautions. "Make sure the students you invite can be trusted," she had cautioned. "And let them know the place where we're meeting only at the last minute!"

Despite her warnings, a few days into the seminar, things went wrong. The police arrived in the middle of the night, only to find an empty house. Just in time someone had warned the group that the Public Security Bureau (PSB) were on their way to the training site. Within minutes Anna and her students had dispersed into the darkness—thankfully she had taught everyone to leave the site in five minutes.

But once they left the house, they were faced with another danger. The temperature was below zero, and a thick layer of snow covered the ground. In groups of two or three, the students and teachers fled in different directions. For two hours Anna plodded through the cold, wet, heavy snow. When she and the few others with her spotted a dim flicker of light ahead, they were so exhausted that they took a risk and knocked on the door.

It was nothing short of a miracle that the house belonged to a Christian, and the owner risked his life by allowing them to spend the night there. If the police had simply followed the footsteps in the fresh snow, it would have been very easy for them to track down the fugitives.

As her frozen feet slowly warmed up beside the fire, Anna was more than grateful to the friendly farmers who had welcomed them. Knowing her Bible well, she blessed the household with the words of Jesus, "Whoever receives one little child like this in My name receives Me" (Matt. 18:5 NKJV). She told them, "Because we are working to save the children in China, I believe that by welcoming us in, you have received Jesus here tonight."

Anna and her friends were not discovered by the PSB, but the churches in the area were less fortunate. Many of them, an estimated 90 percent, were searched. One Christian man ended up in prison. People who trusted Anna and her co-workers and cooperated with them cried in disappointment when things went wrong.

It broke Anna's heart to see others suffer. She never discovered who had informed on them and found comfort only in the fact that Jesus had also been betrayed by one of His own disciples. He understood her pain.

During the long trip home, she told her co-workers, "We must be even more alert. Let's ask the Lord to give us discernment. It looks like we're going to need it."

Signs of Encouragement

One day at a follow-up training seminar, Anna met a believer, Sister Hai, who had been trained in one of her seminars.

"How has the training helped you?" Anna asked Hai.

"It has increased my burden to reach out to the children in my own village. What's more, you've given me the books I need to prepare myself for our meetings on Wednesday afternoons."

From the start of her ministry, providing teachers with literature and training materials had been part of Anna's vision for reaching China's children. Since no publications for children were available in China, she'd had to start from scratch herself. But over the years, with help from Christians around the world, Anna had found a way to distribute juvenile curriculum to the farthest corners of her country.

"Thank you for what you are doing, Anna," Sister Hai said. "I have also learned to create materials myself." Then she shared a story that greatly encouraged Anna. It had happened in Hai's own house, among the children she taught.

"It was a cold and windy day," Hai began. "But that didn't stop Lin and her little brother from attending the meeting. Wednesday afternoons are always special for these two little ones because they get to come to my house."

Sister Hai described the way Lin firmly held her little brother's hand. The two children had walked quietly along the dirt road, trying not to draw attention from passersby. They walked briskly to keep warm. When they arrived at the house, they sneaked in through the back door. Even the smallest children knew this was a secret meeting. If the police found out about it, they would all be in trouble.

Sister Hai had taken all kinds of security measures. Someone was already positioned as a lookout, ready to warn everyone else if trouble arose. The children arrived intermittently to avoid attracting the attention of the neighbors, so it took quite a bit of time for everyone to get there. This gave Hai the opportunity to chat a little with each child while she provided cups of hot tea to warm them up after their long, chilly walk.

"We were studying the life of Jesus, and I told the children the story of the storm on the lake and how Jesus came to the rescue of the disciples," Hai explained. "When He is with us, when He is in our boat, we don't need to be afraid. But it was kind of hard to talk about the sea or a large lake here in central China, because most of the children have never seen such a mass of water, so I had cut out pictures from a magazine to show them."

Hai's students knew only too well what storms are like. They had heard them raging through their village many times, ripping branches off trees, destroying bamboo fences, and leaving gaping holes in the corrugated iron roofs of their houses. These children had all lain in their beds at night and listened to storms raging outside, so they grasped exactly what it might have been like to be as scared as Jesus's disciples.

Halfway through the story, the meeting was disturbed. Shin, one of the girls who stood guard outside, burst through the back door. "Quick!" she shouted, "Hide the stuff. The police are on the way."

Immediately everyone sprang into action. Hai disappeared through the back door, fleeing to a friend's house on the other side of the village. She hid in their barn until the next day. Only then did she hear what had happened to the children.

Mai, one of the older girls, had taken the few books Hai had been using and put them in a hiding place in the wall, behind a cupboard. The other children sat around in groups and pretended to be talking together. The blackboard was wiped clean, and the flannel picture board Hai had used to illustrate their story was hidden with the books. The children had practiced all this before. They had locked the front door and barred it. But the two policemen who burst into the room didn't have much trouble breaking it open.

"Where is Sister Hai?" one officer shouted.

Nobody said a word.

"What are you doing here? You were having a meeting, weren't you?" A policeman grabbed Lin's arm and twisted it painfully, trying to force her to answer the question. As much as it hurt, Lin bit her tongue and remained quiet.

"In the car, all of you!" one of the policemen commanded, "You're going to the police station." Outside, an open truck waited and all thirty-seven children were loaded on the back. It was a good thing it had been quite cold inside the house, because they had kept their coats on. They huddled closely together. This helped keep them warm and make them feel they were not alone.

Suddenly, Lin's voice broke the silence. "If one day we'll be in jail . . ." she began to sing quietly. One by one, the other children joined in. They all knew the song; it was one of the first songs Hai had taught them and was one of their favorites. The singing helped. Instead of worrying about what was coming, it made them focus on Jesus.

"How great is our God!" someone started another song when they had finished singing the first. "How great is our God, how great is his name!" the whole group joined in. Louder and louder they sang.

"Stop it!" a sharp voice commanded from the front of the truck. "Stop that singing! You are giving me goose bumps," one of the police officers shouted at the children, covering his ears with his gloved hands. His command was obeyed, for a while at least. But as soon as the truck was unloaded and the children were shuffled into the police station, one of them started singing yet another song. "In the name of Jesus . . ." thirty-seven high-pitched voices sang. "In the name of Jesus, we have the victory!"

"I told you to stop singing!" The angry policeman repeated his command. In a rage he began to kick and beat some of the children. "Who taught you these songs? Who taught you to believe?" he demanded.

Now it was the children's turn to shout. "Jesus!" they replied in one accord.

Later Hai was told that the loud noise coming from the police station startled a passerby. Curious, the man, a Communist cadre in the community, decided to investigate. To his shock, he saw thirty-seven children shivering in the cold.

"You can't lock up little children!" he protested angrily. "It's too cold to keep them in a place like this. Why are they here? What did they do to deserve this?"

Nothing the policemen said could satisfy the man. "You have to release them," he ordered. "Otherwise I will report you. Let their parents come and pick them up."

Anxious to save face, the policemen quickly drew up a statement. They would release the children but not without a written statement signed by their parents, stating, "We hereby declare that we do not believe in God."

Some parents were not Christians, so when they came to pick up their children, they had no problem signing the letter. But for Lin's mother, it was a different matter. She had lost her husband a few years previously. Especially after his death, she had experienced the loving care of her heavenly Father every day. She could not live one day without Him.

With tears in her eyes, she told the policemen, "I can't sign your statement. Jesus is more precious to me than anything else in the

141

world. You may not believe in God, but I do. I know Him, and I trust Him to find a way to release my children, so I cannot sign this letter." With that, she left, praying silently that God would protect and deliver her son and daughter, and trying very hard not to reveal the pain she felt in her heart.

"That evening," Sister Hai concluded, "relatives went to pick up Lin and her little brother, who were the last two children remaining in the police station. Without protest, the policemen handed the children over to them, glad to be rid of them. And so God had answered the prayers of their hurting mother."

By the time Hai had finished recounting her story, Anna was sobbing quietly. She had heard many similar stories before, but this one touched her deeply. Perhaps it was the timing that caused her to react so emotionally. It hadn't been so long since her own brush with the authorities. In any case, God knew what she needed, and He had used Sister Hai to encourage her.

A Worthy Sacrifice

As she made her way home from a series of training seminars, Anna was deeply in need of encouragement. She knew God had called her to do the work she so tirelessly pursued, but sometimes the cost seemed very high indeed. Not long before, she had battled with the question of whether she was too demanding of her co-workers. On the one hand, some of them had refused to take money when she offered it to them, even though she knew they needed it badly. "Please, Sister Anna," they said, "please, give us the privilege to serve the Lord like you do."

On the other hand, some of them thought she was unrealistic in her expectations. "Sister Anna, you are asking so much of us!" one trainer complained during one of their sessions.

And Anna knew it was true. Many of her teachers had given up well-paying jobs. They spent months away from their families, traversing their vast country, hiding in shabby buildings for days. So much trouble, just to reach the children of China with the gospel. *Just?* Anna's own thoughts startled her, and she was quick to correct herself. Hadn't that been the vision all along? Reaching the children of China was a God-given goal, worthy of their sacrifice.

Anna's memories carried her to an emotionally charged evening many years ago. Some years after she began her ministry, she had met her husband. From the start, he shared her vision but realized he would not be able to join her on most of her trips. So they agreed he would stay home and take care of the administrative work, while Anna traveled. One night Anna and her husband had knelt down beside their bed. After days of struggle, they had reached a conclusion. "Lord, we give up our right to have children," they had prayed together, firmly clasping each other's hands, "but we ask You to give us all the children of China instead."

Even before that, when she was still single, Anna had prayed the same prayer alone. Praying it later on, with her husband, it had seemed to be an even greater sacrifice. They both loved children, and there was no physical reason why they couldn't have children of their own. But they knew having a family would stand in the way of the vision that God had given them—reaching hundreds of millions of Chinese children with the Christian gospel.

Yes, she was asking a lot of her colleagues, she realized. But she was not asking more of them than she was willing to sacrifice herself. And most of her workers recognized that.

Thinking of her dear husband made her conscious of how much she missed him. She had been traveling for many weeks, and she could hardly wait to get home and be with him. He was such a great help to her, keeping track of finances and administrative records, encouraging her, and supporting her in countless other ways. How she thanked the Lord for giving her a partner in ministry who was willing to make sacrifices of his own because he loved Jesus more than anyone else!

Anna had one last thing to do before returning home. She had to visit some of her workers in prison. Unfortunately, visiting prisoners had become a familiar responsibility for her. Most of her co-workers had been in prison at least three times, spending days, weeks, and sometimes even months behind bars. Nearly all of them had been beaten or otherwise abused in the process.

That particular visit turned out to be a source of great encouragement. Her students smiled at her through the bars that separated them. "We know Jesus is with us and that we're on the right track," they told Anna. "We've had several opportunities to share the gospel right here."As she walked away, Anna realized that her work was paying off, even in ways she hadn't foreseen. She always gave her students a simple, three-part message: confess your sins, learn your lessons well, and praise the Lord. There in the prison, as she talked to her young co-workers who had been arrested during a recent Sunday school training seminar, she could see that they were putting into practice the principles she had taught them. Anna's heart was lifted by their strong faith and their perseverance in the face of adversity.

As she traveled home, Anna practiced what she so often preached. She too confessed her sin. She asked God's forgiveness; lately she had been more focused on the price she was paying than on Jesus, who had called her. She had gotten so tired that she had begun to feel sorry for herself because her life was hard and she lacked so many comforts that others in her family enjoyed.

Yet God had been so good to her. He had given her many of the things she'd requested. The first children whose lives had been changed through her ministry were now pastors of churches, sharing the Good News with other children. God was using boys and girls trained in Anna's Sunday school classes all over the country. They were reaching out to their unbelieving parents with the gospel.

Anna had hundreds of faithful helpers who shared her vision and were willing to sacrifice. All the major networks of house churches in China had gratefully accepted her help and asked her to train their children's workers. Her students were sharing the gospel with twenty-seven different ethnic minority groups. Yes, she had much to be thankful for. She had no reason to complain. Anna's spirits rose as she began to praise the Lord for His goodness. Her Father in heaven, for whom nothing is impossible, was answering her prayers for the children of China.

At long last she arrived home. "Thank You, Lord," she sighed, when she felt the welcoming arms of her husband around her. Her tired face spoke volumes to him, and he joined her in a prayer of thanks. For so many reasons, he was glad Anna was back. He had missed her loving presence in their home, her radiant smile, and her good cooking. And he could not wait to hear what had happened on this trip. But first, for Anna, it was time for a cup of tea and a warm bath.

This story is based on Anna's oral report to the author. Though the description of her ministry is true, with her permission some of the details were filled in using imagination. To protect Anna's identity, some details had to be changed and other biographical information was omitted.

Thinking about Confession

1. During hard times, Surinder recalled appropriate and encouraging Scriptures. How do you suppose she came to have those passages stored in her mind?
2. Read Psalms 32 and 38. Describe how the psalmist felt *before* he confessed his sins. Can you relate to that?

145

3. Read Nehemiah 9:1–3. What was involved in the Israelites' confession of sin? Anna taught her students to do three things daily as part of their quiet time. What were they?
4. Why are these practices good for all of us, not just for people who are in difficult circumstances?
5. Read Hebrews 12:1–2, 14–15 and 1 John 1:5–10. Why is confession an important part of our walk with God? Why is it an important part of our relationships with other people? What results did Surinder and Anna see after practicing confession?
6. How will you apply the lesson of confession found in this chapter?
7. How will you pray more specifically for our suffering sisters?

6

Bless, Do Not Curse

On January 20, 1994, Rev. Haik Hovsepian was brutally murdered in Iran, leaving his wife and four children behind. During the family's deep sorrow, Christian hymns were of great comfort to them. Gilbert, Haik and Takoosh's second son, composed some songs to express his grief. With their great musical talent, the family's performances and stirring testimonies have often moved audiences. Following is one of the songs Gilbert Hovsepian wrote after his beloved father was martyred.

> In my darkest hours of life
> I was down and tired and lost
> I was desperate for your light
> that could give me a new insight

On my knees I cried and cried
Called your name with broken heart
I said Jesus you're my friend
Help me I've come to dead end

In my tears I came to you
I was broken but I knew
In your presence things will change
I just need to pray and wait

Lord you heard my prayers soon
Talked to me that afternoon
Once again you showed your love
Sent your spirit from above

Now I know you care for me
Anytime you're there for me
When I pray you hear me, Lord
If I wait you'll give your word

You're my father you're my God
You're my strength you are my guide
Jesus Christ you're on my side
I am blessed you're in my life

In your presence I find peace
That's what I don't want to miss
In your presence I find joy
That's why I'll sing and adore

Ethiopia: Tsige

"Please, Tsige, get help! Run or you'll get hurt even more!"

Hesitating only for a few seconds, Tsige escaped through the
back door of their house and ran through the darkness. It was
July 17, 2002. She didn't know it at the time, but those were her
husband's last words to her.

Twenty-one years before, Tsige had married fellow teacher Dantew in the Ethiopian town of Bali. They had since had two sons, Dawit and Zelalem. In 1991, when the boys were four and six years old, the young family moved to Merawi, a town situated some sixty miles north of the capital Addis Ababa in northwestern Ethiopia. Both Tsige and Dantew had continued their teaching careers and become active in their town's small evangelical community.

Since 1987, to the dismay of the dominating Ethiopian Orthodox Church, two evangelical churches had been established in Merawi. Tsige, Dantew, and their two sons were members of the Full Gospel Church where Dantew had become a leading elder. The Protestants were well aware that the Orthodox leadership considered their fellowship a heretical sect and derisively called them *Pentes*, an invective that was not reserved just for Pentecostal believers. Sporadically members of the two Protestant churches in Merawi were beaten, robbed, and socially ostracized, but it was not until July of 2002 that things really got out of hand.

That May local authorities had allocated land to the Merawi Full Gospel Church for a church compound. On July 15, when the congregation started to fence in their new property, a mob was incited by local Orthodox Church leaders, and they tore down the fencing. The church members started to construct the fence again the next day. In the evening, a larger, more agitated mob attacked the compound, tearing down the fence and vandalizing a storeroom on the property. When the evangelicals' request for police protection remained unheeded, they fled to their homes. After hearing gunshots, they locked and barricaded their doors and prepared for the worst.

Half an hour later, a large, unruly gang surrounded Tsige and Dantew's home, throwing stones and breaking down their fence and main gate. Enraged rioters smashed doors, tore windows out of their frames, and ripped away pieces of the roof.

149

A stone hit Tsige in the face, right below her eye. She screamed in pain. Her two teenage sons hid under the bed while Dantew begged her to try to escape and summon the police. Terrifying as it was, she knew it was the wisest thing she could do.

After taking her life in her hands to escape the rioters on her own property, Tsige finally arrived at the police station, only to find it unmanned. She ran frantically through the streets, looking for someone who would help, but she searched in vain. Many hours later, after the mob retreated, she dared to make her way back to her house under the cover of darkness.

What Tsige found there broke her heart. After charging into the house, the attackers had discovered Dawit and Zelalem hiding under the bed with a female servant.

"Leave them alone," the Orthodox priest who directed the attack had ordered. "It's their father we want."

The assailants proceeded to attack Dantew, beating him and finally felling him with an ax blow to the head. This left him bleeding and in agony with a fractured skull. After they had ransacked the house, stealing or smashing everything that was of any worth, the attackers left, but guards remained behind to prevent anyone from assisting Dantew. A neighboring doctor asked the guards to allow him to treat Dantew's injuries, but he was turned away. Dawit and his brother spent an excruciating night with their dying father. When the guards finally left and Tsige came back, she found her husband alive but very weak. He died on the way to the hospital.

"Oh, Dantew," Tsige wept, "it would have been better if God had taken me, not you! You are needed so much at our church."

For Tsige this marked the beginning of a very painful period of her life. The house where she and her family had once been so happy needed to be repaired before she could sell it. But even after the repairs, because of the savage death that had taken place there, it was hard to find buyers. Tsige finally was forced to sell the house at a substantial loss. In the meantime, her two sons left home for further studies in Addis and Bardar.

Once the house was sold, Tsige moved to Bikolo Abye, a town seventeen kilometers from Merawi. She had taught there for several years, even before Dantew was killed. Now that her husband was gone, it made sense to live closer to her work.

But Bikolo Abye is a lonely place for Tsige, who is one of two evangelical Christians in town. She has repeatedly applied for a transfer to Bardar, to be closer to her eldest son who attends university there, but her efforts have been fruitless; the conservative Orthodox officials at the education office continue to reject her application.

Because she is a known evangelical Christian, her landlord also discriminates against her. He refuses to allow another Christian woman to live with her and share expenses. "If she moves in with you, I'll take my house back and evict you both," he has warned Tsige. Permission to build her own house has been repeatedly denied too, again because of the hostile campaign against Protestant Christians.

Tsige feels isolated and lonely, but she is grateful for her sons, who provide her with comfort and joy. Dawit translates the many cards and letters Tsige receives from Christians around the world who know about her situation and pray for her. Sometimes, through Open Doors, she welcomes visitors who come to encourage her and pray with her. Her loving, calm personality is immediately noticeable to those who meet her. "Even though her circumstances are painful and challenging, she really lives a victorious life in Christ," a colleague told me not long ago.

Tsige has forgiven the people who killed her husband. She knows that forgiveness is the way to healing, and she has said so repeatedly. But the daily confrontation with some of the offenders is more difficult to cope with. A few of her students continue to harass her. "I caught some of them cheating during an exam and

I warned them," she confided recently to a colleague. "Because of that, they tried to beat me up after the exam. The Lord protected me, but I'm never really out of danger."

Tsige knows that blessing her hostile students instead of cursing them is a biblical command. It isn't easy, but it is the path to ultimate victory. "Bless, do not curse" has become Tsige's motto. She has to repeat it every day as she looks into the angry eyes of her Orthodox students. She tries to educate them as best she can, hoping that by blessing them their hateful hearts will change.

Even though our trials cannot be compared to the suffering of our persecuted brothers and sisters, during our more than thirty years with Open Doors, Johan and I have had our share of wounds and bruises too, although ours have been emotional not physical. Some came as the result of our own mistakes; some were caused unfairly by others. It is bad enough to be treated unjustly yourself; it is even worse when someone is hurting your husband. In retrospect, it is easy to see the devil's hand. He has tried to break us through grief, anger, bitterness, or hardening of our hearts. But in the midst of the battle, it is easy to forget the spiritual aspects and to react "in the flesh" and fight back.

Many years ago, one of Johan's colleagues hurt me deeply with his words and actions. For months on end, he was the first person I thought of every morning. One day I went to a conference and heard a sermon on forgiveness by Sally McClung. "Forgiveness is a choice and a process," she explained. "Tell the Lord every day that you choose to forgive the person who hurt you." Though it was difficult, and the pain in my heart continued unabated, from then on whenever thoughts of that troublesome man haunted and distracted me,

I prayed, "Lord, I choose to forgive him, and I bless him in Your name."

When Jesus gives us difficult instructions in the Bible— such as loving our enemies, forgiving as we are forgiven, and blessing and not cursing—He does so for our own good. I realized that when, months later, I bumped into the person who had treated me so badly. To my surprise my anger for him was gone, and it had been replaced by compassion. The battle was won. I had made the choice to forgive, and as time progressed, God completed the process in my heart by healing the pain.

That's not the only time Johan and I have had to forgive. There have been many other occasions. It's never easy, but it is part of following Jesus. One thing is clear—there is far too much cursing going on in today's world. If we Christians don't react in the opposite way, all hope for change is lost. We need to forgive and not hold grudges. Hard as it is sometimes, we must choose to bless and not curse.

Like Tsige, a courageous woman named Marlene also lost her husband in a violent attack. In obedience to Christ, she too chose to forgive instead of hate, and she did so under very distressing personal circumstances. Both these women serve as wonderful examples to us all.

Colombia: Marlene

"Hasta luego," Marlene said, waving good-bye to her husband, Fausto. Deep in thought, she went back inside. Sometimes she still had to pinch herself to make sure she was awake. If the change she had seen in her husband was just a dream, she never wanted to wake up.

As she entered her house, her mind drifted back to scenes from the past. For years, every time her husband had left the house, she'd felt panic rise inside her. "Please, Fausto," she had pleaded with him when they were first married. "Please, stay home tonight. Think of me and the baby!" But he had always refused to listen to her. In his mind only wimps listened to their wives, so her begging had no effect.

From Marlene's perspective, she had every reason to be worried. They were living in Bogotá, the capital of Colombia, the fourth largest country in Latin America. Colombia has long been involved in a seemingly interminable civil war between the government, rebel guerrillas, and right-wing death squads. Most sides have links with drug traffickers, who rake in enormous amounts of money and finance the operations. Western media have called Bogotá "the kidnap capital of the world," and Marlene knew that whenever their city was featured in the international news, it was usually not because of its beautiful scenery. She was also well aware that her husband had enemies who would much rather see him dead than alive.

Friends and foes alike, everybody who knew Fausto feared him. At a young age, he and his brothers Caleb and Mario had joined a paramilitary group. For years the three had reveled in violence, establishing themselves as the scourge of the neighborhood. An insatiable hunger for power drove them to spread terror throughout Bogotá.

When he was still a teenager, Fausto noticed Marlene one day on the street. Slender and petite, her long, glossy hair reaching her shoulders, she was more than attractive to him. He made up his mind that he had to have her, and after a while, she agreed to marry him. She had done so, however, more out of fear than love.

Fausto was not very tall, but his well-developed muscles revealed his brute strength. His bushy hair and burning eyes added to her feeling that he was not someone to be trifled with. After

154

they married, Marlene often wondered if her husband was really able to love anyone. Hatred seemed to consume his whole life. She knew he had killed people; in fact, he sometimes told her about what he called "cleansing sprees." When she asked him one day what he meant, he shrugged and said, "Oh, it just means that we had to kill some people. We think they were collaborating with some of our enemies, so we took them out."

Too shocked for words, Marlene decided not to ask any more questions. By now she knew very well that she had married a murderer. *But is that really the right term?* she asked herself, trying to make sense of it all. *Maybe killing people is the only way to survive in a country like this.*

Killing wasn't Fausto's only vice. He was unfaithful to Marlene. Coming to terms with this was more difficult for his wife than thinking about the murders. Every year since their marriage, she had given birth to a baby. The more children she had, the more nights Fausto stayed away from home. She suspected him of having a mistress, but again, she didn't dare ask. She had come to grips with the fact that their union was far from a partnership, and she knew better than to inquire about his whereabouts or, worse, to call him to account. If she wanted to raise her family in relative peace, it was best to be quiet.

Marlene was not the only wife struggling with a wayward husband's lifestyle. She knew that many of her friends were in the same position as she. Even though they rarely discussed their husband's dealings, she could read the story on their fearful and sad faces. As she went about her daily chores, solely responsible for the raising of her children, she often wondered sadly if lonely, endless drudgery was all she could expect out of life.

One day a policeman showed up at the door. "I need to speak to Fausto," he announced. Fausto was asleep in the back room, and when Marlene went to wake him up, he was infuriated. "I told you not to disturb me!" he snarled at her. But when she told him

155

who was there to see him, he quickly pulled on some trousers and went out to talk to the officer.

Marlene was curious, so she eavesdropped on the conversation.

"I need money," the policeman said. "And you haven't paid me my service fee. We made a deal, remember? Give me the money now, or you'll be in trouble. I won't turn a blind eye to your dealings anymore unless you pay me."

Sulking, Fausto walked out the door with him, heading somewhere to scrape together the money.

So that's why Fausto never seems afraid, Marlene said to herself. *The police are protecting him because he is bribing them. Meanwhile, they're only too happy to have Fausto and his brothers killing rebels for them. One thing is clear—he never leaves home without his bag.* Marlene knew very well that Fausto's bag contained a revolver.

Then one astonishing day, everything changed.

A Beautiful Transformation

One evening in 1994 Fausto and his mistress were wandering around the streets of Bogotá in a drunken fog. When they passed an Evangelical church, Fausto had an idea. "Let's go in and play a joke on the pastor," he suggested. They walked in and sat down in the front row, biding their time. But before Fausto found an opportunity to interrupt the service with his mockery, a strong force took hold of him. Dumbfounded, Fausto listened as the pastor addressed the subject of marital infidelity.

How could he know these things about me? he wondered.

Right then and there, the Holy Spirit convicted Fausto of his sin, and he knew that he had to give up his mistress, his alcohol, and his violent way of life. When the pastor asked those who wanted to break away from their sinful habits to walk to the front of the church, Fausto was the first one to stand up. Weeping uncontrollably, he gave his life to Jesus and repented of his sinful and violent past.

For the first time in his life, Fausto encountered, in Jesus, someone who really loved him. God knew every wicked thing Fausto had ever done, and yet He somehow loved him anyway. Fausto was amazed by the Lord's power and grace. It was too strong for him to resist.

From that moment on, Fausto became a soldier in a different army—God's army. And in his bag he carried a different weapon. He got rid of his revolver—he'd had enough of killing. His gun was replaced by a Bible, and his message to others was one of forgiveness and life instead of hatred and death.

The first two people he tried to convince of the love and truth he'd found in Jesus were his brothers, Caleb and Mario. They couldn't help but notice that the hardness in Fausto's face had softened. Gone was the hatred that used to flash in his eyes. Now, when his brothers came to Fausto's house, to their amazement they found Fausto playing with his son Fabio. Or he was helping Marlene or his daughter Diana with household chores. This was a very different Fausto than the one they had known before. And it was his changed life that convinced them that he was telling the truth about Jesus. It wasn't long before his brothers decided to follow Jesus too.

Marlene was easy to convince. She had fallen in love with the new Fausto and felt like she was married to a different person. She gladly accompanied him to church on Sundays. And as she began to understand the message she heard there, she accepted Jesus Christ into her life. The children also loved their transformed father. For the first time ever, he seemed to notice them and listen to them. The five older ones, Mariana, Diane, Suzy, Jennifer, and Fabio, were old enough to understand what had caused the change. Only Andres, the baby, was still too young to appreciate the difference.

"Fausto, I must tell you something," Marlene confided in her husband one evening. "I think I'm pregnant. This will be the first child we've conceived since we were born again. I think that's so special, don't you?"

Taking his wife in his arms, Fausto prayed. "Father, we thank You for this new baby. We ask You to keep your hand on it as it is woven in Marlene's womb. We thank You, Lord, for giving us a new life together, and we thank You for this new baby who represents our new life in You."

Soldiers in a Different Army

If this was just a dream, Marlene did not want to wake up. But it was not a dream. First of all, the soft baby cries coming from their bedroom were clear proof of the new life God had given to them. Baby Doris, whose face was the image of her father, was the delight of their whole family. None of the other children had received so much love when they were babies, Marlene realized. She and Fausto had been incapable of wholeheartedly loving their children before. Now that had changed.

Fausto was still gone a lot of the time. But instead of setting out to kill, he now went on a different mission—to bring life. His work continued to be dangerous, but gone were the days that Marlene pleaded with her husband to stay home. Now she endorsed his new work; he was fighting for the souls of others. That's what he was going off to do as she waved good-bye to him.

Fausto and his brother Caleb had decided that the only hope for their country was the love of Jesus. It had changed their lives, so why couldn't it change the lives of others? Their former comrades needed to hear their message. Even the groups who had been their enemies needed to know about Jesus. The two brothers had become evangelists, consumed with a desire to preach the gospel to Colombia's guerrilla fighters and paramilitary groups. Single-handedly they distributed more than a thousand Bibles to them. Before long, an impressive number of their former colleagues had accepted Christ.

Desertion was risky and dangerous, but many of those new believers left their armed groups. And it didn't please their commanders to see their ranks depleted. Tensions increased. Not only had Fausto and his brothers deserted, but they were also responsible for the decreasing number of fighters. One day a letter was shoved under the door of Fausto and Marlene's house. "Stop visiting our troops or we will kill you," it read. "Leave the city or your days are numbered!"

It was not the first warning they'd received. Ever since Fausto had become a Christian, he had received various kinds of death threats. But during 1999 those threats greatly increased in frequency. He knew that the killers seeking his life wanted him dead, and that they were fully capable of getting it done. It was no longer safe for him or his family to stay in the city. He explained to Marlene that they would have to move.

Before they could leave, as if to underscore the urgency of their departure, an armed group attacked their house, shooting indiscriminately at it from outside. Windows were shattered and bullet holes pocked the exterior. It was a miracle no one in the family was injured. Shortly after that terrifying incident, Fausto, Marlene, and their children joined the ranks of Colombia's hundreds of thousands of displaced people. Some estimate the number of refugees from violence to be as many as two million people.

Christian friends offered to drive them, even though the trip was dangerous and traveling with seven small children across the mountain ranges that surround Bogotá was arduous. Through guerrilla-infested country, they made their way, cringing every time they were forced to stop at a roadblock. Marlene tried to distract the children by telling them interesting facts about the areas they passed through. But no matter how hard she tried, nothing Marlene said diminished the tension in the car. Everyone was strangely quiet. Only the baby seemed oblivious to the danger around her.

"God Has Forgiven You"

At last the family arrived at their destination—a town on the plains where friends had located an empty lot for them. They would have to start from scratch, but they could camp there and eventually cobble together a house. The area had no electricity and was surrounded by jungle, but at least their enemies would not be able to find them here, or so they hoped. After the family had somewhat settled in, Fausto found a new place to continue his ministry.

More than fifteen thousand refugees had resettled in the vicinity. Many of them were evangelical Christians, but thousands of others had never heard the gospel. Living conditions were often appalling. With sticks, trees, and bed sheets for walls and plastic tarps for a roof, men had thrown together makeshift homes for their families. Pieces of cardboard were laid out on the floor to serve as mattresses. When it rained, the whole ramshackle camp was transformed into one enormous pool of mud.

Every day Fausto took a cotton bag filled with Christian literature and went off to preach the gospel. One day he bought a piece of bread from a man in one of the camps.

"Where did you get this bread?" Fausto asked, surprised to find such a treat here in the refugee camp.

"I baked it myself," Antonio answered. "The Agape Team gave me an oven so I could make some money baking and selling bread."

"*An Agape Team?* I know them!" Fausto reacted enthusiastically. By now he was well acquainted with the Agape network. They had representatives all around the country, helping Christians who were caught in the violent crossfire. Shortly after his conversion, Fausto had attended an Agape training seminar. Whenever he ran out of Bibles and evangelistic materials, he knew he could go to them and ask for a new supply.

160

"I'm so glad to hear they are working in the area," he added. "But tell me, brother, what brought you here?"

When Antonio told him his story, Fausto's heart sank.

"We used to live out in the jungle about two hundred miles from here," Antonio explained. "One day our two teenage daughters disappeared. When they didn't come home, I went to look for them. I was almost paralyzed with fear over what might have happened. For three months I zigzagged through the jungle, searching, inquiring everywhere if anyone had seen them. I returned home a few times to see if my wife had received any news. I did everything I could, and finally I located them."

Antonio went on to say that his daughters had been kidnapped by guerrillas. Away from their families for months on end, guerrilla fighters habitually kidnapped young girls to satisfy their sexual needs. They also gave these captive girls military training, requiring them to take up weapons and join their ranks. For three months Lisa and Dolores had been raped, beaten, and forced to do all kinds of chores. The sisters had kept their eyes open for an opportunity to escape, but they didn't know their way around the jungle. When their father finally found them, they were both pregnant. One night he somehow managed to rescue them from the paramilitary camp.

"It was impossible to stay on our farm," Antonio continued. "Without question, the guerrillas would have come to look for us, and I hate to think what would have happened once they found us. We packed some belongings and moved here a few months ago. The girls have had their babies and seem to be coping remarkably well. But the whole ordeal has cost me my wife," Antonio shook his head sadly. "She just sits and stares absently into the distance. I can't seem to get through to her. She won't talk to me or anybody else."

Fausto was at a loss for words. Fighting back tears, he just shook Antonio's hand, repeating, "I'm sorry. I am *so sorry!*"

161

Fausto was too overwhelmed with sorrow and guilt to continue his work that day, and he went home in despair. "I just heard the saddest story," he began, relating to Marlene what had happened to Antonio and his family. After he finished, he sat silently for a few minutes. "I'm going to cut some wood to make a fire," he muttered, rising slowly to his feet. Clearly Fausto needed some time alone. He knew that what had happened to those two teenage sisters was happening all over Colombia, to Christian and non-Christian families alike.

Walking off into the jungle area surrounding his house, Fausto cried out in anguish to God. "O Lord! Please forgive me for the pain my brothers and I have caused!"

When he finally returned, Marlene could see the pain in his eyes. "God has forgiven you, Fausto," she said, stroking his rough face with her hand. "Now you've got to try to forgive yourself."

Bloody Revenge

Fausto's brothers continued to share the gospel. Mario had moved to another large city. Despite frequent death threats, he told people about the change Jesus had made in his life. On the morning of September 7, 1999, his bullet-riddled body was found. Mario was the same age as Jesus when he died—thirty-three.

Caleb had become an itinerant evangelist, moving from place to place to evade capture or worse. The morning his brother Mario was killed, Caleb was selling pastries in a small plaza. As he walked past a group of men, he heard one of them call out to him, using a nickname by which he'd been known before. Without responding, Caleb continued on his way. He realized that only people who meant to harm him knew him by that name.

"No, that's not him," he heard someone in the group say. "If he were him, he would have stopped in his tracks."

Caleb escaped. Mario didn't. Then, that very same day, Fausto ran into problems of his own. While he and his family were eating their evening meal, someone started banging on the door, shouting, "Fausto, come out here! We need to talk to you."

"Please don't go, Daddy!" Suzy pleaded. She was sitting next to him at the table, clinging to his arm. Doris, the baby, began to cry, and so did Andres. Quickly Fausto weighed his options. He looked across the table into Marlene's clear, brown eyes. They both knew what the disturbing noises meant. The men congregating outside were not in a friendly mood. If Fausto refused to go out and talk to them, they might come inside and harm Marlene and the children.

Forcing himself to be calm, Fausto walked to the door and opened it. He looked straight into the barrel of a gun.

By now Marlene and all of the children were in tears. "Please, don't take him! Please, please, have mercy! Think of us!" they pleaded.

"Don't worry," one of the men shouted as he seized Fausto by the arm. "We'll bring him back tomorrow."

Diane and Fabio slipped outside into the dark jungle and followed the men from a distance. Later they were sorry they did, because what they saw will haunt them for the rest of their lives. Silently they watched in horror while their father was brutally tortured by his abductors. And when one of the attackers lifted a large machete in the air, ready to strike Fausto, Fabio could no longer contain himself. "No!" he screamed. Once the guerrillas realized that the children followed them, the men threw Fausto into a car and drove away into the dark. The brother and sister made their way home. Sickened and weak with sorrow, they haltingly described to Marlene the brutal torture they had witnessed. Huddled together in the big bed with her, afraid to be alone in the dark, they tried to sleep. But Marlene was too anxious even to close her eyes. She hoped against hope, praying with all her heart that Fausto would come stumbling through the door. Injured, yes, but alive.

It was not to be. Early the next morning a neighbor notified the family that Fausto's mutilated body had been found. Next to his corpse was his bag, filled with his beloved Bible and dozens of tracts. Even that last evening of his life, he had not left home without them.

Marlene's first reaction to her husband's brutal death was anger—anger and deep hatred toward those who had taken his life. "Why would you do such a thing?" she cried out in despair. "How sick are you? How cruel and inhuman?" She wanted to run after the killers and take revenge. Of course it was out of the question—if Fausto couldn't defend himself against them, how could she? They would kill her too, without a second thought, and then what would become of the children?

When Fausto's brother Caleb arrived, Marlene poured out her heart to him. At times she screamed, completely losing control of herself, and at other times she just sobbed quietly. She asked all the questions that had haunted her through the seemingly endless night. How was she supposed to take care of seven children all by herself? Why wasn't Fausto more careful? He knew this could happen some day! How would she be able to feed her family, let alone give the children an education? Where would they live? There was no way they could stay in the house—they couldn't afford it, and it wasn't safe for them anyway. When Fausto left his paramilitary group, their income had dwindled, but apart from his evangelistic work, he had always found odd jobs to do. They had been poor, but there was always food on the table. Who would help her now?

Caleb sat quietly. While she raved and ranted and raged, he just let her pour out her pain and confusion. He knew she needed to express herself to someone. And he didn't have much to offer her anyway, apart from a listening ear.

Thinking about Fausto and what she had learned from him eventually helped Marlene calm herself. She knew that if he'd been there, he would have told her that anger and bitterness didn't offer answers to any of her questions. And she knew that was right, even though an insistent desire for revenge tugged at her soul. Fausto had practiced revenge for many years, killing everyone who crossed him. Ultimately it had been the love and forgiveness of Jesus that had transformed him, and only Jesus could possibly change his murderers. Marlene was going to have to bless them and not curse them. It was a choice she knew she had to make.

Tearing herself away from the children and the house, she walked outside. She needed time alone, time to think, and time to pray. She found a quiet place to sit on a fallen tree. Her fists clenched, she just sat there, glaring at the sky. Finally the tears came. As the battle continued to rage in her heart, she wept bitterly. Then, while crying her heart out, she finally looked up to heaven and gave in. She almost choked on the words, but she said them anyway: "Lord Jesus, I want to forgive them. Please help me!"

Just then Marlene somehow remembered the words of Jesus, recorded in Luke 6:27–28. "But I tell you who hear me: Love your enemies, do good to those who hate you, bless those who curse you, pray for those who mistreat you." She knew immediately that Jesus had heard her prayer.

In silent gratitude, she went back inside. Before long, Marlene's house was filled with people. The entire extended family came to grieve the loss of their two fallen relatives, both lost in one day. Marlene buried herself in Caleb's arms. "Now you are the only one left to keep the light of Jesus shining," she sobbed.

Caleb was weeping too. "Not the only one, Marlene," he said through his tears. "Fausto left you seven children. God can use them."

The funeral was sad and victorious at the same time. Caleb and some family members carried the two caskets containing the bodies of Fausto and his younger brother Mario out of town and into a beautiful cemetery. Beneath an overcast sky, autumn-colored trees lined the paths along the way, and friends and loved ones placed flowers on the caskets. A freshly dug grave marked the place where the brothers would be buried.

Members of the Agape Team arrived just in time for the funeral. There were more tears, but there were also smiles because, at the very moment the caskets were lowered into the ground, a beam of sunlight broke through the clouds. It seemed like a sign to everyone that Fausto and Mario had made it safely to heaven. Jesus had paid the price for their sins. The two brothers were forever out of harm's way.

A New Beginning

"What can we do for you, Marlene?" Ricardo, the Agape Team leader, asked as family and friends gathered in Marlene's home after the funeral. "We think Fausto was a martyr for his faith in Jesus, and we want to help you from a special fund we've set up for people in your situation."

Marlene already knew the answer to their question. Her mind had worked overtime ever since Fausto had been killed. She knew what she wanted. She had talked to Caleb, and he agreed with her. "Ricardo, we want you to give us Bibles," she replied, her voice full of conviction. "We can't think of a better way to honor Fausto's memory than by distributing Scriptures to the guerrillas, including his killers."

Ricardo was speechless. How could a family react like this so shortly after such a loss? This was the grace of God—that much was clear to him. *Those who have forgiven much*, he thought, *best understand the power of forgiveness. They had seen the power of forgiveness in Fausto's life. He had been forgiven much. They knew forgiveness was better than revenge.*

"We'll gladly supply you with Bibles, Marlene," he promised, "but we need to do more. We'll ask people around the world to pray for you and your children. And you're going to need a way to earn some money. How about if we give you an oven? We can teach you how to bake bread so you can sell it at the market."

"Marlene also needs another place to live," Caleb added. "Can you help her find a house?"

A few months later an Agape Team returned to visit Marlene and her children. They had just moved into their new home—a makeshift house of three rooms constructed of red bricks, topped by a roof of corrugated iron. It was a small house in a resettlement camp, and it had electricity. Marlene happily showed her guests around. She had been told that the house was a gift from Christian believers around the world.

A commercial oven took up most of the kitchen area. On a small table in the living room, Marlene had found a prominent place for Fausto's Bible. His picture was conspicuously placed on the TV, right next to the front door. A few chairs and a cupboard were all the furniture in the main room. Outside, the family's laundry was drying in the sunlight. A large oil drum full of water sat on the patio. Next to it a plastic container of cleanly washed cooking pots were awaiting use at the next meal.

"The children still can't believe this mansion belongs to us," she told the Agape Team. "They keep asking, 'How can we pay the rent for this place, Mommy?' I tell them, 'The Lord provided a place in heaven for your daddy, and He has provided us with this house here on earth.'"

Seven years have gone by since Fausto was killed. Marlene's journey through life continues to be full of difficulties, though there are happy days as well as sad ones. Mariana, her oldest daughter, is married now, and it was a wonderful occasion for the whole family when she gave birth to her first baby. And after struggling to make a living with baked goods from the oven, Marlene was able to exchange it for three sewing machines. With high hopes, she has finished a seamstress course and is now ready to start a

167

new business endeavor, in which she and two other local women will manufacture clothes to be sold locally.

Raising a family in a violent country like Colombia is full of hardships. Some of Fausto and Marlene's children have experienced pain that is too private to share in a book. It devastates Marlene to see her children suffer abuse. All of them have wished, at one time or another, that their father were there to give them advice.

"I know I'll continue to face problems and challenges," Marlene told a visiting member of the Agape Team recently. "But I have often felt the love of Jesus for me and my family, despite our suffering. He has helped me forgive my enemies and pray for them. And I know that our family has become the apple of His eye. Every day I sense that God is keeping us safe, hidden in the hollow of His hand."

Thinking about Blessing and Forgiving

1. Read 1 John 1:9 and Ephesians 1:3. What two things has God done for believers that believers can pass on to everyone?
2. Read Romans 12:14–21 and Luke 6:27–36. How did Tsige and Marlene live out these Scriptures?
3. Read Matthew 6:12–15 and Luke 6:35–37. What are the results of forgiving?
4. In what situations do you have an opportunity to bless instead of curse?
5. In light of all the above passages, how can you better pray for your persecuted sisters?

7

Never Lose Hope

Since the first Protestant missionaries arrived in 1880, many Koreans have become Christian believers. After the country was divided and North Korea became Communist more than fifty years ago, the church of Jesus Christ in the north has been severely persecuted and innumerable Christians there have been martyred for their faith. Remembering the past continues to give Christians in that desperate, needy country hope for the future. The words of a great old hymn help them remember that throughout the ages, as Jesus promised, "the gates of hell" cannot and will not be able to prevail against the church.

> Faith of our fathers! Living still
> In spite of dungeon, fire and sword;
> O how our hearts beat high with joy
> Whene'er we hear that glorious word!

Faith of our fathers, holy faith!
We will be true to thee till death!

Faith of our fathers! We will strive
To win all nations unto thee,
And through the truth that comes from God
Mankind shall then be truly free.

Faith of our fathers! We will love
Both friend and foe in all our strife;
And preach thee, too, as love knows how,
By kindly words and virtuous life.

Frederick William Faber (1814–1863)

North Korea: Lee

In North Korea there is room for only one god—the "Great Leader" Kim Il Sung. It is estimated that some two hundred thousand people are languishing in prison camps spread around the country, and tens of thousands of these are Christians. Author Soon Ok Lee met with some of these captives during her own six years in prison. In her book *Eyes of the Tailless Animals*,[4] she writes that imprisoned Christians, who worked all day as slave laborers, were forced to keep their faces downcast, eyes on the ground. It was forbidden for them to look up toward the sky for one reason only. Their captors knew that they believed in the God who made heaven and earth.

During her imprisonment, Lee was not a Christian, and she saw many Christians die. "Yet they never denied the God who is in heaven. All they had to do was say they don't believe in religion, and they would have been released."

One night in February of 1992 Lee witnessed a gruesome scene. The imprisoned workers were almost done for the day, and she saw eight Christian prisoners carrying a big kettle holding molten iron. "An officer called to them, using vile words," she writes. "'Tomorrow is the day of re-education training. As you know, it's held because of your stubbornness. . . . Tomorrow is "cleaning the mind" day. You will go and tell everybody that there is nothing in heaven to believe in; there is no God. Otherwise you will be killed. Understand?'

"When none of the eight Christian prisoners said a word, the man began to yell at them. He became furious and started cursing. At the top of his voice, he screamed 'You sons of b——es! All eight of you come here and put your faces down to the ground!' The Christians followed his orders but remained silent. Other prisoners were called to the scene. They were forced to fill buckets with molten iron from the oven and pour it over the kneeling Christians. If they refused, they would die the same cruel death."[5]

Lee goes on to describe how she saw the bodies of the eight Christians shrink and shrivel from the melted metal's intense heat. She and the other prisoners screamed in horror as the eight martyrs died. "I looked at their shrunken bodies and wondered in my heart, What do they believe? What do they see in the empty sky? What could be more important than their lives?" Lee did not understand why these people were not afraid to die. "Their unbelievable faith brought a big question into my heart. 'What did they see and what am I missing?'"

Her question was answered after her miraculous release from prison in 1992, after which she put her faith in Jesus Christ. She came to know the God who lives in heaven but also, through his Holy Spirit, in the hearts of his followers on earth. She discovered that Christians have hope, no matter what their circumstances.

As for me, for reasons I don't really understand, some of my
prayers get answered quickly, while others—often about things

that are very important to me—seem to remain unanswered. About ten years ago, our two sons told their father they were not ready for the commitment to God they saw in his life. For many long years and during many sleepless hours, I have prayed that our sons, like their older sister, would fully commit their lives to the God in whom they profess to believe. Just as this manuscript nears completion, one of them told us that he had decided to fully commit his life to God.

"Though I love you very much," he wrote, "I want you to know that I am not doing this for you. I feel I owe it to God and to Jesus." He has counted the cost and is finally ready to make this life-changing decision. Nothing could give Johan and me more joy. Often it was hard to continue praying and believing God would answer. Still, I forced myself not to give up hope, because my hope was based on the assurance that God will keep His Word and complete what He started in our sons' lives. When we don't give up hope, we are able to persevere. The Bible assures us there is more to life than what we are experiencing right here, right now.

I asked a dear friend in Vietnam what it was like to live under the pressures of a Communist government for twenty-five years. When she shared some of the problems she had faced, she kept repeating two words, khong sao*—"It doesn't matter." She was able to look beyond the present because she understood the words that Paul wrote in Romans 8:18: "I consider that our present sufferings are not worth comparing with the glory that will be revealed in us." She saw the present, but her eyes were firmly fixed on the amazing future Jesus has promised to us all.*

I am so grateful for the example my persecuted brothers and sisters have set for me. Because they know God and have learned to rely on Him, they don't give up hope. Neither should we.

When I met Helena in a Central Asian country, I saw God's hope in her. Helena's hope was based on the past because she had placed her faith in the death and resurrection of Jesus Christ. Helena has hope for the future because she believes that Jesus is coming again to make all things new. And Helena also has hope for the present, for the here and now. She knows that God is able—more than able—to change our present circumstances.

Central Asia: Helena

Helena's family was no different from most other families in their small town (names of the country, towns, and cities in which these events have taken place are withheld in this chapter for security reasons). Born while her country was still part of the vast Soviet Union, Helena was her parents' second child—she has an older brother and a younger sister. Quiet and obedient, Helena was an easy child to raise. During her childhood, nothing distinguished her from other children in her town. Like everybody else, she grew up in a nondescript, gray cement high-rise apartment building. Helena's greatest childhood dream was to become a teacher one day.

Her family was not rich, but they had enough. Under the Soviet system, everybody had a house to live in, all children could receive an education, and the government provided medical care. Public transportation was cheap, so occasionally, on holidays, her parents took her to see interesting sites beyond their own community. For example, she never forgot their trip to a twenty-five-hundred-year-old city, which had become a tourist attraction. The city walls and towering minarets were impressive. The Islamic history was interesting, especially because, like most people in their region, Helena's parents called themselves Muslims.

Under Communism, everyone was taught that there is no God. So in practice, being a Muslim meant little. The family did not attend a mosque; they did not learn the Qur'an. During the month of Ramadan, other Muslims around the world fasted from sunup till sundown, but not in the Soviet Union. It would have been dangerous for Helena's parents to observe Ramadan under the atheistic regime. Sometimes they had a party when the month of Ramadan ended, but that was the extent of their celebration.

A Quest for Spiritual Answers

Helena was a young teenager when a historic change took place in the world—the Iron Curtain fell. After years of occupation by the Soviet Union, her country and many other neighboring states in Central Asia gained independence. Citizens in those former Soviet republics felt as if their chains had fallen off. No longer were they told what to do, what to believe, what to read, and what to watch on television. A new wave of hope and freedom flooded people's hearts. Helena felt as if a whole new world had opened up. Their country had its own president, its own parliament, and its own language, with the local vernacular no longer taking second place to Russian. Citizens were free to travel abroad if they could afford it, and foreigners were allowed to live in their country.

Inquisitive and intelligent, Helena graduated from high school with great success. To attend university, she moved to a city nearby. Now not only was her country independent, but she enjoyed her own new freedom, living on the university campus. Her dorm was as gray and unattractive as the apartment building she had grown up in, but Helena loved living in the big city.

Not long after she came to the university, however, serious questions began to form in Helena's mind. She wondered about the explanation she had always been given for the origin of life. Had the world really been formed by random chance and come into being through the "big bang" as she'd been told in school? And what about her? What was the purpose of her life? What would happen after she died? Neither her teachers nor her parents could provide answers that resolved her questions. Somewhere deep inside, Helena was convinced there was a God and she should be able to speak to Him.

One day, when she was nineteen, she found the answer to her questions. Helena had noticed a change in some of her friends. She'd heard rumors that certain students on campus now believed in the "Russian God." Nobody quite knew how it had started, but it was obvious that religion had become a hot topic of discussion at Helena's university.

But even in a country that had a nominal Muslim tradition, such a discussion was not without its risks. After the collapse of the Soviet Union, Islam had become a more significant part of her people's national identity. Officially Helena lived in a secular state, which promoted a moderate form of Islam. Still, she knew only too well that, after independence in 1991, the indigenous people of her country were regarded as Muslims and that belief in the "Russian God" was considered all but treasonous.

"Helena, there's something I want to talk to you about," her friend Sonja said one day. "I've found the answer to some questions I've been struggling with for years. Remember how our teachers used to tell us that there's no God? I always wondered if that was true."

"Me too," Helena nodded. "I've always had a feeling there must be more to life than what we were taught in school."

"Well, there is!" Sonja said with a happy smile, and then pulled a small book out of her bag. "Here," she said. "I want you to have this. It contains portions of the *Injil* (the New Testament) in our own language." Then Sonja began to tell Helena about her new-found Christian faith.

Helena listened politely to her friend. It was obvious that Sonja was thrilled about what had happened to her. But was this what

175

Helena had been searching for? Would she really be able to find answers to her questions in this book?

As if she could read Helena's mind, Sonja continued, "This book talks about all kinds of things, but the most important lesson I learned from it is about Jesus. He's the Son of God—the God who created the universe and the earth and you and me."

"Wait a minute," Helena interrupted. "What are you trying to tell me? Do you mean to say that Darwin had it all wrong? Are you really serious, Sonja?"

"I couldn't be more serious, Helena," her friend answered emphatically. "This book tells us that God is the one who created the world. It didn't just happen by chance. And then He sent His Son Jesus into our world to die for our sins. In Jesus, the God who created everything actually became a human being! Helena, can you believe that?"

Helena didn't answer. How could she? She needed time to think, time to read the book Sonja was giving her. For one thing, she was trained to use her mind and not to trust her feelings, and Sonja was very emotional about all this. Like a cascade, Sonja's flow of words continued. "What kind of God would leave His place in heaven to come and save us? He is so different from all the other gods I've ever read about. And even though He was human, He never sinned once. That's why He could be the perfect sacrifice for our sins."

"Please, Sonja, slow down! You're going way too fast. What did you have to do to get to know this God?"

"Nothing, Helena! That's what's so wonderful about Christianity. I discovered that I don't have to do a lot of things, like praying five times a day or fasting, to be saved. I don't have to earn my salvation. I just have to admit my sin, believe in the Lord Jesus, and ask His forgiveness. Don't you think that is good news, Helena?"

Sonja's enthusiasm was infectious. But for Helena, it was too much information in too little time. Helena was not at all convinced that this new Christianity of Sonja's was right for her. Before she could respond, Sonja had still more to say.

"You can keep the *Injil*. Read it, please, and if you're interested, you are welcome to come to my house group." Lowering her voice, she began to explain how she and a few of her friends met together every week to study the *Injil* and pray together.

"But, please, Helena, don't talk about our group," Sonja warned. "We have to be so careful. The government doesn't want to register our meetings, so if they find out where we meet, we could get into serious trouble." Then she took Helena's hand, looked into her almond-shaped eyes, and said, "I hope Jesus will become your Savior too, Helena."

With that, Sonja rushed away, leaving a startled Helena behind.

In the days that followed, in the quietness of her room, Helena read the Gospels. In spite of her reservations, the life and teachings of Jesus Christ gripped her heart. Before long, she went to one of the house group's meetings. There she met others whose lives, like Sonja's, had been changed. As they studied the Word of God together, the light began to dawn. After some weeks of study, it struck Helena that not just fishermen like Peter and John, but also intelligent people like Paul and Luke, had put their faith in Christ. Eventually she did what Sonja had told her to do. In a quiet time of prayer, she confessed her sin and asked Jesus to forgive her. She admitted that she needed Him to change her heart and fill her with His love.

"Inner peace"—that is the best way she could describe the new awareness that had come into her life. Her search for truth had finally led her to some answers. She had found them in the pages of the New Testament. It wasn't long before the house church, which met in different homes each week to avoid discovery, became the highlight of the week for Helena. The other Christians became Helena's best friends. Whenever they faced a difficult exam or problems with their families, they prayed for each other. As time went on, more and more students joined them. Communism had left a vacuum in their lives, and Jesus had come in to fill the void.

The Burden of Blame

Just as Sonja had told her about Jesus, Helena now began to talk to others about Him. She had to be careful doing so, because witnessing—or as it was called, "proselytizing"—on campus was forbidden.

Initially, her parents didn't object when she told them that she had become a Christian. Their view seemed to be that as long as she kept quiet about it and practiced her faith only in the city and not in her small town, things would be all right. But Helena did not keep quiet. She talked about her new faith with students and teachers alike.

When her mother found out how outspoken Helena had become about her beliefs, their relationship deteriorated rapidly. Her mother was ashamed of her daughter. More to the point, she feared the neighbors' gossip and her son's rage.

"Do you know what Helena is doing?" her brother confronted their mother one day. "She's spreading this Christian stuff all over the university—teachers, students, she's telling everybody about it! You're going to have to kick her out of the house, or we're all going to be in trouble."

"As if we weren't in trouble already!" Helena's mother could hardly contain her angry tears.

Helena knew that her mother's life was difficult. For economic reasons, her father had gone to work in Kazakhstan, and since his departure, her brother had been drinking heavily. And now that Helena had become a follower of Jesus, her mother felt as though she had lost her too. Helena wished she could help her mother, but by now she seemed to have become the scapegoat for every problem in their family, unjustly bearing the burden of blame for her mother's heartaches.

One night the sound of shattering glass in the living room awoke Helena with a jolt, and she raised herself up onto her elbows from her mattress, trying to figure out what had happened. She was home for the weekend, visiting her mother, brother, and sister, and it didn't take her long to realize what was taking place in the adjacent room.

"Oh, no, not again," she sighed.

Her brother often came home drunk. In his intoxication, he would grab and destroy anything he could lay his hands on. Helena's parents had few belongings to begin with, and he had already ruined most of them. Avoiding her brother's rage, Helena stayed in her room. She knew very well that it would only make matters worse if she went to investigate. Instead of confronting him, she did what she had done so often before under similar circumstances. In the darkness, she whispered a prayer. "Lord Jesus, please stop him from doing any more damage. I know that some of this is happening because he's so angry with me! And please help me too. I want to follow You, but it's so hard. Please just give me enough strength to face tomorrow!"

As she lay there in the dark, listening to the now subdued voices coming from the living room, she was frightened, but at the same time she was also grateful. Jesus had taught His followers that it would be tough to follow Him, but He had also promised that He would never leave them or forsake them.

Certainly she wasn't the only one who faced problems. She knew some Christian believers who had already served time in prison for their faith. Others were regularly summoned by the police to come in for questioning. Several Christian leaders had been sentenced to pay fines. As soon as the authorities realized that a Christian was sharing his or her faith with others, trouble inevitably followed.

One of the youngest members of their group, Olek, was regularly beaten by his mother. He had told his story at a recent meeting, explaining how he tried to pray quietly while his mother battered him. He worked hard at keeping his lips from moving so she couldn't see what he was doing. But despite his precautions, he described the way his mother had suddenly struck him on the back of his head, shouting, "Stop praying!"

How did she know I was praying? he wondered.

While he talked, Olek's eyes were alight with joy, and there was always a smile on his face. Often Helena had noticed the friendliness and love that seemed to emanate from this young man. He was only nineteen years old, and in spite of his violent home life, the presence of Jesus was evident in his demeanor.

As Helena lay in the dark thinking about these things, she was grateful for the change in her own life. And she had read in the *Injil* that nothing was impossible for God. Some of the parents of her friends had come to believe in Jesus. Someday her parents would change, she promised herself. The same God who strengthened Olek was her God too. With these comforting thoughts in mind, she finally fell asleep.

The light of the sun shining through her small window woke her up the next day. Helena mustered up the courage to get up and face her mother. She found her sobbing in the kitchen. The blackened water kettle on the gas stove was steaming, but she didn't seem to notice it. "He ruined our television," were the first words her mother said. "There isn't much left for him to put his hands on now. Our lives are such a mess! And it's all because of you, Helena!"

One Step at a Time

Helena's problems at home weren't her only challenge. One day she was summoned to the office of her university's dean. Feeling uneasy, she made her way there, only to find him in an angry and threatening mood. "I've been told that you're disobeying our rules," he said in a harsh voice. "You know we don't allow Christian propaganda at this university, yet you seem to think you have to bring up the subject of the Russian God with every person you talk to."

Helena couldn't deny what he said, so she kept quiet.

"Here, sign this paper or I'm going to expel you from school," the dean continued, noticing that she hadn't denied his charges. Quickly and quietly, Helena read the piece of paper that was rudely shoved onto the table in front of her: "I admit that I have trespassed the rules of my university regarding religious propagation. I promise that I will not talk about my faith with other students again. I understand that if I continue to do so, I will be expelled."

Intimidated by the dean's stern voice and overbearing posture, not to mention the threat of being expelled from her classes, Helena compliantly signed her name on the document. Her hand shook as she tried to move the pen. And that night, sleep evaded her. *How could I sign that paper?* she asked herself. "Lord Jesus, please forgive me!" Her prayers were full of remorse. "Please let them lose that paper. I don't want to deny my faith in You!"

God answered Helena's prayer. Apparently the paper got lost, because nothing more was said about it. Helena continued to share the good news of Jesus and didn't run into trouble again. She was a good student, and after graduation she managed to obtain a teaching position at a local school—the fulfillment of a childhood dream. But unfortunately Helena had to move back into the family home.

Although she was still estranged from her mother, she tried to be as helpful and as kind as she could. Whenever she had an opportunity and when he was sober, she tried to talk to her brother. "Jesus can set you free!" she told him. But her words seemed to fall on deaf ears.

Still, Helena could not keep quiet about her faith. She shared the love of Jesus whenever she had an opportunity. Careful not to offend people, she asked God to guide her. "Please lead me to people whose hearts You have prepared," she prayed. Noticing the joy and peace in her life, people even came to her house to ask about Jesus, and many of them became Christians through her witness.

A new house church was formed, and although it was impossible for them to meet in Helena's house, they met for fellowship elsewhere and eagerly studied the New Testament. Helena was the instrument God used to bring the Good News to spiritually hungry, needy people who, until she spoke to them, had no hope of knowing Him on earth or of spending eternity with Him in heaven.

Then one day all hell broke loose.

His footsteps thundering through the hallway, the director of her school stormed into her classroom. "I want to see you in my office immediately!" he shouted. Shaken and scared, Helena quietly followed him down the corridor.

"What is this?" her boss demanded, his face flushed with anger. He threw a book on the table.

"It . . . it's the *Injil*," she stammered.

"It's the book of the Russian God, you fool! Why have you betrayed the Qur'an? Why have you sold out your faith?" He didn't wait for Helena to answer. "There's no need to deny it." He continued his tirade. "I know all about the secret meetings you've been attending. You've brought disgrace on my school and you've put me and my job on the line! If the authorities find out, I'll have nothing but trouble on my hands. Now get out of here! You're fired!"

Helena was trembling all over, and she just wanted to run away. In a daze she picked up her belongings from her classroom, and without a word of explanation to her students, she made her way out the door and rushed through the dark building. As she ran, she pulled on her favorite blue fur-trimmed jacket, and without even taking the time to zip it up, she rushed out into the cold air. A flood of tears streamed down her face.

"Lord Jesus, please help me. What do I do now?" she whispered. She tried to delay the moment she would have to face her family. "What am I going to tell them? They'll think it's a scandal. They are going to be so disappointed in me!"

Helena had no idea what she would say, but a phrase suddenly came into her mind, seemingly from nowhere: *one step at a time.* The more she thought about it, the more she realized that those words applied not just to her present situation, but to the uncertain days that lay ahead.

"What are you doing home so early?" Helena's mother asked.

"I . . . I left my job," Helena said.

"You left? What do you mean, you *quit* your job? Why on earth would you do that? What happened?"

"Well, I didn't exactly quit," Helena began, but she didn't get far into her explanation before her mother started screaming at her, "You deserter! You have turned your back on all of us!" Her mother's biting words hit her like physical blows. It was one thing to be accused by her director, but to hear the same accusations from her own mother was far more devastating.

"You seem to have forgotten how hard we worked to make sure you got a good education! Is this your way of thanking us for getting you into a teaching position? Are you really willing to squander all that for the sake of this 'foreign religion' of yours? You've disgraced our family," her mother ranted. "What are we supposed to do now? The leaders of this community don't just hate you; they hate us too. We are all going to suffer because of you."

"Mother, I'm sorry, but—"

"Shut up! Don't think for a minute that you're going to get away with this. Your father and I will make you pay back every penny we've invested in you!"

On and on she went, and Helena knew very well why her mother was so infuriated—her parents had bribed the school leader and the local officials to make sure Helena got the job. And to make matters worse, since they couldn't afford to pay for the bribe outright, they had struck a deal. They were to pay the rest of the kickback money in installments.

As her mother moved closer, Helena cringed. The fire in her mother's eyes was terrifying. She tried to back away, but it was too late. Unleashing the anger within her, her mother slapped Helena as hard as she could, right across the face. Then she grabbed her daughter by the arm, pulled her closer, and started battering her with hard, fast blows. "I will beat this Russian God nonsense out of you!"

Wildly Helena's mother pounded out all her grief, bitterness, and frustration on her daughter's body. But she still wasn't satisfied. Beating Helena or piercing her soul with outrageous accusations was not enough. They'd been through this kind of scene before, and it never seemed to make much difference. Helena hadn't yet given up her faith.

Finally her mother spat out the worst abuse of all: "Why don't you just kill yourself? That would solve all our problems!" The lines in the older woman's forehead deepened as she spoke, and her eyes reflected nothing but darkness.

Helena intuitively pressed the palms of her hands against her chest. The pain she was feeling inside was too much to bear. She felt as if her heart were breaking. How could a mother ask her own daughter to commit suicide? Dumbfounded, Helena cowered in a corner, immobilized as if she had been nailed to the floor.

"Did you hear me? I told you to kill yourself! Are you listening?" By now, her mother was screaming hysterically. "Don't you see that it would be better for all of us? You wouldn't have to suffer anymore, and neither would we."

Finally Helena summoned the courage to speak. "But, Mother, how can I do that," she answered, nearly choked by her raw emotions. "I can't take my own life. That's not what Jesus teaches us in His Word."

"I don't care what this Jesus of yours says!" her mother screamed. "Can't you just this once think about the good of your family instead of worrying about your own soul?"

Hope for a Better Future

That day was only the beginning. Losing her job opened the door to more severe persecution for Helena. A few days later, her parents marched her to the center of the town square. In front of an angry, jeering crowd, they publicly disowned their daughter. "We are no longer responsible for her bad behavior and for her disgraceful rejection of us and our religion."

"Have her arrested!" someone shouted. "Call the militia and get them to lock her up!"

As she made her way back to her parents' house, Helena knew that it would be impossible for her to live at home any longer. She had no choice but to leave. And, just then, for a fleeting moment, Helena considered suicide. *If I do it,* she promised herself, *I'll do it in the city, not in this town. I won't give them the satisfaction!*

It wasn't the first time she had thought about taking her own life. She had battled with those same dark thoughts years before, at one point consuming an excessive amount of medication in hopes that she would fall asleep and never wake up. But now, as a Christian, her experience with such ideas was much different. Her faith gradually replaced despair with hope for a better future.

Thinking about the past helped Helena to see things in perspective again. She knew that God had prepared a place for her in heaven, but that He was also able to prepare a better life for her on earth. She knew her mother was still under Satan's influence but that God could set her free. He could touch the hearts of her parents, her brother, and her sister. By the time Helena had reached a friend's house, thoughts of death and self-destruction had vanished from her mind. *Never lose hope*, she encouraged herself.

Once or twice, the dark cloud of suicidal feelings overshadowed her again in the days that followed, but Helena's Christian friends helped her to see things from the right perspective. Taking her own life was simply not an option. Satan might want her dead, but God wanted her to live for Him until He decided her task was finished. Besides, killing herself would not solve her family's problems. Coming to Jesus was the only answer for them. No, she must not lose hope. Her family needed her now more than ever. She might not be able to speak to them, but she could pray. And she would no longer be able to pray if she took her own life.

Helena decided to find a job in a neighboring country for a while, and she located one in Kazakhstan. Because there was freedom of religion there, she joined a local church, hoping to find a new group of friends to share her Christian journey with her. But somehow it wasn't the same. She missed the warmth of her own fellowship at home, and she longed to talk to Sonja and her other friends.

Sometimes Helena walked alone until she came to a place in the countryside where no one could see her or hear her. After tucking her long hair into the hood of her coat and shoving her gloved hands deep into her pockets, she would stand beneath the cold winter sky and cry out to God. She begged Him to intervene. She pleaded with Him to let her go home. She asked Him to touch her family and change their hearts. She prayed and cried until peace and hope overtook her anguish and sadness.

After about four months, Helena decided to contact her family. She sat down and wrote a letter to them, telling them how deeply she loved them and missed them. She asked her mother to forgive her and to accept her back. She waited two months for an answer. No response arrived. When after six months she still had not received a reply, she decided to return to her country and talk to them face-to-face.

Helena heard that in the city where she had studied, a training seminar was being organized for new believers. Yearning for fellowship with her old Christian friends, she decided to go. And once she'd made the decision, she couldn't wait to see everyone. Maybe her mother had missed her after all. Maybe her boss realized that he'd made a mistake in firing her. Hope carried her home, but disappointment awaited her there.

"Pray for My Family"

The seminar was wonderful. Seventeen young believers, many of them her old friends, met in a private home. Just to be with them again, to sing together, to study the Word of God—it was food for Helena's hungry soul and water for her thirsty heart. But in the midst of the meeting, they were suddenly startled by loud banging on the door.

"Open up!" a man shouted. And once the door was opened, six policemen burst into the apartment.

"What are you doing? Where are your books?" they demanded.

None of the believers knew quite how to answer. Roughly the officers searched everyone present, including the women. They knew this was a grave insult to local custom, but that was of no concern to them. Afterward, the whole group was marched off to the police station.

"You're going to be here for a long time," one of the policemen snarled. He and the other five officers fired question after question at the young believers. Despite their fears, God did what He promises in His Word. He was with them and He gave them the right words to speak. In fact, they decided to use the opportunity to witness to their aggressors.

"We are loyal citizens of our country," one of the young men said. "We aren't trying to oppose anyone's authority. Several times

187

we have tried to register our meetings, but we always get no for an answer."

Then the young Christians began to describe how Jesus had changed their lives. They explained how He had died for their sins. The officers were quiet, so one believer went on to explain how they had experienced God's love. God had given them joy and hope for the future. They even invited their captors to open their hearts to Jesus. "He can change you too," a young girl said with a smile.

"Stop this nonsense!" one of the policemen shouted. "You'd better be careful, or we'll plant drugs on you. Then you'll never get out of here."

Glancing at one group leader, Helena shuddered. Some of them had wives and young children. She knew the authorities had resorted to this tactic before to harass Christians. *Oh God*, she prayed silently, *please protect us. Don't allow them to do that!*

For six hours the questioning continued, and for six hours the believers explained their faith to their captors. And thankfully, despite the threats and bullying they had endured, all seventeen Christians were released. Two days later, four of them were fined by the city court. They had to pay the equivalent of thirty-seven U.S. dollars.

For Helena, however, the matter did not end there. One of her best friends, a young man who had taken over the Christian group in her hometown, came into the city to warn her. "Helena, I heard you've been hoping to come back home," he told her. "Please don't! The time is not right. Have you seen our local newspaper? Just yesterday there was a story in it about you." He took a carefully folded newspaper clipping out of his pocket. When Helena saw her picture, her hands trembled. She read the story in disbelief.

She was portrayed as an indecent woman, an ingrate who had betrayed her family, an outcast who should be forever shunned. Helena could only imagine what her mother had thought when she read the article—and of course she would have read it. Even if she had somehow overlooked it, some local gossip would have brought it to her attention.

"You were also mentioned on television," her friend told her. "Please listen to me, Helena. Don't come home to your parents now. It will only make matters worse."

"So, what should I do?" she asked tearfully. "I need a job. I wish I could have my old job back, but that seems impossible."

One after the other, her friends tried to help. Sonja offered a place to stay. "My student room at the university is pretty small, but you are welcome to share it with me."

Another friend thought it might be better for Helena to stay in the city for a while. Since she couldn't go home anyway, she might as well try to find work close to the place she was staying.

"We love you, Helena," her friend Gaby said softly as she put her arm around Helena's shoulder. "You're very precious to us. I am sure God wants to use you to help new believers grow in their faith. You could use your teaching skills to lead another group. Why don't we pray for you?"

"Yes, by all means pray for me," Helena interrupted. "But I want you to pray for my family too. Please pray for my brother and sister. They need Jesus so much, and I'm longing to see them. And we all know that nothing is impossible for God—" Helena's voice broke. She was too emotional to say any more, but she didn't need to. Many of her friends shared the same burden for their own family members.

Sonja was the first one to pray. She pleaded with God to show Helena what she should do, to tell her when it would be safe to go home. Others followed, asking the Holy Spirit to touch the hearts of Helena's family members. Then they all began to focus on the power and the greatness of God. They knew that Jesus had come to seek and to save those who are lost. He had come to heal the sick and the brokenhearted, to deliver the oppressed, and to give hope to the hopeless. They sang, they bowed down, and for a while they knelt silently in quiet adoration. And when they finally stopped and prepared to return to their homes, Helena felt that somehow an enormous burden had been lifted from her shoulders.

A Glorious Return

Late in the afternoon of December 31, 2002, Helena boarded a bus. She was feeling a bit shaky, but at the same time she and those who prayed with her believed that it was finally the right time for her to go home. It had been a few months since she had returned to her country from Kazakhstan. Surely by now the effects of the newspaper article had worn off a bit.

Her brother answered her knock on the door. To Helena's surprise he was both friendly and sober. He welcomed her in, took her coat, shawl, and gloves, and put them away. Careful not to mess up her mother's clean linoleum, Helena yanked off her snowy boots. The atmosphere was a bit tense when she walked into the living room, but Helena was amazed at how calm she felt.

The whole family was seated on the floor. Even her father was there. Steaming bowls of *plov*, a traditional rice dish with chicken and local spices, were placed on the tablecloth that was spread on the floor. Flatbread, dried figs, sweets, nuts, and a plate of sliced tomatoes flavored with dill complemented the main dish. To Helena's surprise there was no vodka on the table. Careful not to force her affections on them, Helena went around and politely shook hands with everybody.

"Please join us," her mother said, tearing off a piece of bread and dipping it in a bowl of sour cream. Her tone of voice was friendlier than Helena had dared to hope. Quietly Helena put her cold feet under the table. After an awkward silence, her brother asked her how she was doing, and then he filled her in on what had been happening in town while she was away.

190

Suddenly Helena felt overwhelmed by the presence and authority of the Lord. Without asking permission, she prayed and asked Him to bless the food and the conversation. Then she asked her family to forgive her for any hurt she had caused and for any hard words she had spoken in the past. "We have to forgive each other," she said. "If we do, then God can live in this house."

Nobody reacted badly to what she said, and everyone remained friendly. Her father talked about his time in Kazakhstan, her mother told Helena about the new job she found, and her sister clearly had a story of her own to tell—she was in love. The longer they talked, the more pleasant the atmosphere in the room became.

Shortly before midnight, Helena's father opened a bottle of vodka. Together, they all toasted the New Year. Her sister's boyfriend had joined them for the occasion, and afterward the couple went off to celebrate somewhere else. After their parents went to bed, Helena and her brother were the only ones left in the room.

"Helena, I am fed up," he confided. "I don't want to be addicted to alcohol for the rest of my life. I want to change, but I don't know how. Can you help me?"

"I can't set you free," Helena replied, trying hard not to sound too excited, "but I sure know someone who can!" As their discussion continued on into the night, he revealed other areas in his life that had left him unsatisfied. While praying silently throughout the conversation, Helena gradually felt his heart warm to the message of Christ. By the morning hours of the New Year, her brother had made the choice to follow Jesus as his Savior.

In time Helena's parents also changed. "I feel they are almost ready to accept Jesus," she told Sonja some months later. "My relatives accept me now, and in fact they're eager to listen to the Bible stories I tell them. At last Jesus lives in our home."

Helena has now moved back to her hometown, and her younger sister has accepted Christ. God continues to use Helena to spread the gospel. When she relates her story to others, Helena still feels the pain from the past. She often cries, especially when she talks about her mother. But when she considers the spiritual progress in the lives of her family members, her hope in the living God is renewed. And when she recalls the times that she nearly lost hope, she reflects on a passage of Scripture that has become dear to her heart: "God did this so that . . . we who have fled to take hold of the hope offered to us may be greatly encouraged. We have this hope as an anchor for the soul, firm and secure" (Heb. 6:18–19).

Thinking about Hope

1. Where does the hope of Soon Ok Lee, Helena, and all believers lie?
   Matthew 6:19–21
   Romans 8:18–19
   Ephesians 1:18–19
   1 Timothy 1:1
   1 Timothy 4:10
   1 Timothy 5:5
   1 Timothy 6:17
   1 Peter 1:13
   1 John 3:1–3
2. Contrast what Helena could and could not put her hope in.
3. Where do you put your hope?
4. Is there a situation in your life in which you feel hopeless? What do we learn about God in the following passages that will increase your hope in this situation?
   Psalm 33
   Isaiah 40:31
   Jeremiah 29:11
   Luke 18:27

   Romans 15:13
   Hebrews 13:5–6
   1 Peter 1:13
5. How does the Bible say we can nurture our hope in God?
   Psalm 119:49–56
   Acts 24:14–16
   Romans 5:1–5
   Romans 15:4
6. How will you now pray for your suffering sisters? You might find Psalm 71 and 2 Corinthians 1:3–11 helpful in guiding your prayers.
7. How will you apply the lessons you have learned from the stories about Soon Ok Lee and Helena and the Scriptures you have just studied?

8

Don't Waste Your Sorrows

African people do not just sing with their voice, they use their whole body when they worship God. And they keep singing when life is difficult. In both north and south Sudan, the singing of the Sudanese Christians intrigued me. During the difficult, dangerous, and uncertain years of civil war, which caused many casualties and internal displacement, Christians continued to sing and dance before God. For them it was a way to express their feelings and to process their grief. A Sudanese colleague, who suffered physical abuse and imprisonment, sent me the following song.

> O God our Father, we are weeping too much;
> Almighty God and Father, we are in deep sorrow.
>
> I have completed all my years running;
> I have completed all my years running;

I have completed all my years being chased by
  animals in my own land.
O God our Father, our footprints will be counted in
  grass;
Almighty God our Father, our footprints will be
  counted in grass.

When I lived in my own land, I lacked nothing;
When I cultivated my sorghum, it was snatched by
  animals;
When I think of a far country, I will be a beggar in a
  foreign land.

We have completed all our years running.
O God our Father, our footprints will be counted in
  grass;
We have completed all our years being chased by
  animals in our land.

What can I say about this untimely death of the
  world?
O God our Father, our bones will be picked up from
  the grass.
O God our Father, I bring all these before you;
On this earth I only trust in God.
Almighty God our Father, my case I will present to
  you;
O God our Father, my case I will present before
  you.

China: Shen

Every now and then a tragic situation affirms a sad truth that
we've heard all around the world: *not all persecuted believers
stand strong in times of testing.* Consider "Shen," for example.
Shen was a Chinese Christian woman who has faced some terrible circumstances. She is married to a dedicated Christian

believer named Yun, and when word reached us that Yun had been arrested for Bible distribution in China, we began to pray for them both.

As soon as I heard what had happened, I longed to see Shen. I wanted to talk to her, encourage her, and pray with her, but she refused to see me. And whenever I asked people how she was doing, they always said the same thing: "The news isn't good. Shen isn't coping very well."

After her husband's arrest, Shen stopped going to church. She blamed the Christians for her family's troubles, and her initial anger gradually hardened into bitterness. People tried to comfort her. Church members visited her, sacrificially sharing their own scarce food and scant money. Most of the time they received only a cold shoulder.

To be fair, Shen had ample reason for her disappointment. She had been eager and enthusiastic when she first received the gospel. It had given her and her young husband hope and had offered them a new reason for living. Jesus had not only forgiven their sins, but He had changed Yun from a selfish person into a far more kindhearted husband.

Before long the young couple was active in their house church and Yun began traveling to share the Scriptures with others. Then one day he brought home a stack of Bibles. He had been asked to transport them to Christians in another part of the country. "They need God's Word so badly," he told his wife, "and someone needs to deliver it."

Shen did not object. Jesus had died for them and had changed their lives, so giving something back to Him seemed like the least they could do. Having a generous spirit and being willing to pay the price for loving Jesus were recurring themes in their house-church meetings. With that in mind, Shen waved good-bye to Yun and then prayed faithfully for his safety on his risky mission. She continued to intercede for him in prayer every day he was gone.

In spite of Shen's prayers and hopes, Yun did not return from his trip. The PSB had apprehended him on the train, arrested him, and locked him up. After everything was said and done, Shen's husband was sentenced to seven years in hard labor, and she was left to care for their infant daughter alone.

Some women in such circumstances become stronger Christians as they face their sorrows. Others, like Shen, succumb to the pressure. The Bible tells us that God wants to prepare us for conflict and war. In Psalm 18:33–34 we read, "He makes my feet like the feet of a deer; he enables me to stand on the heights. He trains my hands for battle; my arms can bend a bow of bronze."

Are we willing to give Him our hands so He can make them strong? Or will we keep them hidden behind our backs? Shall we open our hands to receive whatever God chooses for us? Or shall we clench them into angry fists because we don't understand why He occasionally allows pain and sorrow to come our way?

One of the great advantages of getting older is that you can look back and—at least for some times of testing—see God's purpose in the difficulties you've endured. For example, it was far from easy for me, as a twenty-year-old, to say good-bye to my fiancé, Johan, as he left to serve God in war-torn Vietnam. Brother Andrew's remark at Johan's farewell service, "God tells us to go, but he doesn't promise that we'll come back!" didn't make the parting any easier. Yet today, in retrospect, I can see how that year of separation laid a firm foundation for our marriage, which has lasted now for more than thirty-five years.

A few years later, in 1972, Johan and I took our children, my parents' only two grandchildren, to Vietnam with us as we made our way there to serve as missionaries. That was very painful too, especially for my father and mother. But it was at our isolated Asian mission station, during a year of political turmoil, that I learned some very valuable lessons—important lessons that prepared me for decades of future service with Open Doors.

As the wife of a man who travels often, I've faced many hours of loneliness; as the wife of a ministry leader, it has often been difficult to know my place in the ministry. Yet these heartaches helped me understand something of the battles and sorrows faced by women in the persecuted church. My own troubles enabled me to empathize with them and to share a little bit in their suffering.

And then there was the pain that often accompanies motherhood. Johan and I have wonderful kids who give me great joy, but when our two sons rightfully decided to make their own choices in life—and, in the process, not to fulfill all their mother's expectations—I was filled with sadness. Many tears and sleepless nights later, I realized that this experience was teaching me to let go of my sons. I was also learning to work on a weakness in my character—a craving to be in control. It taught me to persevere in prayer and not to give up hope.

As long as we are on this earth, no matter where we live, what we do, or who our loved ones are, there is no way to avoid pain. It's how we handle the pain that makes the difference in how our lives turn out. If we are willing to give our sorrows to God, they won't be wasted.

I thought about Shen when I talked to Grace in south Sudan. Grace's life has been anything but easy, and she has experienced more than her share of heartache, disappointment, and loss. But she has opened her hands to Jesus, and in doing so, she has become strong. Grace did not waste her sorrows but instead turned them into opportunities to bless others.

Sudan: Grace

Beneath the hot African sun, Grace hurried across the courtyard to the teahouse. Guests were coming, and she needed to get everything ready. With open windows to let in the breeze, the spacious, round mud-brick building with its thatched roof fit right in with the other *tukuls* on their compound (*tukuls* are conical huts made of mud bricks or stone, thatched with straw, and common in south and west Sudan).

In the teahouse, Grace and her family received visitors. That afternoon she quickly touched up the interior and rearranged the cushions on the chairs and sofas that lined the yellow plaster walls. As she straightened some of the pictures and plaques, her eyes rested on her husband's favorite, a piece of black slate. In large white letters, it read: "By God's grace I am what I am."

Better than anyone else, Grace knew the truth of those words. Elisha had been a professional builder in their earlier years of marriage, but the love of God had taken hold of him and he had become a pastor in the 1980s. Now he was a bishop, overseeing thirty pastors and twenty-seven congregations in the region.

Grace had married a man of vision. They were surrounded by severe human need of every kind, and Elisha continually sought ways to establish new churches and initiate new projects. He was alert to his people's deficiency in Christian training, and he used his many contacts in the community and abroad to initiate both Bible classes and vocational training programs. Grace was proud of Elisha, but she knew it was only through God's grace that he had become the man he was.

Before long, the guests arrived. Grace was accustomed to receiving people from different parts of the world, and this time it was a mixed group, coming from Europe and Africa. Quietly she served them tea and left most of the talking to her husband. It was his job to inform the visitors about the present situation in Sudan, the largest country in Africa.

After a few words of welcome, Elisha thought it might be a good idea to provide his guests with some background about himself. He was a good-looking man and over six feet tall. Like much of south Sudan's population, he was obviously African, not Arabic.

"My arrival into this world was quite dramatic," he began. "I was born on May 10, 1955. While my mother was in labor, fighting erupted in Yei City Square. As soon as I was born, she wrapped me in a cloth and took me into the bush for safety. That fighting marked the beginning of a power struggle in our area between north and south Sudan that has continued until this day. North Sudan is mostly Muslim, whereas the south has a Christian heritage. But the south also has oil, gold, and diamond reserves and is far more fertile than the north, so Sudan's conflict is not simply one of culture or religion.

"We have suffered a great deal," he continued, absently stroking his bald head. "In the mid-1960s, missionaries were expelled from Sudan. The public schools became Islamic—in fact, I was given the name Mohammed Ali when I started my studies. My father was upset by this turn of events, so he joined the guerrillas and took me with him. At twelve years of age, I became a child soldier. A year later, in God's providence, I was allowed to attend a Ugandan Christian school. That's where I became a Christian.

"We south Sudanese Christians feel as if we are the last remaining wall between Islam and the rest of Africa," Elisha said. He went on to offer more background information about the civil war, their lives, and their ministry. Then, smiling proudly at his wife, he described the impact of women's work. "The income-generating projects that my wife has started have served to motivate, empower, and unify women. They have brought spiritual healing to our community. The women are preaching Christ through their actions."

Several of the guests commented on what Elisha had said, and a few of them asked questions. One woman turned to Grace and said, "Can you tell us about some of the difficulties you've faced in your women's ministry?"

Dressed in an elegant yellow and brown cotton dress, with her dark hair braided in cornrows around her head, Grace was a portrait of African dignity. So far, she had said nothing, but she didn't have to think long before she answered. "When I look back at my life, I can see that nothing came easy," she told the visitors. "Everything I have ever done has been difficult."

Childhood in a War-Torn Country

The civil war in Sudan had started more than ten years before Grace was born, but regardless of the conflict, her caring, middle-class parents tried to make life as pleasant as possible for their children. Her father was a teacher, and he was able to provide for his large family. With three brothers and five sisters, Grace always had playmates. She was never bored, but she was often afraid.

At night Grace could hear the percussion of artillery in the distance. On her way to school, she frequently saw soldiers clad in their green army uniforms, Kalashnikovs or AK-47s slung over their shoulders. She overheard her parents' anxious conversations about how the soldiers living in the bush often extorted money from farmers. She knew that young boys were sometimes kidnapped and forcibly trained to fight against the army from the north. Her oldest brother was a young teenager, and even though Grace was only a child, she understood that her parents were worried that some day he would not come home from school.

In 1972 there was a break in the civil war. In Addis Ababa, north and south Sudan signed an agreement by which the south was granted a measure of autonomy and religious freedom. Not long after that, Grace's father received a promotion. The whole family moved to hot, humid Juba, a provincial center in the heartland of the south, where he became an education officer.

Those were happy times for the family. Many girls her age did not have the opportunity to study, but Grace was fortunate. After completing her primary education, she went to high school and learned practical skills, such as typing. Even though she had to walk half an hour in the blazing sun every day and jump across muddy ruts that filled with water and flooded the streets during the rainy season, she enjoyed going to school and delighted in her studies.

Grace's mother talked to her children in the Bari language, and in school Grace spoke Juba Arabic, the lingua franca among south Sudan's tribal groups. But with keen foresight, her father also taught his children English. This was a huge blessing for Grace when the Sudanese People's Liberation Army (SPLA) later made English the region's official language.

During her teenage years, the seed of the Christian gospel message, sown during her childhood, slowly but surely took root in Grace's heart. She began to understand what Jesus had accomplished on the cross of Calvary. She decided that whatever happened, she wanted to follow Him and be used by Him. In spite of the break in the civil war, serious problems continued in Sudan. Racism and hatred between the different ethnic groups cost many lives. Her people needed hope, and Grace knew, young as she was, that Jesus could give it to them.

Then tragedy struck. Grace's father was only in his fifties, but he fell ill and had to give up his job. The family watched helplessly as he became weaker and weaker, and before long he was completely bedridden. Doctors were unable to diagnose the cause of his illness. They tried all kinds of treatment, all to no avail. Despite the prayers of his family, he died, apparently of heart failure.

Grace's mother decided to move her grieving family back to their native town in Central Equatoria Province, a few hours' drive south of Juba. And not long after their move, the civil war erupted again. In 1983 Colonel Jafaar Nimeiri, the military leader of north Sudan, declared Sharia (Islamic law) to be the law of the land, breaking the Addis Ababa agreement in which south Sudan was promised religious freedom. John Garang, a member of the large Dinka tribe and a graduate of Iowa State University in the United States, reactivated the SPLA. Within two years Garang's guerrilla group had enlisted twenty-five thousand armed soldiers. By 1989, before tribal infighting weakened their position, the SPLA had more than 90 percent of south Sudan under its control.

A Marriage Made in Heaven

Gradually, Grace's grief over the loss of her father diminished. The church their family had joined in Central Equatoria Province was lively and full of young people. Practicing with her church choir was a weekly highlight for Grace, especially because Pastor Elisha, their friendly youth minister, directed it. His shining eyes, broad, gap-toothed smile, and positive attitude endeared him to all his parishioners. He was so amiable that it was hard not to like him. Elisha was several years her senior, and Grace wondered why he was still single. Surely many girls must have wished that someone from his family would come knocking on their door to negotiate a marriage.

Grace didn't see herself as especially attractive. She was shorter than average, and her round face with its high cheekbones seemed too ordinary. In her opinion, many of her friends were much prettier. Grace was quiet, contemplative, and sensitive, and she never stood out in a crowd. So it was a pleasant surprise when Elisha himself showed up at her mother's *tukul* to seek his bride and negotiate her dowry.

Because of the civil war and Sudan's dire economic straits, it was four long years before Elisha and Grace were finally able to marry. But the time was well spent. During the long courtship, their love for each other grew as they worked together in ministry. Grace used her administrative gifts as a church secretary, and she worked in a local office to earn some extra money.

When the dowry was paid and their wedding day finally arrived, it was everything Grace had dreamed about. According to local custom, several goats were slaughtered and a wonderful meal was prepared. The meat was spiced with onions, tomatoes, and garlic. Several dishes seasoned with sorghum were served, along with a cabbage and tomato salad, and a green, spinachlike vegetable called *dodo*. Elisha's and Grace's families exchanged two sets of goats—the legal validation of the wedding. Drums and stringed instruments accompanied singing and dancing, and the party lasted all day and all night.

Grace had good reason to be happy. Unlike many women in her country, she knew her husband loved her. "You are mine forever," Elisha told her as he held her face gently between his hands. "Nobody will ever take you away from me!"

Despite Elisha's optimistic words, both he and Grace knew that in different areas of their vast country, women and children were sometimes abducted by Arab raiders or African tribesmen and taken away as slaves. These captives were exploited and often brutally abused, sometimes forced to serve their masters in unspeakable activities. And there was no way Elisha could promise that such a thing would never happen to his wife.

Cupped Hands Full of Tears

To the great joy of the newlyweds, Grace soon found that she was pregnant. After months of eager anticipation, she gave birth to a son. The infant brought joy to their lives and seemed to make the ever-present smile on Elisha's face even broader. But their joy soon turned into sadness.

After tucking the baby in bed one evening, Grace was enjoying a chat with her mother under the leafy mango tree outside their hut. Suddenly she was alarmed by a strange noise coming from inside.

"Oh, God! My baby!" she cried, rushing to his side. A woman, who was a tenant in their compound, was in the room, a place where she didn't belong. And she was bending over the baby. Startled and defensive, the woman began to make excuses. "I heard a strange noise, so I came in to see what was the matter," she mumbled as she bowed her head and slunk out of the room.

Shaking with fear, Grace picked up her baby. She noticed that some sort of foam was coming out of his little mouth. Clearly he was sick and struggling.

"Elisha!" she screamed at her husband. "Quickly, go and get help!"

Because it was late at night by then, all the local medical services were closed. Elisha frantically rushed around town searching for help, but he was unable to find anyone who knew what to do. At two o'clock in the morning, he and Grace watched helplessly as their tiny son died in his mother's arms.

Grace was devastated. And when she learned the likely cause of their baby's death, she was even more shattered. All the symptoms pointed to the likelihood that Grace's tenant had poisoned the little boy—most likely out of envy. Among some of the Sudanese tribes, such poisonings are not so unusual.

As for Grace, she felt like a piece of her heart had been ripped out, leaving a gaping hole. It took her a very long time to work through the questions of why this had to happen. Grace cried until she had no tears left. "If I could hold my hands like a bowl, it could not contain all the tears I've shed," she said years after the tragedy.

"Let's Start Marching!"

Slowly Grace recovered from her grief. Despite her pain, she continued to be very much involved in Elisha's ministry. The more she worked, the better she felt. And as time went by, an idea began to unfold in her imagination. "Why don't we organize a day of celebration for our church?" she suggested. "Youth choirs from other churches could perform, people could give their testimonies, and we could encourage everyone to invite non-Christian friends."

"Sounds like a good idea," Elisha said. "I think you should go ahead and do it."

Grace quickly went to work. She formed a group of volunteers to organize the events of the day. They contacted area churches, arranged for food, invited choirs to participate, and asked a few Christian young people to share their testimonies.

Less than a week before the event was to take place, Thomas, a former member of their church, came to see Grace. "You'd better cancel the meeting," he warned her. "The Muslims are planning an attack on the church the day of the festival." Thomas's story sounded plausible enough. Grace and Elisha knew him well. He had once been part of their church's youth group but some months before had converted to Islam. They knew he had contacts with the Islamist leadership in the area.

"What should we do?" Grace asked Elisha.

"Pray!" was his answer.

Grace called her volunteers together for a day of prayer and fasting. Time was short, so they decided to pray through the night. The longer they prayed, the more Grace was convinced that they should go ahead with the celebration. Encouraged by the story about King Jehoshaphat, recorded in 2 Chronicles 20, she came up with a plan to march through town a few hours before the meeting on Saturday. When the other leaders agreed, she called the young people together. "Don't come to the celebration if you're afraid," she cautioned them. "We won't look down on you if you decide to stay home."

On Saturday morning a huge and energetic group gathered outside their church. But the senior pastor asked to talk to Grace privately. "Thomas came to see me this morning," he said, his face lined with worry. "He told me that if we go on with the meeting, the Muslims are going to throw bombs into the church."

Grace called the group leaders aside, and their pastor repeated the frightening news. "What shall we do?" Grace asked.

"Let's start marching!" someone said.

"Yeah, it's time to go," somebody else agreed.

So that morning a colorful throng of young people, members of different churches, marched for Jesus through the streets of their town. They beat their drums, they waved palm branches, they worshiped the Lord, and they invited everyone to the festival. "Everybody is welcome at our Jesus Celebration. Join us there today!"

To their surprise, the church was filled to overflowing with far more people than anyone expected. Because of the threat and the public attention, a wealthy Christian, who happened to be in town, heard about the meeting. He decided to purchase lights for the church, so even at night everybody could see what was happening in the front of the sanctuary.

"It feels like Jesus is visiting us here!" Grace shouted to Elisha during one of the songs, trying to make herself heard above the clapping of hands, the throb of drums, and the ululating of the women (ululation is a high-pitched sound that African women often make, intermittently putting a hand over their mouth for effect). Moving with the rhythm of the song, Elisha smiled broadly at his wife. Several people accepted Christ that day as their Lord and Savior. No bombs were detonated and no grenades exploded.

That evening after dark, a young man sneaked through the gate of the pastor's house. It was Thomas, and he had come to ask for forgiveness. He confessed that the Islamic authorities had threatened him, forcing him to terrorize the Christians so they would cancel their meeting.

"God certainly knows how to give the devil a taste of his own medicine," Grace said to Elisha as she crawled under the mosquito net and into bed that night. "I am so glad He gave us peace to go ahead anyway."

"And I am so proud of you," Elisha answered, taking Grace into his arms.

Preaching the Gospel

Elisha became increasingly busy with his ministry and community work. When she could, Grace accompanied him on trips, but she often found herself alone at home. The pain of losing her son still ached inside her, and more severely when Elisha was away. Several of her brothers and sisters now had families. As she watched her little nieces and nephews, it was hard not to be envious. Children were a measure of worth in Sudan, and Grace wondered why God hadn't answered her prayers for another child. Hurtful remarks from her in-laws about her inability to conceive only compounded her sadness.

Meanwhile, in war-torn south Sudan, life was far from normal. More and more, the drone of Antonov planes caused people to run for shelter. Bombings and air raids went on nonstop. Gunfire could be heard at all hours, day or night, as the battlefront edged closer and closer to town.

One day a man walked through the compound's gate and pounded on the front door. "Where is your husband?" he demanded. Grace was alone, and although the visitor was wearing a green army uniform, his olive complexion told her that he was an Arab, not an African. The harsh tone of his voice frightened her, and she steeled herself for what was coming next.

"You'd better tell me the truth, woman. Lying won't do you any good."

As calmly as she could, Grace responded, "My husband is out preaching the gospel." Everyone knew that both the Khartoum government and rebel forces had positioned countless troops in the bush around town, readying themselves for a contest to see

209

who would control the city. She went on to tell him that Elisha had received permission from the local government to leave town and preach in the bush. Once he had received the necessary papers, he had said good-bye to his wife, promising to be back in a few days.

Grace was telling the truth. An evangelist at heart, Elisha always took every opportunity to share the message of Jesus. This time he had taken the Jesus film as a tool to reach local people who had never heard about Jesus. But Grace's unwelcome visitor suspected that Elisha sympathized with the SPLA, was in touch with their leaders, and was using his position as a church leader to cover his underground activities.

"My husband went to share the gospel of Jesus Christ," Grace repeated, speaking the truth once again, firmly and clearly. Still the man did not believe her.

"I'll be back," he said coldly.

He did come back, night after night, often bringing others with him. Grace struggled with increasing fear, and friends from the church slept at her house, ready to come to her aid in case the unwelcome visitors tried to harm her. During those days, the soldiers' intrusions became more and more threatening. But every evening Grace gave the same answer. Her statements never changed. "My husband went to preach the gospel. He has permission from the local authorities."

Finally, to Grace's enormous relief, Elisha returned home unharmed. But the news he'd heard in the bush was not encouraging. They were in for trouble. A big battle was brewing.

Refugees in the Bush

By 1990 Sudan's civil war had dramatically intensified. Fighting erupted in the streets, and the situation became extremely dangerous. Grenades were exploding everywhere; sniper fire was taking the lives of innocent civilians. Local families spent hours in makeshift bomb shelters—little more than deep holes dug into the ground—hoping to shield themselves from flying shrapnel and exploding bombs.

One day Elisha received some inside information that a huge battle between the government and the SPLA was imminent. "Quickly," he told Grace, "pack some clothes and some food. We need to get out of town."

As much as she wanted to protest, Grace knew her husband was right. It was clearly too dangerous to stay. Many of their neighbors had already fled into the bush, and if Grace and Elisha didn't leave now, they might never have another opportunity.

They headed out on foot, and Grace valiantly tried to keep up with her husband's hurried pace, striding for hours through thorny shrubs. After hours of walking, Elisha cut some elephant grass and laid it out on the ground. That would be their bed for the night. Too tired to think or worry, Grace fell asleep. But when the orange morning sun woke her the next day, she was faced with a hard reality. Grace and Elisha could now count themselves among Sudan's millions of displaced persons, refugees without a home.

After they had found a refugee camp far enough from the fighting to settle down for a while, they discovered just how many new challenges they faced. They had never lived in the bush before. Which roots and plants were edible? How could they grind maize without a grinding stone? Without a river nearby, where would they wash their clothes? How could they cook without cooking pots?

Thankfully, Grace and Elisha weren't the only city people in the camp. Many others like them were totally unprepared. But by learning from one another and pooling their knowledge, the resourceful refugees soon acquired the skills they needed to survive in the harsh environment of the African bush. They looked for stones to use for grinding; animal dung served as fuel; water was boiled in tin cans. They lived in tents made from bamboo sticks that held up a grass roof.

Elisha learned to capture bush rats and large birds, adding protein to their deficient diet of roots, cassava, and whatever fruit they could find on trees. Little by little, life regained some sense of normality, but many nights they went to sleep hungry. *Thank God He never gave us another child*, Grace thought at times. *He knew what He was doing. He could see what lay ahead.*

Realizing it might be years before they could return home, they moved on to a village near the Congolese border called Laso. Elisha managed to build a *tukul*, and as best she could, Grace settled into her new life. Always thinking ahead, Grace had taken as much wool and as many knitting needles with her as she could manage. Now they came in handy. She knitted baby clothes and took them across the border to sell or barter for food. Grace was gifted at organizing people, and she did her best to make life easier for the many refugees surrounding them, helping women learn ways to support themselves.

Laso was in SPLA–controlled territory, and the rebel army's commanders soon realized that Grace was a lady with special skills. When they heard she could type, they began to bring her documents. Many of these contained classified material. Grace obeyed their orders, but as she typed, she became aware that she was reading confidential information pertaining to the SPLA's battle plans. At the time it didn't occur to her that knowing about such things might complicate her life in unwelcome ways.

Called to Serve

The civil war raged on, and by about 1990 more than a million people had already died. Casualties of war and famine would eventually swell to two million before a cease-fire held. Juba, Yambio, Kaputa, Yei, and many other towns in Central Equatoria Province were now in the Khartoum government's hands.

Elisha and Grace's family members were scattered. Some of her sisters' families had found refuge in Europe and the United States, and her mother had fled to Uganda. But Elisha and Grace didn't want to leave. With their country at war, the Sudanese people's spiritual needs were as great as their physical needs, and Christians who could teach the Word of God were scarce. The battle wasn't just about power, land, or oil; a spiritual war was raging too. Religious freedom for the people of south Sudan was at stake.

One afternoon soldiers came to the *tukul* in Laso. "Where is Pastor Elisha?" one of them demanded. When Elisha appeared, they quickly came to the point. "We need your wife," they said. "We want to give her military training. She'll be back after twenty-one days."

Elisha had no choice but to let Grace go, and she assumed she'd be doing more administrative work for a few days. Even though Elisha didn't always agree with the SPLA's tactics, like most south Sudanese, he supported the primary causes of the freedom fighters. And as an internal refugee, he longed for the war to stop so they could return home.

Twenty-one days went by, but Grace did not return to Elisha. Instead, the army took her to the battlefront near Juba and Torit, where she underwent military training alongside the men. Perhaps the SPLA thought they had to protect the confidential information Grace had typed by keeping an eye on her twenty-four hours a day.

For weeks she and the other recruits were marched through the bush. They lived on wild fruits and roots of plants. Sometimes they were given corncobs to make porridge. Grace's rifle magazine doubled as a cooking pot. At night she and the others had to construct their own grass shelters where they would sleep. Sometimes the bush and elephant grass tore their clothes, and somewhere along the way, Grace's shoes completely wore out.

Grace was nearly dead physically and emotionally, but her spirit was very much alive. Her relationship with God kept her going. "Jesus, help me!" she prayed many times a day, determined to keep her eyes on Him and not on her circumstances. Her faith became her lifeline, and the presence of Jesus was very real to her. She knew He was walking right next to her, and sometimes it almost seemed as if He had been carrying her when she could no longer walk on her own.

Even after the troops arrived at their final destination, Grace's life did not get any easier. At the battlefront, she was placed in command of a group of soldiers. Her organizational skills were always in demand, and she continued to receive on-the-job management training. Whenever an SPLA dignitary came to visit the troops, she was put in charge of logistics, planning and preparing the meals.

Grace was small and prone to illness, not at all cut out to be a soldier, yet she learned to fight alongside the men. She hated being trained to shoot other people and was grateful she never actually had to kill anyone. Though several men in the army were dedicated Christians, the ruthlessness of some of the other soldiers appalled her.

Those were difficult days for John Garang's SPLA. The defection of Dr. Riek Machar and most of his Nuer tribesmen, forming the Southern Sudan Independence Movement (SSIM), had weakened the SPLA.[6] The fall of the Mengistu government in Ethiopia, a staunch supporter of the movement, was also a crucial setback. As a result of all this, the rebel army was losing ground in south Sudan.

Even though they fought together against their enemy, Grace could see that the soldiers were far from united. The intricacies of lineage, tribe, clans, tribal subdivisions, different religions, and the hierarchy of the leadership—all of these caused undercurrents of dissatisfaction within the SPLA movement. It was a world Grace often longed to run away from.

"Lord, I can't do this anymore!" she cried out one day. "Please get me out of here!" It was certainly not the first time she had prayed that prayer. But at long last, she was about to see God's answer.

Elisha missed his wife terribly. He longed to have her at home with him, but he knew the SPLA would not easily let her go—she knew too much and was too great an asset to their cause. Then he had an idea. The SPLA had many critical needs. Perhaps if he could offer them something they desperately needed, they might be willing to provide something in return.

It was common knowledge that the soldiers were short of diesel fuel for their trucks. So with the help of Grace's brothers and her uncle, who was also the bishop in the church and a man of great influence, a deal was made. This uncle contacted one of the leaders of the SPLA and made an offer. If they would release Grace, he would give them twelve barrels of diesel fuel for their trucks.

It worked. The army leaders accepted the offer. Then Grace heard some news that took her totally by surprise. "You are summoned back to Torit. Our commander wants to see if you are fit to graduate as a captain."

Hoping against hope that her prayers were about to be answered, Grace packed her stuff and started on her journey. In Torit, to her great relief, Grace received her final rank and was allowed to return home to Laso. At last, after being separated for more than a year, Grace and Elisha were reunited.

The two of them had always shared the gospel wherever they went. And now, in their new life among other refugees, those around them were more than ready to listen to the good news about Jesus. The Khartoum army, which marched in the name of Islam, was hated. That brutal Islamist regime tried to force conversions among the Christians and animists in south Sudan, but as a government, they did nothing for the people. The countless women, men, and children who had never heard the Christian gospel were open to its message of hope. They put their trust in the God who had sent His only Son simply because He loved them—the despised, poor, beleaguered inhabitants of south Sudan.

As a result of their success in soul winning, Elisha and Grace's task of providing for the spiritual nurturing of all the new believers was overwhelming. "We need Bibles, Grace," Elisha told his wife. "I'm going to go to Uganda to find help. These new believers have got to be grounded in the Word. If we don't teach them the principles of the Bible, the seed that's been sown in their hearts will wither before it has a chance to take root."

Elisha was gone for several weeks, but when he came home he was energized and optimistic. Through a providential turn of events, he had met "William," a Christian man who served with Open Doors. In due time, thousands of Bibles were supplied to Sudanese believers, and at a later stage, hundreds of pastors received theological training. In William, Elisha found a real friend, a ministry partner on whom he could rely.

The Return to Yei

After years of waiting, Elisha and Grace were finally able to return home. Government soldiers had withdrawn from the area, and Yei was now in the hands of the SPLA. Grace was thankful, but buried deep in her heart was a hidden sorrow. She had to face up to that pain once and for all.

After all the years since the death of their precious little son, Grace had never again conceived. By now she realized that she and Elisha might never have a child of their own. She knew that in their culture it would be normal for Elisha to take another wife; in fact, her in-laws had made that very clear to her. Grace knew that her husband would love to have children too, but he never blamed her. When she finally brought up the subject, he took her hand and simply said, "We'll face the pain together."

After they returned home, Grace hardly had time to think about what she was missing. Thousands of refugees were returning from the bush. The church was starting to function again, but they almost had to start from scratch since the fighting had destroyed so many of the homes and buildings in town. To deal with the countless war orphans, an orphanage was established in their neighborhood, and before long, Grace and Elisha had welcomed three of the children into their home. Once again thinking about God's wisdom and sovereignty, Grace could see that although her womb might never carry another child, her heart and her arms could always be full of children.

At the same time, Elisha's partnership with William was flourishing. Before long Elisha was appointed as bishop for their region. While he was away, teaching or distributing Bibles to needy congregations, Grace used her experience to organize the women's ministry in their church, and she welcomed the many women and children who came to her home for assistance.

While in the bush, she had heard stories of families who had been evicted from their lands and homes, their *tukuls* and crops set afire by the Khartoum army. She had met women who had been kidnapped and later escaped, and she had listened to victims of rape. Those tragic tales were now repeated almost daily in her own house. Untold numbers of women were trapped in a cycle of despair. In Grace's desire to help, she called for a time of prayer and fasting.

The Start of a Great Ministry

Later on, as a group of the women prayed, one of them had an idea. The church owned some property near the river Yei, and the river contained sand, a much needed commodity in Sudan for rebuilding roads and structures So Grace organized a work force—she called it the Women's Project. The participants did not have wheelbarrows or other equipment, but with cans, small

217

containers, or anything else they could find, they began to scoop sand from the riverbed.

Gradually the pile of sand grew higher and higher. It was tedious, hard work. Thirty women started, but by the time the project began to generate money, only seventeen were left. A man working for a nongovernmental organization (NGO) was so impressed with the women's hard work that he became their first customer. After his first purchase of sand, Grace could pay her workers. She was careful not to spend all the money, however. She needed funds to finance other projects that could provide help for more Sudanese women.

Since numerous people from abroad had started to visit their area, another idea for a profitable women's business came to light. The women started to construct a guesthouse. An aid worker donated one thousand dollars. Workers began to cut away the high elephant grass, clearing the ground to put up the first guest *tukul*. Many more bright yellow conical cement huts with thatched roofs were built in the years that followed. Grace used some of the money she'd made from the sand business to buy mattresses. The more paying guests came, the more *tukul*s could be built. The Women's Project was thriving.

Then Grace heard that her husband's friend William had given a bag of Kenyan seed to some impoverished pastors. Growing vegetable gardens had helped the pastors feed their churches' families, and they also sold some of the produce in a local market. "Please! Could I have a bag of seed too?" she begged William. "Growing vegetables could generate more income for the Women's Project."

That one bag of seed resulted in a wonderful harvest of onions, tomatoes, garlic, and cabbages—and more seeds. By now the women were getting really excited. Ladies from other churches joined the workforce. News about other possibilities spread, and the Women's Project, now the Christian Women's Empowerment

Project (CWEP), became a means for sharing the love of Jesus with those who did not know Him.

With the help and advice of different agencies, the work of CWEP was reorganized. Different projects were assigned to different church groups. Every group of women decided on what they wanted to do. And while they put together their strategies for success, Grace brought together trustworthy leaders from several churches to train them spiritually.

They initiated new projects. They extended small loans. Women became involved in vegetable production, goat rearing, tie-dying colorful fabrics, making handcrafts, producing shea butter ointment, sewing children's clothes to sell locally, making soap, manufacturing bricks—new ideas continued to materialize. Now, less than ten years after the sand business was initiated, the whole district around town is involved, and the CWEP has opened branches in other regions.

A lot has changed, but the vision remains the same. "My main aim in starting the Women's Project was to share the gospel with women in need," Grace tells her visitors. "Our primary focus should be on preaching the Word of God."

She gets excited when she tells about the widows who are now able to provide for their families. Grace smiles when she reports that through their brick-making project, street kids are finding jobs and their addictions to alcohol and drugs are being broken. But she firmly believes that in the long run, lasting fruit will be realized not only when women's outward circumstances change, but when their spiritual lives are transformed from the inside out. And only Jesus can do that.

Glory Belongs to God

For a long time Grace and Elisha had looked forward to a special celebration. More than twenty pastors from all over south Sudan had completed an advanced theology course and were graduating. A few hundred people gathered under two large mango trees at a Bible training site that Elisha and William had recently developed.

Grace was up at the crack of dawn, organizing lunch for more than two hundred people. When the first guests arrived, a cow and several goats had already been slaughtered, bread dough was rising, and cabbage, tomatoes, and onions were being cut up. When Grace was sure everything was under control, she took her place among the guests of honor.

After a while, it was Elisha's turn to speak. "This is a miracle," he began joyfully. "And for a miracle, no one takes the glory. It belongs to God!" Thinking back over her life, Grace knew that this was true for her too. Only God deserved the credit for whatever she had been able to achieve.

While they gathered in the shade, peace negotiations between the government of Khartoum and several liberation movements from the South were going on in Kenya. Several of the morning speakers talked about a new day dawning for Sudan. For the first time in years, there was hope for peace. But Elisha and Grace were very aware that the new Sudan would have challenges all its own.

For now, Islam had failed to win the war with guns, but everyone knew that the Islamists would never give up. From all over the Islamic world, money was already pouring in for schools and health services. Grace and Elisha needed to reach their communities with the Christian gospel before the Muslims reached them with the Qur'an. Perhaps the battle for the hearts and minds of Sudan's people would no longer be fought with guns, but it would be fought with ideologies. Grace knew that she and her husband were at the forefront of that battle.

Still, she smiled as she looked at the beaming faces around her. Grace knew that beyond the shadow of a doubt, the church in her country was much larger and stronger than it had been twenty years earlier when she'd married Elisha. The struggle was not over, but her hands had been trained for battle (see Ps. 18:34) through all the difficulties she'd encountered. Her hardships had made her creative. The suffering she'd endured had taught her to comfort others. Grace had not wasted her many sorrows, because through all her heartaches, she had learned to rely on Jesus.

Thinking about Suffering

1. What do the following verses teach us about God?
   1 Samuel 2:6–8
   1 Chronicles 29:10–13
   Isaiah 46:9–10
   Matthew 10:29–30
2. God knows about our suffering. What would He like us to learn from it?
   Matthew 5:10–12
   Romans 5:1–5
   2 Corinthians 1:3–7
   2 Corinthians 12:7–10
   2 Timothy 3:12
   1 Peter 4:12–19
3. Contrast the differences in how Shen and Grace responded to suffering. Why do you suppose Shen reacted the way she did?
4. How was God able to work through Grace?
5. How will you respond to suffering?
6. What have you learned in this chapter that will help you as you pray for your persecuted sisters?

9

Reach Out to Others

In China many rural house churches conduct their own basic discipleship and evangelism training. Young people, barely in their twenties, gather for biblical instruction, after which they immediately leave for the mission field. In teams of two, they are given enough money for a one-way trip to their destination and the name of one Christian contact or some church member's relative in a village. From there they reach out and share the Good News with their target community, often at great personal cost and hardship. An Open Doors co-worker witnessed the final commissioning of a group of students after a training session. Following one last exhortation and a final prayer, they sang this song before going their separate ways.

Entering a new day
With sweet joy in my heart
The first words from my mouth are
"O Lord, I thank you."

Pour down your anointing
Bathe me in your love
Call out my name
And lead me into your life.

Grant me wisdom, courage, and strength
To stride over high mountains, traverse great rivers,
    gallop across vast lands
Determined to spread the Good News in every
    village,
In the valleys and by the brooks.

Step-by-step I walk on
Step-by-step till the very end
A new day, a new era
O Lord, I speak forth of You.

Lu Xiaomin, *Songs of Canaan*, 26

China: Xinran

Xinran and Wang had traveled all night. Since Wang was a well-known house-church leader, it was too dangerous for us to meet them in their hometown. Clearly Xinran was tired, although she did her best not to show it. Neatly dressed, her thin black hair tied back, she smiled warmly at us from across the table.

Wang told us about his life and his ministry. After he'd talked for a while, it was time for us to hear from Xinran. Her eyes lit up when I asked her to tell us about herself.

"I am a nurse in the local hospital," she began, "and I love my work."

I was surprised to hear her telling us about her career. Her husband had just described his many travels, including a narrow escape when the Public Security Police raided one of his clandestine training places. For four years he had been living the life of a fugitive to avoid arrest.

During Wang's years on the run, from time to time Xinran met him in secret locations. Risky as it was, sometimes she even brought their son along. After four years the PSB finally caught up with Wang, arrested him, and sentenced him to prison. He has since been released, but because of his history, he will always attract scrutiny from the Chinese authorities.

Xinran didn't say a word about the hardships she'd suffered as the wife of a well-known Christian leader. She preferred to talk about her work at the hospital. "I have so many opportunities to share the gospel," she smiled. "After I've finished for the day, I often visit the wards. One of the surgeons tells his patients that he can heal only their bodies. But he goes on to say, 'If you want healing for your soul, go find Sister Xinran.'

"When Christians are admitted to the hospital," Xinran continued, "their believing friends come to visit. Whenever we can, we try to have a Christian meeting on the ward, using opportunities such as Christmas and Easter to share the gospel. Last year more than five hundred people accepted Christ!"

I couldn't believe my ears. Was this really happening in a government hospital in Communist China? Wang must have seen my questioning look. "Of course what Xinran does is forbidden in our country," he explained. "And it's a miracle that she gets away with it. The hospital's management team like her, so they turn a blind eye. They know that she often helps poor people who can't afford their medicine. Her superiors also know that her words soothe the patients' inner pain. As much as I would like to have her traveling with me, Xinran is doing an amazing job of evangelism right where she is."

I couldn't keep my eyes off Xinran. Here was a woman who had suffered intense loneliness and loss. Johan and I knew that after Wang was taken to prison, the PSB had ransacked her house. They had taken for themselves whatever they wanted, vandalized the rest, and left behind a litter of broken furniture and the contents of looted drawers and cupboards. When friends came to her aid, they were surprised to find that Xinran was very much at peace. "We've always said that everything we own belongs to Jesus," she told them. "So I've never allowed myself to get attached to things. I miss Wang's presence in the house a lot more than I miss my furniture."

How did Xinran remain so calm and collected in the face of such enormous challenges? It seems obvious that reaching out to others enabled her to cope and that ministering to them helped her not to focus on her own problems.

In some ways, I feel ill equipped to write about reaching out to others. In recent years more than one of my friends has lost her husband to death. Others have experienced the trauma of divorce. A few months ago one friend lost her thirty-four-year-old daughter following heart surgery. A woman from our church has suffered from kidney failure for decades, and just this week she was told that part of her leg needs to be amputated. Another colleague is fighting for his life as cancer destroys his body. When I think about all these beloved people and the heartaches they bear, my own difficulties seem almost trivial.

God gave me a perfect match for a husband. I've never lost a child and have never been seriously ill. But at times I have been faced with emotional pain, rejection, loneliness, and lack of support. And more than once I've been tempted to slump on the couch and feel sorry for myself.

Don't get me wrong. I'm not suggesting that any of us should deny pain or escape it by keeping ourselves overly busy. There is a time to mourn and grieve. But through the lives of Xinran and Alia, I think we can all learn, even when we are faced with the worst hardships or heartbreaks, that we need to give of ourselves anyway. As we reach out to others— and I've seen it proved true at home and abroad—God reaches out to us and ministers to our deepest needs.

Iraq: Alia

Alia was weighed down with depression. As she rode toward her home along a palm-lined boulevard in a prosperous Baghdad neighborhood, she didn't notice when the bus passed the giant bronze statue of Saddam Hussein on Firdos Square. It was the prospect of walking into her empty house—once again—that made her feel so sad. The seemingly endless war between Iraq and neighboring Iran had taken her husband, Yousif, away from her. He had been drafted and was serving in the army, and she missed him painfully.

Six years before, while they were both attending university in Mosul, she had fallen in love with Yousif Matty, a solidly built student with wire-rimmed glasses and a moustache. His powerful personality and great sense of humor attracted her. After their wedding in 1980, both Yousif and Alia found good jobs in Baghdad.

Then all too quickly, Yousif was conscripted into the army. Although he was trained as a geologist, the army assigned him a job as a radar technician in Basra, where he had to identify enemy planes. He was allowed to return home for a family visit only four days a month. And that certainly didn't make for the kind of marriage Alia had always dreamed about.

227

In Mosul Alia had earned a B.A. in physics, which qualified her to be head of production at a local factory. She was thankful for her good job, but the war and Yousif's absence had robbed her of her upbeat and optimistic perspective.

The youngest of five children, Alia had grown up in a well-to-do family in Kirkuk, a few hundred miles northeast of Baghdad. They were a happy family—Alia's father was a businessman and the family lived in a spacious, comfortable house. As the baby in the family, Alia was spoiled and protected. Not only were all her needs met, but many of her wants as well.

On Sundays her whole family had attended the ancient Chaldean Catholic Church. Centuries before, it had separated from the Roman Catholic Church, while retaining its Eastern form of liturgy recited in the Aramaic language. After they were married, true to tradition, Alia and Yousif continued to attend church there, but Alia found no solace or help in the liturgy or tradition.

A Changed Life

One evening there was a knock on Alia's door. "Oh, Ayad!" she cried out as she embraced her handsome brother. "I'm so glad to see you!" Like many Iraqis, Alia's brother had found work abroad. Now he was on his way home to visit his parents in Kirkuk.

Alia was overjoyed to have her brother's company, and she went out of her way to cook him a nice meal. As they sat at the dinner table and tried to get caught up with each other, it was clear to Alia that her brother had changed. He had never been especially interested in religion, yet now he couldn't stop talking about the church he attended in London.

"Come with me this weekend, Alia," he said with a smile. "There's an evangelical church in Kirkuk, and I want to take you there. When you see the difference with your own eyes, you'll understand what I'm so excited about—Christianity is about having a relationship with Jesus Christ, not just about form and tradition. Jesus has changed my life, and you need Him too, Alia."

More than a little curious, Alia accompanied Ayad to church the following Sunday, and she wasn't disappointed. The lively worship in the Kirkuk sanctuary was certainly different from anything she'd experienced in Chaldean Catholic services. Everyone was friendly, including the pastor's wife. After the service, the older woman made a point of talking to Alia. "I hope you'll come again next Sunday!" she said as they parted.

From then on, Alia often spent weekends in Kirkuk. A warm friendship developed between her and the pastor's wife. One day, sensing Alia's depression, her new friend finally said, "Alia, you need Jesus."

"But I've gone to church all my life," Alia protested. Even though she struggled not to admit it, she knew the pastor's wife was right. She did need Jesus. She knew that her brother had found something wonderful in Him, and she wanted it too.

The pastor's wife opened her New Testament to the Gospel of John, chapter 1. The passage spoke of Jesus, who had been sent as God's heavenly Light into the darkness of the world. She read verse 12 aloud: "To all who received him, to those who believed in his name, he gave the right to become children of God."

Then she urged Alia, "Don't you want to do that, Alia? Don't you want to believe in Jesus, to receive Him into your life and to become God's child?"

"Yes, I do," Alia nodded. She prayed with her new friend, asking forgiveness for her sin and accepting Jesus, the Son of God, as her personal Savior. Even before she opened her eyes again, she knew she had been touched and warmed. Alia's house was full of lovely possessions, but her heart had long been empty. From now on, Jesus would live there.

When Yousif returned home on military leave, Alia had a lot to tell him. She was disappointed that he didn't understand what she

was talking about. It would be several years before he acknowl-
edged his spiritual need and accepted Jesus Christ.

A Growing Family

After she and Yousif had been married for two years, Alia gave
birth to her daughter Noor (light), who brightened Alia's days.
Of course, being the mother of an infant also added to her daily
burdens. When she was well enough to go back to work, she had
to arrange for someone to stay with Noor. Coming home from
work was much more pleasant now. Alia's house was no longer
empty. Every evening as she walked through the door, her little
daughter greeted her with a smile.

Eleven months after Noor's arrival, another baby girl was born.
Her proud parents called her Farrah (joy). Alia's joy increased,
but so did her responsibilities. Yousif was still serving in the army,
and Alia found it harder to cope with her job while the Iran-
Iraq war dragged on with no end in sight. She longed to have a
normal family life, without continuously having to say good-bye
to Yousif. Scores of young Iraqi men had been killed, and every
time Yousif left, she couldn't help but wonder if she would ever
see him again.

"Mommy, Uncle came home!" Noor called out to Alia one day.
It was Yousif she was talking about, and Alia was troubled that
her husband was a stranger to his own children. After a couple
of days, Noor called him Daddy, but by then it was time for him
to leave once more.

After some years, Alia's position in the factory changed, leaving her less time for her family. She had to leave home at six in
the morning and did not return until five in the afternoon. She
hated leaving her children with others, and to complicate matters
further, she was expecting another baby. When Farrah was three
years old, Alia gave birth to a little boy. Yousif was overjoyed to
have a son, and they named the baby Mejid (glory). He was a

delightful little boy, but Alia was more and more overwhelmed by her heavy workload.

By now the constant pressure was seriously wearing her down. When she looked in the mirror, she was appalled to see her lank hair and pale complexion and the dark shadows under her eyes. She bore little resemblance to the trim, high-energy young woman she had once been. Her new faith had given her hope, but she was still faced with more than her share of difficulties. *Is God trying to teach me something about suffering?* she wondered. She moved closer to her parents, made some changes in her work responsibilities, and somehow managed to get through one day at a time.

Finally, in 1988, the senseless war, which ultimately claimed an estimated 1.5 million lives, ended with a United Nations mandated cease-fire. To Alia's immense relief, Yousif returned home. And by that time, he was a changed man. He too had come to know Christ. The young family grew in grace and enjoyed together the teaching, fellowship, and friendship they found in the Kirkuk Evangelical Church.

The First Gulf War

When Yousif returned from his military service, his salary stopped, so he needed a job urgently. To Alia's relief he was hired as a geologist for an oil company, but life was not normal for long. They had just moved to a different house in Kirkuk when Saddam Hussein summoned his armies to invade Kuwait. It wasn't long before President George H. W. Bush rallied a coalition of Western allies and launched an offensive against Iraq. Yousif was conscripted again. With a heavy heart he left his three young children and his wife, returning reluctantly to his former duties as a radar technician.

This time the battlefront was not at some remote place in the desert. Bombs began to fall on Kirkuk. During the first week of the war, Alia's water service was cut off, and the electrical power failed. For forty days she heard no news from her husband and was uncertain whether he was dead or alive. And Yousif wasn't her only worry. Day and night helicopters roared overhead, accompanied by the sounds of heavy shelling and exploding bombs. Her face etched with tension, Alia moved her three little ones into the basement, where they hunkered down and pleaded with God for protection.

The war with America and its allies soon ended, but afterward Kirkuk was far from a safe city. Kurds in the north were now fighting with Shiites in the south of Iraq. In the meantime, Yousif had not returned home, and Alia was increasingly desperate. The streets were full of tanks and soldiers. She decided to take the children to her brother's house for shelter. Not long after they arrived, to Alia's amazement, Yousif appeared at the door.

"How did you know we were here?" she asked, a big smile softening her weary face.

"I figured you must have come here since you weren't at home. You have no idea how glad I am to be back!" He shook his head and rubbed his stubbly chin. "It's a miracle I made it! You wouldn't believe the destruction! Almost all the bridges are out. I hitchhiked home, riding in so many different cars on so many different roads! This war was bad enough, but the aftermath may turn out to be even worse."

As the couple talked for hours about all they'd been through, Alia told Yousif that her parents had died while he was away, and their house—her childhood home—was vacant and available to their family. After some days of hard work they settled into the roomy mansion. At last the children had plenty of room to play. The elegant wooden furniture, the Persian carpets on the tiled floors, and the peaceful setting were all very much to Alia's liking. The electricity had come back, and now she even enjoyed the luxury of having her own washing machine and electric oven.

"I could spend the rest of my life here," she told Yousif with a happy sigh. For a while it looked as if she might be able to do just that. The oil company had rehired Yousif, the children had started school, and their family was able to spend every evening together.

Kirkuk is situated on the border between north and south Iraq. Many Kurdish people lived in the city's poor Kurdish zones, and Saddam Hussein was no friend of theirs. Suddenly one day, the sound of helicopters and gunfire rattled the windows.

"Alia, come and see!" Yousif had rushed outside, and Alia quickly joined him at the front gate. Together they stared in horror as scores of terrified Kurds fled from the shelling to safer areas in the city. One young boy carried his wounded grandfather on his shoulders. Mothers clutched their babies, their older children clinging to their skirts, screaming in fear. Young Kurds supported crippled old relatives who were unable to run.

"Why is Saddam trying to kill these people?" Yousif raged. "Is it only because they want to speak their own language?"

That evening he and Alia prayed for the desperate Kurds they had seen that day. As they prayed, an unmistakable impression came into Yousif's mind. He was sure God was speaking to him through His Holy Spirit, and he immediately told his wife.

"Alia," Yousif said somberly, "I think God is calling us to go and tell the Kurdish people about Him." Alia did not know what to say.

As Saddam's ethnic cleansing continued, thousands of Kurds fled across the border into northern Iraq. Baghdad brutally crushed Kurdish attempts to establish their own state, and eventually the United Nations established a security zone.

Yousif and Alia were unable to forget the terrified Kurds they had seen fleeing Kirkuk. By now those few had multiplied into tens of thousands of needy refugees. "I wonder if any of them know

Jesus," Yousif said to his wife. "Listen, Alia, I have to go try to help them. I know that's what the Lord wants me to do."

Yousif purchased some Christian books and began to make monthly visits to the north. Quickly he discovered that the church in northern Iraq was composed of minority groups: Assyrians, Chaldeans, and Armenians. Each of these minority groups had their own church and kept their Christianity very much to themselves and their own community, and there was no Kurdish-speaking evangelical church to be found.

A Time of Preparation

Alia shared Yousif's burden for the Kurds. Together they often prayed for the Kurdish people he met on his trips, and they both longed for the Kurds to come to know Jesus. But whenever Yousif suggested that they move their family to live among the Kurdish people, Alia protested. "That's too hard for me," she objected. "I don't know anyone there. I'm an Iraqi, Yousif. I can't be Kurdish. Plus it would be too much of an adjustment for the children."

But one day, as she read her Bible and prayed, she heard God speak very clearly to her heart. "Go and tell the Kurdish people that I love them."

Six months after they had moved into her old family home, Alia was out running errands, and while she was walking down the street, once again she heard the Holy Spirit's voice speaking to her: "Alia, do you want to follow Me or not?"

"Of course I do, Lord!"

But now a fierce battle began in her heart. Satan did everything he could to distract Alia from God's call. One by one, as if in a movie, he showed her all the things she loved so much about their home. In her mind's eye she saw the furniture, the new television, the washing machine, and all her clothes. *You'll lose every bit of this if you move north*, she thought. *You won't be able to take anything with you, and once it's gone, you'll never get it back.*

God had been Alia's lifeline during so many difficult years, and she had made it her habit to turn to him in prayer. Now she cried out, "Jesus, if You really want me to do this, then please give me the strength to obey."

As soon as she spoke the words, Alia felt a change in her spirit. The devil had tried to bind her, she realized, but now she was free.

Shortly afterward, a friend warned Yousif that his life was in immediate danger. Saddam's security forces were aware of his frequent trips to the north. His involvement with the Kurds was considered treasonous, and his name had been added to Saddam's hit list. An inside military source let Yousif know, on no uncertain terms, that soldiers had been ordered to arrest him the very next day.

As darkness fell, the Matty family walked away from their beautiful home in Kirkuk. Alia was able to take along only two suitcases, leaving all the rest behind. But God had prepared her heart before she was put to the test. Without protest she gathered her children and followed her husband out the door and into the darkness.

A New Life in Dohuk

It was a wonder that the Mattys even made it across the border. The south did not want them to leave, and the north did not want to let them in. Only Yousif's good relations with the border guards made it possible for their family to pass through the checkpoint unhindered.

Life in the UN–protected no-fly zone of northern Iraq was every bit as difficult as Alia had envisioned. For one thing, it was extremely expensive to rent a house, so they could afford only a one-room apartment. Cooking, sleeping, eating—everything had to happen in the same room. What a change from their spacious villa in Kirkuk! Having no electricity or fuel was another real hardship; for two years, they lived after dark by the light of a kerosene lamp. The family had only one heater, which kept them warm and also heated their bathwater. Alia washed the dishes and did her laundry in cold water.

Despite their stressful living conditions, Yousif and Alia began to invite people to their home. Over a cup of tea or a meal, they shared the good news of Jesus with the predominantly Muslim Kurds. Then shortly after their move to Dohuk, a Western relief organization's delegation came to the area.

"Is there a church here to help us with the distribution of goods?" their representatives asked the local people repeatedly. They always got the same answer. "No," the Kurds replied, "but there's a family who tells us stories from the Bible. Maybe they can help you."

Before long the Mattys didn't have to invite people to their home; needy people continued to show up at their door. Not only did the poor receive food for their bodies, but Yousif and Alia used every opportunity to introduce them to Jesus, the Bread of Life, the only One who could satisfy their hungry souls.

Alia knew she had married a man of vision, but after their move to northern Iraq, it was sometimes difficult for her to keep up with Yousif's many plans and schemes. While he traveled all over the country to distribute relief goods and preach the gospel, Alia gave English lessons, using the Bible as a textbook. Soon their apartment was far too small and they had to move again. Meanwhile, Yousif had decided that they needed to open a bookshop where people could come and go unnoticed, while having some freedom to talk about the gospel.

Yousif and a missionary friend decided to work together. They rented an apartment as their headquarters, and before long it was filling up with books—Western friends were only too willing to provide them with stock. They rented a narrow, rectangular-shaped store in one of Dohuk's shopping areas, where they made Arabic and Kurdish books available for purchase or loan. The shop also had a small library of Christian videocassettes, and customers could watch them on the shop's VCR.

All too soon the bookstore's Christian activities were brought to the attention of radical Muslims, and Yousif started receiving threats. Vandals set fire to the bookstore and damaged many precious Bibles and other merchandise. But Yousif wasn't easily put off. "We'll just have to open more bookstores," he told Alia. "Having only one store makes us too vulnerable because all the opposition can be focused on us here, and that's not good."

Yousif wasted no time. He soon had enough books to stock three stores. Apart from Dohuk, new shops were opened in Erbil and Sulimaniyah.

While Yousif continued to move around, Alia found her ministry closer to home. Her warm hospitality gained her many friends among the Kurdish women. Sometimes alone, at other times with her children, she visited their homes too. When tensions mounted between radical Muslims and Christians, she sensed that her friends were hesitant to receive her in their homes. Everybody saw Yousif and Alia as Christian missionaries, and in certain quarters their activities were not appreciated. But when Alia told Yousif what was going on, her visionary husband simply came up with another plan.

"Radio is the answer!" he declared. He contacted his friends abroad to ask for their help and quickly transformed their basement into a studio. Now unnoticed by overly curious neighbors, Kurds could listen to the Christian gospel in the safety of their own homes.

By Life or by Death

But the more Kurdish-speaking Christians got together for prayer and Bible study, the more persecution increased. Alia had to steel herself before she picked up the phone. She could no longer count the times a voice on the other end had threatened to kill Yousif. Even though her husband didn't think of himself as a hero and was often afraid, he never let fear paralyze him. With the approval of regional governments led by various Kurdish factions, he took the Jesus film to remote areas, but he never stayed long in any one place.

Alia fought off her worries about Yousif, but her greatest anxiety was for their children. A recent letter had almost paralyzed her with fear. "We will attack your children," it read. "And we will kidnap your son." As usual, the devil was directing his fiery arrows at the most vulnerable part of her heart.

In Yousif's absence, Jesus was the only one she could turn to, so Alia poured out her fears to God. "What can I do, Lord?" she cried. "Please, Father, protect Mejid! He's just an innocent little boy. You're the One who called us here; You have to take care of our children. Cover them with Your blood and send Your angels to protect them."

Threats and attempts to intimidate the Mattys continued, and at times Alia angrily lashed out at Yousif, asking him why they were subjecting themselves and their children to such a dangerous, inhospitable situation. Then one afternoon while Alia was shopping for groceries at the colorful local market, a stranger approached her. The woman wore a long-sleeved dress that flowed gracefully down to her ankles. Her hair was covered with a scarf.

"Can I talk to you?" she asked Alia softly.

Assuming the woman knew her and wanted to inquire about the Christian faith, Alia began to tell her about Jesus. The woman started crying. After talking with her a little longer, Alia offered her a Bible.

"No, thank you," the woman graciously refused the offer. "I already have one. Look, I understand why you are here. And I just want to tell you—we love you. Please don't leave; stay in our country. We need you here."

Startled by the woman's unexpected words, Alia asked, "Who are you? Where do you live?" The woman never told her. But more tears poured down her face as she looked into Alia's eyes. "I love you and I love your children, and don't ever forget it," she said in a quiet voice before disappearing into the crowd.

For two months, whenever she went to the market, Alia searched for the mysterious woman, but she never saw her again. It would have to be enough to know that God had sent a Muslim lady to encourage her and to remind her to stand with her husband. This unusual encounter convinced Alia that she could not ask Yousif to choose between his family and his ministry. He should not have to walk the hard road alone. Even though life in Kurdistan was harsh and hurtful, at least they had each other. Most of all, as the woman had said, the Kurdish people needed them.

Trouble on Every Side

By this time the Matty children had come to know Jesus, and He had given them a burden to reach their little friends with the Good News. Noor was only eight when she asked her father for Bibles to give to her teachers and friends at school.

One day Farrah opened the window of their apartment and shouted at one of the children playing in the street. "Do you know who Jesus is?"

"Yes," the answer came, "He is Isa from the Qur'an."

"That's not true!" Farrah shot back in Kurdish. "He is the Son of God."

"*Kaffir, Kaffir*, you are lying!" Insults were exchanged until Alia became aware of the conflict and told her daughter to stop shouting and close the window.

Not many days later, Mejid came home crying. That wasn't especially unusual, but this time he seemed more upset than ever.

"What happened, darling?" Alia asked.

239

"Murat started to beat me up on the way home," he sobbed. "When his friends saw it, they all came after me. It was terrible, Mommy. Look!"

Alia's eyes filled with tears when she saw her son's bruises. She knew her daughters were ridiculed at school too and were sometimes mistreated as they walked home.

"We can't go on like this!" she protested to Yousif that evening. "It's asking too much of them."

"Maybe we should ask our American friends for help," he said thoughtfully. "I know for a fact that many of them homeschool their children. Maybe we could do that too, if they'll provide us with curriculum."

Homeschooling proved to be an ideal alternative. Alia was an excellent teacher, and before long Yousif began to envision a network of Christian schools that could benefit thousands of other children in Kurdistan, Christian and Muslim alike. But before Yousif could focus on his plan, tragedy struck. Their co-worker Mansour Hussein Sifer was murdered in the bookshop in Erbil. Yousif and Alia were devastated by this atrocity, which not only cost them a close friend, but also reminded them of their own vulnerability. They did what they could to help Ruth and Kevin, Mansour's widow and sixteen-month-old son. (For this story see chapter 14 of *Hidden Sorrow, Lasting Joy*.) Not long after Mansour's murder, their ministry in Dohuk came under attack.

By then the Matty family had moved to a two-story apartment, in which the first floor housed the studio and ministry equipment, and the second floor served as the family residence. A large metal garage door was the only entrance to the building, and knowing they were prone to attack, the family took great care to keep the door shut at all times.

Alia was alone at home with the three children when she heard angry voices outside yelling, "*Allahu Akbar! Allahu Akbar!*" The voices were coming from the street, and when Mejid looked outside, his face paled when he saw a local child—someone he'd thought of as a friend—about to throw a rock at the house. Within minutes the sounds of shouting and shattering glass filled the air.

"Mejid," Alia yelled, "get away from the window!"

By now Noor and Farrah were screaming. With all the strength she could summon, Alia cried out, "God, help us! Jesus, save us! Please, God, *please tell me what to do!*"

"Mom, we're finished!" Noor sobbed. "The garage door is open!"

In that terrible moment, a familiar Voice calmed Alia's spirit. *No one can touch you. Trust Me.*

All at once the noise outside died down. Alia peeked through a window in time to see a mob of more than sixty young males standing near the open garage door. One by one, they were dropping the stones from their hands and walking away. After the crowd had dispersed, a neighbor approached the house and closed the garage door.

That evening, when Yousif heard what had happened, he was overjoyed that his family was unharmed. He was even more grateful when the neighbor told him, "I couldn't figure out what was going on. Those guys came over to kill your family and steal your radio equipment. But for some mysterious reason, even though the garage door was wide open, they did nothing more than throw a few rocks at your house. And then they left."

Yousif and Alia knew the reason very well—God had answered their desperate prayers and had protected them.

Threats of physical violence, directed at the Matty family and the western Christians who supported them, increased during the ensuing weeks. One day a violent mob attacked the church they had started. Since it was no longer safe to meet there, Yousif had to suspend its services. Days later, when another mob gathered outside their house, poised to attack, Yousif knew it was time for them to find a safer place to live.

A Time of Seclusion

For three months the Mattys lived in a friend's basement, and their time in hiding seriously stretched their faith. The ministry seemed to have ended. The local government did what they could to pressure Yousif to leave northern Iraq by refusing to give him permission to move to a safer house, using the excuse they could not guarantee the family's safety. Even close friends couldn't understand why the Mattys chose to stay in northern Iraq when they had an invitation to pastor a Kurdish church in the United States. Yet every time Yousif asked God for His will, he received the same answer: *Stay where you are. These people need you. This country needs you.*

During a particularly demoralizing week, Gerry, a visitor from Holland, arrived unexpectedly at the Matty's hiding place. In the past Gerry's organization had helped Yousif with books and radio equipment. But since it had become extremely difficult to cross the border into Kurdistan, no one had seen Gerry for a long time.

"How on earth did you get here?" Yousif exclaimed, stretching out his arms to embrace his Dutch friend. "And how did you find us? If ever we needed encouragement and prayer, it's now. I am so glad to see you!"

The two men talked long into the night.

Moved by Yousif's plight, Gerry started a letter-writing campaign on behalf of the Mattys. Letters and postcards were delivered to the hidden family from all over the world, assuring them of other Christians' prayers and good wishes.

Then Yousif had an idea. "Why don't you ask your friends to send emails to our local governor?" he asked Gerry. "Tell them to say, 'How do you think you can protect four million Kurds if you can't even guarantee the safety of one harmless pastor and his family?'"

Yousif was soon summoned to the governor's office.

"Please tell your friends to stop sending me emails," the governor begged him. "There are so many emails in my mailbox that my server is jammed. Just tell them we're not going to send you into exile and that you have my permission to move to another apartment."

That proved to be a turning point. After the Mattys got settled in a place of their own, it took several months to reestablish their ministry. But with the help of their many friends, Yousif and Alia regained their confidence that God would use them to minister to the Kurds.

Alia went back to doing whatever her hands found to do. She started to minister in a center for handicapped people, teaching them to sew and embroider. When they were skillful enough, she showed them how to make school uniforms, bed covers, and pillowcases for a local orphanage. And when Alia showed the Jesus film to her students in the handicapped center, many of them were moved by Jesus's suffering. They were able to identify with Him and to understand better the stories Alia told about Him.

Concern for Women

It wasn't long before Kurdish believers found their way to the Mattys' new home. Yousif studied the Bible with several men who were new converts. Although their wives were willing to visit Alia and welcome her to their homes, to their husbands' disappointment, the women were reluctant to make a commitment to Christ. Alia understood that they needed time to see whether their husbands really had changed. Many of them had been hurt in the past and refused to make a decision.

"In my country, women walk ten meters behind their husband, unless they are walking into a minefield. Then the ladies go first!" Yousif said it as a joke, but Alia knew there was truth in his words. She could only imagine how difficult life was for so many of the women around her.

Over the years, she'd heard many stories of abuse. Women came to her with their most intimate hurts, mostly because they had no one else to talk to. When Kurdish men mistreat their wives, the women get no sympathy from their mother or sisters. Culture dictates that they have to stay married, no matter what is done to them. "He owns you," they are told. "And you'll just have to put up with him."

From the beginning Alia had been told that it would be ten years before her Muslim friends would really trust her. Now, after a decade in Kurdistan, God began to answer her prayers for the women she had come to serve. One of these women was Selwa, who was married to a Christian convert named Mustafa.

Selwa's parents and brothers often came to her house, threatening to take Selwa away from her husband. "Turn back to Islam," they warned Mustafa, "or we'll come and take our daughter home with us. You know very well that now that you've become a Christian, she can divorce you!"

Over the years, Selwa had gone to Alia's house for regular visits. She'd heard the Christian gospel explained over and over again, but Selwa never showed any particular interest in it. But when her parents decided to drive her away from Mustafa, to everyone's surprise she took a stand.

"I can't obey you," Selwa said the next time her parents showed up at the door. "Yes, it's true that my husband is a follower of Jesus. But here's the part you don't understand. Because of the change I've seen in him, I want to become a Christian too. And no, I will not divorce him!"

Many other Kurdish women also chose to follow Jesus after they became convinced their husbands really had changed. And they admired Alia. They had been watching her for years, and several of them explained that they'd been won over to Christianity not so much by what Alia said as by the way she lived her life. There was peace in her home, she did not shout at her children, and it was obvious that her husband loved and respected her.

Muslim women knew their husbands were free to bring home other wives, and it was often a cause of great concern. After both she and her husband had come to Christ, one woman confided to Alia: "Now I can put my head down on my pillow at night without fear, just like you, Alia."

Over the years, Alia had set up numerous Bible study groups for women, preparing Christian leaders to disciple others, just as Yousif had done with the men. After thinking about these women and their unique needs, she told her husband about a dream she had. "Yousif, why don't we build a center for women?"

Vision for the Future

When American troops invaded in 2003, more bloodshed and devastation rained down on Iraq. But there was good news too. Saddam Hussein was ousted, and the border between north and south Iraq was opened up. After more than ten long years of separation, Yousif and Alia were reunited with their extended families.

During their years in northern Iraq, Yousif and Alia have accomplished more than they ever imagined or thought possible. They have established three Christian bookstores, three Christian radio stations are in operation, and three Christian schools have been opened.

And Alia's Community Center for Women opened in 2005. Apart from training local women in special skills, Alia continues to work hard so the center will provide a haven for Kurdish women, a place where they can relax, play sports, find a listening ear, and—most important of all—hear about Jesus.

Threatening emails continue to arrive in Yousif's inbox. Now they come from Al-Qaeda–related groups. Not long ago one of Yousif and Alia's dear friends was murdered. But hardship and persecution have never stopped the Mattys from doing what God has called them to do. In fact, if you ask Alia, she will tell you that reaching out to others has helped her cope with her own difficulties.

"Jesus went to the cross for us, for the joy set before Him," she explains. "I want to follow in His footsteps, so I keep my eyes fixed on Him. There's a reward waiting for us if we don't turn back. Remember what Paul wrote? 'Let us not become weary in doing good, for at the proper time we will reap a harvest if we do not give up'!" (Gal. 6:9).

Thinking about Reaching Out to Others

1. In spite of their circumstances, how did Xinran and Alia reach out to others?
2. Read Matthew 5:43–47; 9:35–38; 2 Corinthians 1:3–4; and 1 John 4:7–19. What should motivate all believers to reach out?
3. We read in Philippians 1:12–26 about Paul's life as a prisoner in chains. What can we learn from what he writes?
4. How do these verses challenge your Christian walk?
   Acts 5:41–42
   Acts 10:38
   Galatians 6:9
   Ephesians 5:15–16
5. How will you specifically apply what you have learned here?
6. How will you pray for your suffering sisters?

10

Ask for Help

If one member of the body suffers, we all suffer. But how can we share in the suffering of persecuted believers? One way is to pray for them—it's what they ask us to do all the time. The year 2005 marked fifty years since Brother Andrew made his first trip to Poland. At a large anniversary meeting in Holland, we thanked God for His faithfulness and grace to Open Doors and the Persecuted Church. And as a moving prayer, Graham Kendrick sang the following song of intercession that he had specially composed for our persecuted brothers and sisters around the world.

> As we bring our songs of love today
> Do you hear a sound more glorious?

Like the mighty roar of ocean waves
Many witnesses surround us
It's a harmony of costly praise
From the lips of those who suffer
Of sights and tears and martyrs' prayers
Until this age is over.

How long, Lord, till you come?
How long till the earth
Is filled with your song?
How long until your justice
Shines like the sun?
How long, Lord, till you come?
How long till the earth
Is filled with your song?
How long, how long?

Lord, help us to live worthy of
Our sisters and our brothers
Who love you more than their own lives
Who worship as they suffer
To embrace the scandal of the cross
Not ashamed to tell your story
To count all earthly gain as loss
To know you and your glory.

Nigeria: Nakub

During the night of February 21, 2004, Nakub Zakka couldn't sleep. Earlier she and her family of eight had been enjoying a relaxed Saturday evening together. Everyone had been laughing and talking when, all at once, another sound had intruded on their happy fellowship—the deadly rattle of automatic weapons. The gunshots warned of impending trouble in Yelwa Shendam, their northern Nigerian town.

248

But like most other local Christians, despite the gunfire in the distance, Nakub and her husband, Ciroma, who was the pastor of their local church, ignored the rumors about a possible Muslim attack on Christians. On Sunday they attended church safely. The following Tuesday morning, she and Ciroma walked to church together to attend an early prayer meeting. As they made their way back to their house around 8:00 a.m., they heard the call to prayer—the *Salat*—coming from the local mosque. Suddenly they heard gunfire again, and this time it was dangerously close.

"Run, Nakub, run!" Breaking into a sprint, Ciroma shouted to his wife, "Go back to the church. I'll get the children!"

Ciroma burst through the door of the house and ordered his startled children to get dressed immediately. "Come with me!" he demanded. "Run!" They all rushed back to the church, with Ciroma carrying his three-year-old son in his arms. All along the way they saw men in military uniforms, and for the moment, they gave Ciroma a sense of safety. He felt even better when he saw more armed men surrounding the church compound, noting that a number of Christians had already gathered there for shelter.

But the illusion of safety quickly dissolved into a terrible reality. Seconds later it became clear that the "soldiers" were actually radical Muslims. Before the eyes of the horrified Christians, they began to vandalize the church. Then they rounded up all forty of the women, including Nakub, held them hostage at gunpoint, and herded them off to some unknown destination.

As the frightened women stumbled out of the compound, they were prodded along through ruined streets. Again the *Salat* wailed from a minaret. But in that same instant, another voice crackled over the mosque loudspeaker calling for something other than prayer. It called for jihad against the church. In instant response, gunfire broke out. The women screamed, fearing the worst. And their fears were soon realized—before long, the lifeless bodies of Christian men were scattered across the church compound.

The women were locked up inside the homes of some of the town's most prominent Muslims, pleading with their captors for mercy. "Please, let us go home to our children!"

"No way!" their guards told them. "We can't let you out of here. Our boys are feeling a little crazy right now, and you'd be in a lot of trouble if they got their hands on you!"

The women were detained overnight, but the following morning they were escorted back to the church compound where a grisly scene awaited them. Like the other women, Nakub screamed and burst into tears as she recognized the mutilated bodies of dozens of Christian men, including her beloved husband and one of his closest friends who lay among the dead. She later learned that her three-year-old son and younger brother had also perished in the massacre.

Devastated, widowed, and left alone to provide for her remaining five children, Nakub fled Yelwa Shendam and went to live with her brother in a neighboring Nigerian state. She stayed with him for nearly a year.

Fortunately a member of Open Doors found Nakub shortly after the bloodbath. By then she was in desperate circumstances. Unable to support her children, she was destitute and hopeless. She was still grieving the deaths of her husband, her youngest son, and her brother. Nakub needed prayer, material aid, and counseling.

Nakub is only one of many widows that an Open Doors team has contacted. Under the banner of Project Goliath, we have initiated a trauma counseling seminar specifically for the widows of murdered pastors. Women like Nakub are provided with relief material, such as grains, rice, seasoning, soap, fabric for clothing, and money to pay children's school fees. They are given Bibles. And we pray for them on a regular basis.

Only six months after her introduction to Open Doors, a transformed Nakub met with a co-worker during a follow-up visit.

With sparkling eyes and a broad smile, she eagerly expressed her gratitude. "The trauma counseling seminar I attended has helped me tremendously. I still miss my husband deeply, but the counseling has helped me cope. And through Christ, I've found peace. Every time I pray, God renews the hope that lives within me and He strengthens me—that's why I'm able to smile."

The prayers that others offered up for Nakub were wonderfully answered. She has now returned to Yelwa Shendam and to the church where her husband, Ciroma, used to minister. "I'm determined to support myself and my children. My family has some property here in Yelwa, and I've decided to start farming it before the rainy season begins."

The trauma counseling seminar enables pastors' widows to stay in touch with each other, creating a support system through which they can regularly encourage and pray for one another. Nakub refuses to let her difficult circumstances bring her down or interfere with her spiritual growth, and she continues to be an active member of her late husband's congregation. She knows that Christians around the world have made a huge difference in her life.

So many women, like Nakub, have had to rely on God and on the prayers of others to get through hard times. I have sometimes needed support too, but until one particular incident took place, I didn't always ask for the help I needed. In the mid-1970s an opportunity arose for Johan to participate in Project Rainbow, which involved smuggling thirty thousand Chinese New Testaments to the underground church in China. While he was away, I heard some shocking news.

"Anneke, we got a telex message from the Philippines," a woman at our Dutch office informed me. "Something

*apparently went wrong at the border crossing. Two of our
team members were caught with the Bibles. The message
doesn't say which members were detained or what happened
to them."*

*At first the news didn't bother me. In fact, I was rather
flattered that the staff considered me spiritually mature
enough to handle it, since they hadn't told another
colleague's wife whose husband was also part of the team.
People in the office thought I was strong, and I promised
myself,* I will not disappoint them. *I began worshiping the
Lord, giving Him my trust and praying for the team—
especially for Johan.*

*This spiritual attitude lasted for about three days. Then,
with my birthday approaching and the children constantly
asking the whereabouts of their father, I fell apart. But
instead of admitting that I needed support and the help
of others, I began to get angry. I blamed our colleagues for
insensitivity toward me and, even more important, for their
failure to listen to the voice of the Lord. Surely they had heard
Him speaking to them during our morning prayer meetings,
telling them of my needs. And why hadn't they called our
office in Asia to find out which members of the team were in
trouble? And why hadn't anyone come to pray with me?*

*Then my anger turned toward Johan. Oh, what a life he
had—how exciting to be involved in this risky mission! But
did he ever think about me, alone at home and worried sick
about him? In spite of a note I had put up in our bathroom
some months before: "Self pity is cancer for the soul," I was
feeling very sorry for myself indeed.*

*This did not go on for long before God stepped in. One
night I heard His still, small voice say, "Apparently, you're
not as cool, calm, and collected as you'd like to be. Why don't
you just admit it? How about asking for help? Anneke, you're*

not strong. *You are* proud!*" I didn't hear the voice of God speaking those words audibly, but the message from His Word and His Spirit couldn't have been clearer.*

To my relief, it wasn't long before Johan arrived home safe and sound. As it turned out, the two who had been caught with Bibles simply had to leave them behind, while the rest of the team went on unhindered to deliver their precious cargo. Deemed a successful venture, Project Rainbow was a great encouragement to our Asian team, as it brought to light new ministry opportunities with the Persecuted Church in China. My story had a happy ending, and life soon returned to normal.

Clearly Nakub's circumstances were far more desperate than mine. But we both needed help. And the help we required came both from God's people and through the work of His Spirit. In another corner of the world a woman named Chely faced her own nightmare. The assistance of other Christians eventually turned her circumstances around too. But it wasn't easy, and it didn't happen quickly.

Peru: Chely

David was finally a free man! Chely smiled warmly at the inmates who had formed a line on both sides of the passageway in a farewell salute to her husband. But her eyes filled with tears when she and her family walked away from David's cellblock. It was a very emotional moment to see those rough, hardened men showing such appreciation to David, who had been one of them for so many years.

"God be with you, Colonel," Antonio said, touching David's arm.

"Thank you for teaching us from the Word of God," Ricardo added, stepping forward to pat David on his shoulder.

"Don't worry about us," another one remarked. "We won't stop meeting together."

"You were like a light shining into our darkness," said Hernando, who had once been a notorious drug dealer. Following an old prison tradition, he also tried to touch David. It was thought that by touching a man who was being released from prison, a little of his freedom might rub off.

Eight years and ten days had passed since David had first been imprisoned in Lima, Peru. And during his seemingly endless sentence, Chely had visited him every Wednesday and Saturday. She could not describe the pain she felt that first time when she said good-bye, with her husband waving at her from behind the wrought iron fence that separated him from the free world. She knew very well that he was innocent, which made her pain even more intense. Deprived of David's salary and his authoritative presence, it was challenging for Chely to manage the household alone. In some ways, life had been almost as hard for her as it had been for David.

But now at last, the de Vinatea family came to the large steel door that separated them from the outside world. As the door slowly creaked open, Chely squeezed her husband's hand. How she had longed for this day! It took only one step to get through the steel door, but what an enormous difference that single step made.

Firmly gripping the hands of his wife and his daughter, Pamela, David paused for a moment, took a deep breath, and looked up to the sky. With a smile, Chely glanced over her shoulder into the happy faces of her two grown sons. Even the stray dog, which had become David's companion in his prison cell, looked pleased with himself to be going home with them. Because all family members weren't allowed to visit the prison on the same day, this marked the first time the entire family had been together in eight years.

Outside the prison walls, cheers of joy erupted when a group of waiting friends and family members spotted the robust army colonel with his beaming wife and children walking toward them. Until the last minute, the atmosphere had been tense. The group had been waiting for hours in the hot sun. Now that David had walked out of the prison yard, nothing could spoil their joy. Through the streets of Lima, the party hurried along as quickly as they could to reach the de Vinateas' home.

Surrounded by confetti and balloons, still more people waited for David at the house. Even friends from abroad, who had supported the family through their long ordeal, had come to share in their joy. But when he arrived at his house, David hesitated before he went inside. He lingered at the door for several moments. Finally, overwhelmed by emotion, he stroked the supporting beams of his house in the sign of the cross.

The cross of Jesus had meant everything to him during the many sleepless nights he'd spent on his prison cot. He had clung to the power of Christ's cross when his life was in danger; he had found comfort and forgiveness at the foot of the cross when he was overwhelmed and depressed. Many times he had envisioned himself standing in this very doorway, ringing the doorbell to enter and embrace his wife and children, only to wake up and find himself back in his miserable cell. But today it was not a dream—he was home and the door was open. He saw Chely and the rest of the family waiting for him to step over the threshold, and so he did, to the sound of their cheers and applause.

When the day was over, both David and Chely were exhausted. "I couldn't sleep last night," David told his weary wife. "I dozed off for a bit, but the instant I fell asleep, I saw the prison authorities in my dream. With devilish grins on their faces, they told me there had been a mistake, and I would have to stay inside for the full sixteen years. That woke me up! After all the disappointments we've been through, I began to think that scenario was still a possibility. So I jumped out of bed and got down on my knees to pray. Even during my last night in prison, the Enemy was after me. And as usual, prayer was the only way to deal with him."

A Wonderful Change

During her parents' silver wedding anniversary Chely had met David, a cadet at the Peruvian Military Academy. In 1976 she'd married her handsome army officer. Their beautiful Catholic ceremony took place in one of Lima's largest churches. At the end of the service, in accordance with Peruvian Army tradition, more than one hundred army officers crossed their swords over the newlyweds' path as they left the church.

In 1979 David was promoted to the rank of captain and was selected to study in the Armor School in Fort Knox, Kentucky. By then the couple had two little boys, David and Daniel. During David's two-year course of study in the United States, Chely and the boys were with him. After returning to Peru, several pleasant years passed as David served with the Peruvian army in different capacities. In 1981 he and Chely welcomed their youngest child into the world—a baby girl named Pamela.

Then a wonderful change took place. By 1991 David had advanced to the rank of lieutenant colonel. While he was working in the Infantry School in Lima, a U.S. Army major was designated to work with him through an exchange program. The American colleague was a Christian believer, and he invited the de Vinateas to his home to attend a Bible study with his family. David had heard the Christian gospel some years before, and now that long-planted seed began to grow and flourish. Both David and Chely gave their hearts to Christ.

"I Am Innocent"

David served his country with loyalty and courage. He was recognized as one of the ten best commanders of the Peruvian infantry and had aspirations of attaining high command. With his impeccable record, he was very successful in battling drug trafficking and was instrumental in putting a number of criminals behind bars.

Because he had experienced the power of God's Word in his life, Colonel de Vinatea became involved in a Bible distribution project for Peru's military troops. David was zealous for Christ, and he displayed Scriptures conspicuously on the walls of his office. Then, much to the dismay of his general, he posted a sign on his office door that said, "God rules in this base." It wasn't long before he was summoned into his commanding officer's quarters.

"I don't like that sign on your door!" the angry general told him. "God's not in charge here—I am. Get rid of it."

"Excuse me, sir," David replied. "Yes, you're the commander. You give the orders here, but God really is the One in charge."

This conversation wasn't just about the sign on the door, and David knew it. He took the warning seriously, well aware that he was about to face some difficult consequences for his commitment to Christ. He began to ask himself some hard questions. Was he going to take part in the corruption that was evident all around him, or would he choose to take the side of righteousness and truth? What did he want—to be a ranking general, a millionaire with property, nice cars, and a sizeable bank account? Or did he want to remain faithful to the decision he'd made to follow Jesus and turn away from sin? Once again he committed himself to the Lord and vowed that he would fight the drug traffickers with every legal means at his disposal. And he would not involve himself in illegal tactics. As a Christian, David knew that the ends cannot justify the means.

As time passed, some of David's colleagues admired his sincere and earnest Christian witness, but others despised him. Because of his personal integrity, they were afraid that their own evil practices would be revealed. And so, to protect themselves and get David out of the picture, several officers fabricated a number of accusations against him.

On November 9, 1995, a judge ordered David's arrest while he was working in the army headquarters. A lawyer urged David to flee, but he refused. "Never," he said firmly. "I'm innocent and I will not run away." Instead of leaving the country, he turned himself in to the military police. When he asked for permission to call his wife, they let him use their phone.

"I've fallen into their trap, Chely," he said quietly. "I've been arrested."

Chely was speechless. They both knew of many Christians who had gone to jail for *believing* in Jesus, but now David found himself behind bars for *obeying* Jesus. In July of 1997 he was sentenced to sixteen years in prison, falsely accused of the very crime he had tried so hard to eradicate: participation in drug-trafficking activities.

When her husband was arrested, Chely's life changed overnight. No longer was she the wife of a respected, well-paid army colonel. Instead, she was a social outcast, looked down on by family and friends. While her husband languished in prison, she suffered at home. She had no one to help her with the children. David had been the one to assist them with their studies or remind them to do their chores, and he wasn't there to lead family prayers or say grace at their meals. Chely had to fill his shoes in every area. And she could ill afford to let tiredness, worry, loneliness, or pain overtake her. Her husband and her children needed her, and she had to remain strong.

Christ as Lord

The first years of David's imprisonment were dark and full of despair. For eleven months, he was held in a filthy, rat-infested, maximum-security cell, isolated and deprived of communication with others. When Chely was finally allowed to see him, he poured out his troubles to her.

"You know that when I gave my heart to the Lord in 1991," he told her, "I was like a lot of people. I went to church every Sunday, sang praises to the Lord, prayed, and gave my money—and that was it until the next Sunday. But here in this cell, I found the true Lord and Master of my life, the Lord Jesus Christ. I gave myself to the Lord in a new way—with all my heart."

Yet despite the presence of Jesus, his living conditions were intolerable. Alone and filthy, David was depressed and near despair. He had fallen from a place of authority, where he could control his life, his family, and his subordinates, to complete powerlessness. He could do nothing to help himself, much less care for his wife and children.

After three years, David was transferred to another prison in Lima populated by common criminals, 50 percent of whom were serving sentences for drug trafficking. The conditions at that prison were also horrendous, and to make matters worse, David discovered that some of the drug traffickers and terrorists were the very criminals he had apprehended. Since he was confined with them on the same floor, both he and Chely had reason to fear for his life. Three times he was spared from death during prison riots. Every night he wondered, *Will I be alive tomorrow?* He knew that with enemies around every corner, he could be killed at any time.

It grieved Chely to see her strong and independent husband relying on her for help and comfort. He always tried to maintain his composure, but many times he couldn't hide his misery from his wife. The injustice he had suffered and the long days spent in jail were deeply demoralizing. Chely knew she had to be strong for both of them, and she had indeed become a stronger woman, although she was not without her own sense of helplessness. For the sake of all concerned, she did her best to keep it to herself.

Chely was devoted to David's best interests, and so she accommodated the difficult schedule of twice-weekly prison visits. During the entire span of David's incarceration, Chely left her home at 6:00 a.m. on Wednesdays and Saturdays. She didn't see her husband until 9:00 a.m. On arriving at the prison, she had to wait in a long line with the other prisoners' wives, and during this wait the prison guards typically spewed verbal abuse at the women. Worse yet were the invasive and humiliating body searches. When Chely finally walked through the last iron fence and into her husband's cell, she forced herself to smile, hoping to hide any evidence of the ordeal she had just endured.

And of course the family suffered economically. There were days when Chely hardly had enough food for her children. During this time, she turned to God, unburdening her heart and sharing her needs with her heavenly Father. Prayer became a lifeline. Like David, she also came to know Jesus in a new way, empowered by His strength when she had none of her own strength left. Although she and her husband experienced their pain in different ways, suffering led them both into a deeper relationship with Christ.

If One Member Suffers

All the while, David's legal situation dragged on. For the first four years of David's imprisonment, his lawyers struggled to prove his innocence, but not one charge against him was dropped.

"I don't trust these guys," he told Chely one day. "They're costing a lot of money, but they're not accomplishing anything. By now all our financial reserves are gone. We couldn't afford a competent lawyer even if we found one!"

Chely was frustrated too, so with all the motivation in the world, she decided to study the laws and regulations relevant to David's case. She took it on herself to convince the court of his innocence. As time progressed, she became what amounted to a volunteer lawyer, advisor, and point person in dealing with Peru's various governmental agencies. She also became quite expert in finding her way around the official bureaucracy.

Yet nothing seemed to help. Chely presented convincing evidence, but justice for David was repeatedly denied. In fact, there seemed to be no one, on either side of the court, who was untouched by corruption. As the years went by, the judges, lawyers, and district attorneys who had tried David's case and sentenced him either ended up in jail themselves or were on the lam, evading their own corruption charges.

Exhaustion and discouragement were threatening to break the once strong and powerful army colonel and his family. Friends and extended family became despondent, and one by one, comrades in arms turned their backs on David. Then, after four intense years of struggle, and just when they reached their lowest point, Christians around the world came to the de Vinatea family's aid.

A group of believers from the family's evangelical church decided it was time for Colonel David de Vinatea to be provided with international advocacy and legal aid. Through a Peruvian Christian human rights organization called Paz y Esperanza, the church group learned about Open Doors International and asked them for help. Open Doors had fought for several Peruvian Christian prisoners falsely accused of links with Shining Path terrorists, and after six months of thorough investigation to ensure the validity of his case, they agreed to champion David.

Along with legal assistance, an international writing campaign was also initiated to put pressure on the Peruvian authorities. But most important of all, people began to pray for David and his family. Thousands of letters arrived in Peru for David, a huge outpouring of the concern, prayers, and love of Christians around the world.

This gave a much needed boost to the entire de Vinatea family. In a small notebook David kept track of all the mail he received, recording the names of the senders and their home countries. He showed the list proudly to Chely and his daughter, Pamela, when they came to see him, and his sons leafed through his notebook on their Sunday visits. As a prisoner's family, people in their own country looked at the family with suspicion, yet overseas their father was a hero.

Christians from other lands began to visit the de Vinateas too. The first international team representing five nations visited Luringacho Prison on June 7, 1998, hoping to renew and refresh the exhausted family. Because two inmates had been killed recently in his cellblock, the visitors prayed for protection for David and for the other Christian prisoners. David asked for five Bibles to hand out to fellow inmates. "If I have to suffer more for my religious convictions," David told his visitors, "glory to God! If the judges call me 'mad' for placing God first in my life, blessed be that madness!"

Cry Out to God

Uplifted by the support from abroad, Chely continued to pursue opportunities within the judicial process on behalf of her husband. The family's hopes heightened each time the court reviewed David's case, but every appeal to revoke the sixteen-year sentence was denied. Chely began to dread each upcoming court session, afraid to hear yet another negative verdict. It was extremely difficult for her to see her husband behind bars while true criminals roamed free and guilty prisoners received early paroles. Even an appeal to the Peruvian Supreme Court remained unanswered. There were times when she felt she could no longer bear the pressure.

As the family's economic situation continued to deteriorate, it was the prayers of others that sustained them all. "Pray without ceasing," Chely had often read in 1 Thessalonians 5:17 (NKJV). The many letters David and the family were receiving gave her a better understanding of this passage of Scripture. Due to the different time zones across the globe, people were praying for her family around the clock. In spite of everything, Chely could often feel those continuous prayers lifting her spirit. Every letter, every prayer, every encouraging visit was a breath of fresh air for them, and the Bible verses written on the many cards were like oxygen to their souls.

David responded to his international friends from his prison cell. He always asked the recipients to continue praying for him and his family, and he sometimes quoted Acts 12:5: "Peter was therefore kept in prison, but constant prayer was offered to God for him by the church" (NKJV). Even as legal efforts failed, one by one, he did his best to believe that someday God would open the doors of the prison for him, just as He had once done for the apostle Peter.

Gradually David's conditions in the prison improved. Because of the danger he faced from other inmates, he was placed in a section that was fenced off from the large group cells. This gave him more privacy and safety, and he and his beautiful, courageous wife could share time together in curtained privacy. The cubicle contained a bed, a toilet, and a table, and he was even allowed to have a dog, which gave him some much needed companionship.

Chely was able to cook for David during her visits, and he was permitted to use a radio. Every morning at 3:00 a.m. David woke up to listen to American pastor Chuck Swindoll's *Insight for Living* and Charles Stanley's *In Touch* programs, which nourished him spiritually and intellectually. He recorded the lessons he learned in his notebook and began to cover the walls of his cell with Bible verses. His favorite was Psalm 46:10: "Be still, and know that I am God" (NKJV).

At about this time, David's spirits lifted, and he was inspired to share the gospel with some of the other prisoners. His words did not fall on deaf ears. "A man in prison hungers for the Word of God," David told a group of visitors. "In prison you learn to pray with feeling, to cry out to God." With permission from the prison authorities, David began to meet with a few other prisoners who were appreciative of his spiritual leadership. Week by week, prayer session after prayer session, the men were touched by the message of Christ, and once again David knew that he had something to offer.

Freedom

Years of prayers were finally answered on November 19, 2003. An international coalition of Christian organizations lobbied the Peruvian government to undertake a judicial review of David's case. Due to their efforts, the court altered David's sentence and paved the way for his immediate release. After serving more than half of his original sixteen-year sentence, he was finally blessed with freedom.

Chely had once told a group of women: "When my husband leaves the prison, it will be for the glory of God and the joy of all those that seek His favor." Now the long-awaited day had finally come, and Christians around the world shared in the family's joy and gave the glory to God.

After the euphoria of his release wore off, Chely and David had to readjust to their new circumstances. The family needed a steady income; their two sons, who had been teenagers at the time of their father's arrest, had worked various jobs while continuing their studies to help pay the bills. Financial aid from Christians abroad had been crucial to the survival of the family over the past years, but this stopped abruptly after David's release. David was determined to provide for his family again, and before long, through the efforts of family members, he was able to find a productive job.

Meanwhile, although Chely knew that Jesus had been at her side through the whole ordeal, her burden had been heavy. After

264

David returned home, she began to experience some physical problems, which she attributed to having suppressed any signs of weakness for so many years. Now that her husband was there to support her, she didn't have to appear strong, but her body needed to recuperate.

A trip to the United States and various countries in Europe, sponsored by friends abroad, gave the de Vinateas a fresh perspective, encouraged their hearts, and helped them get their balance as they stepped into the future. Chely shared her experience of the power of prayer as she and David addressed a gathering of people who had supported them with letters and prayers.

"You made a huge difference in our lives, and you can make a difference again in the lives of others!" she smiled. "First and foremost, pray without ceasing. Press on with the battle to liberate our brothers and sisters around the world who are unjustly imprisoned. We must pray and speak out for justice on their behalf. Your prayers will sustain and encourage God's suffering people."

Today, as she speaks to various audiences, Chely de Vinatea acknowledges the pain she and her family have suffered, but hardship is not the final impression of her ordeal that she wants to leave with them. "When we remember the scars," she concludes, "we also remember the power of God."

Thinking about Asking for Help

1. What keeps us (you) from asking for help? Is this a spiritual problem?
2. Some of the greatest people in the Bible asked for help! As you read their stories, make note of who is helping whom and what kind of help is given.
   Exodus 24:13–14
   Deuteronomy 17:8–13
   Ruth 2

Matthew 26:36–38
John 6:1–13
John 11:1–3
1 Corinthians 16:1–3
2 Corinthians 1:8–11
2 Corinthians 9:6–15
2 Timothy 1:15–18
2 Timothy 4:9–18
Titus 3:13
Philemon 17–22

3. Read Galatians 6:9–10. How should we respond when we come across a need?

4. Do we have a responsibility to look for fellow Christians in need to see if we can help them? What will you do differently now?

5. It's likely that our suffering sisters around the world face many of the same obstacles to asking for help that you do. Also some may face cultural barriers that keep them from asking for help. How can you pray for them?

God's Grace Is Sufficient

Like many persecuted believers throughout history, Annie Johnson Flint, the writer of the hymn "He Giveth More Grace," understood both suffering and grace. In 1999 her song inspired and comforted Gladys Staines during the darkest hours of her life after her husband Graham and their two sons were brutally burned to death in India.

> He giveth more grace when the burden grows
>   greater;
> He sendeth more strength when the labors increase.
> To added affliction He addeth His mercy;
> To multiplied trials, His multiplied peace.
>
> His love has no limit;
> His grace has no measure;

His power has no boundary known unto men.
For out of His infinite riches in Jesus,
He giveth and giveth and giveth again!

When we have exhausted our store of endurance,
When our strength has failed ere the day is half
  done,
When we reach the end of our hoarded resources,
Our Father's full giving is only begun.

Annie Johnson Flint (1866–1932)

Australia: Gladys

When Gladys Weatherhead packed her bags in obedience to God's call and ended up in India in 1981, she was unaware of the far-reaching consequences of her move.

Gladys grew up on a dairy farm in Queensland, Australia. From an early age, she was interested in the things of the Lord. Not only did her parents teach her stories from the Bible, but they also introduced her to the world of missions, and Gladys loved the stories they told her. At the age of thirteen, she decided she wanted to serve Jesus as a missionary. She became a nurse, then a midwife, and she later completed a course on maternal and child health.

Her work took her to various parts of Australia, and eventually she joined an international ministry and visited various Asian nations, including India. There she met Graham Staines in the town of Baripada, Orissa. It was their first meeting, although their childhood homes in Australia were only eighty kilometers apart.

More than fifteen years before, Graham had begun his work at the Mayurbhanj Leprosy Mission. A uniquely kind and gentle man, he had spent those years nursing leprosy patients' wounds and seeking to rehabilitate them in society.

On August 6, 1983, Graham and Gladys were married in Ipswich Gospel Hall, Gladys's home church. Afterward she joined her husband in his ministry among the lepers. The Staines's marriage was blessed with three children—a girl and two boys. Along with being a selfless missionary, Graham proved to be a loving husband and father.

One morning in early 1999, during her morning devotions, Gladys was touched by a story she read. As she reflected on it, she felt as if God was asking her if she was willing to give all that she loved to Him—her husband, her children, her possessions. Tears rolled down her cheeks as she pondered this question. Finally she prayed, "Lord Jesus, yes, I am willing. Take all I have for Your use. I surrender them all to You."

Just days later, in the early morning hours of January 23, 1999, Gladys's life changed forever. Graham had taken their two sons, Philip, ten, and Timothy, eight, to a camp in Manoharpur. The three were sleeping in their car outside a small church when, in the middle of the night, a frenzied mob incited by Hindu militants set the car on fire. The charred remains of the father and his two sons were found in the morning, locked in a final embrace.

"We are left alone," Gladys said quietly, breaking the news to her thirteen-year-old daughter, Esther.

Thousands came to the funeral to pay their respects to "Saibo," as Graham was called. No one grieved more than the lepers' community. Only Gladys was able to console them. Throughout the service, she seemed composed and at perfect peace. Many tears flowed as she and Esther found the courage to sing a song together, "Because He lives, I can face tomorrow." Even in the midst of her pain, Gladys knew in her heart that the commitment she'd made to Jesus just days before had prepared her for her nearly unbearable losses.

God continued to strengthen her in very unusual ways as she walked through the valley of the shadow of death. A number of villagers who had fled the fury of the mob told her they had seen a beam of bright light from above shining down on the burning vehicle. "I do believe that my husband and children were specially strengthened by my Lord and the angelic hosts from heaven," Gladys told her friends.

During the following months, Gladys became an international figure. News stories around the world featured her prominently and quoted her statements. "I have forgiven the killers, but the law must take its own course," she repeatedly said in interviews. "We who experience forgiveness from God need to forgive others. Grace is available. Once we forgive, there can be healing."[7]

Gladys admitted that she would never know the answer to the question of why her peace-loving husband and her two innocent children were murdered. But she is convinced that they are with Jesus. Often she has seen them in her dreams, playing together in a vast green landscape.

As time went on, Esther returned to school and Gladys continued her work among the leprosy patients. It was far from easy. She sorely missed her hardworking husband and his spiritual leadership. And it broke her heart to see little boys the ages of her sons, she missed them so terribly. Because of the public attention she had received, she knew people were looking up to her. Again and again she emphasized, "I am not a superhero. I'm just an ordinary woman who needs the grace of God every day to keep going."

Four years after the death of her husband and sons, in an interview with *Christianity Today*, she referred to the hymn by Annie Johnson Flint, "He Giveth More Grace," quoted at the beginning of this chapter. "The fact that His grace is always there for us has been a great source of inspiration and strength for me to cope," Gladys told the interviewer.[8]

I've thought a lot about Gladys Staines and the loss of her husband and sons. And many times, after talking to the

women I've written about, I have wondered: What would I do?
Would I stand the test if something like that happened to me?
*To be honest, in my own strength I wouldn't have a chance.
My faith would never be strong enough. That's why I was so
encouraged when I read the following passage in* Life Lessons
from the Hiding Place.[9] *My friend Pam Rosewell Moore wrote
the book about Corrie ten Boom and describes a conversation
Corrie had with her neighbors in Haarlem. This exchange
took place shortly after her release from Ravensbrück, the
concentration camp where she and her sister, Betsie, were
imprisoned for hiding Jews during the Second World War.*

> *As Corrie recounted their experiences, one of the neighbours
> said, "I am sure it was your faith that carried you through."*
> *"My faith? I don't know about that," replied Corrie. "My faith
> was so weak, so unstable. It was hard to have faith. When a
> person is in a safe environment, having faith is easier. But in
> that camp when I saw my own sister and thousands of others
> starve to death, where I was surrounded by men and women
> who had training in cruelty, then I do not think it was my
> faith that helped me through. No, it was Jesus—he who said,
> 'I am with you until the end of the world.' It was his eternal
> arms that carried me through. He was my certainty.*
> *"If I tell you that it was my faith, you might say if you have
> to go through suffering, 'I don't have Corrie ten Boom's faith.'
> But if I tell you it was Jesus, then you can trust that He who
> helped me through will do the same for you. I have always
> believed it, but now I know from my own experience that His
> light is stronger than the deepest darkness."*

*These words have encouraged me, and I hope they
encourage you. Corrie ten Boom's Jesus is our Savior too.
His grace supports us when the storms of life seem to rip us
apart. Without His grace, which He provides day by day and
moment by moment, none of us would be able to persevere.*

Amira's life affirms that God's grace is sufficient. I am not able to reveal the name of the country in which she lives, but I have her permission to share her story of faith, suffering, and God's presence in her life.

A Middle Eastern Country: Amira

"Go back to your room, Amira! You get no breakfast. You know the rules in this house—no prayers, no food!"

Amira was used to her father's harsh discipline. Without a word, she slipped down from her chair and retreated to her room, feeling guilty. Although she was only eight, she tried to wake up early every morning to pray, something she had been trained to do since she was four years old. But this morning she'd been so tired that she had slept right through the muezzin's call for prayer. Even the creak of the door when her father left for the mosque had failed to awaken her.

Amira had always tried to obey Islam's rigorous rules. She said her prayers five times a day. During the month of Ramadan, she fasted with the rest of her family during daylight hours. And she listened carefully to her father's lectures from the Qur'an.

"Stay away from Christians," he often warned his five daughters. "They've twisted the words of the Qur'an in their holy book, the Bible. You can't trust these infidels. Don't let them influence you."

Of course this constant indoctrination had strongly influenced Amira. Between their house and one of the family's favorite markets stood a Christian church. Whenever Amira was asked to run to the market on an errand, she made a point of taking a much longer route so she wouldn't have to walk past the church. During her childhood, she was more careful about observing Islamic restrictions than any of her sisters. But as she grew older, she began to wonder.

One chilly morning when Amira was twelve years old, as she woke from a sound sleep, she heard the rain beating against the house. Through the open door of her bedroom, she saw her father preparing to leave for the mosque to pray.

"Daddy, why don't you stay at home? You can say your prayers here. It's so cold and wet outside, you'll get sick!"

Amira's compassionate plea could not compete with the religious rule of law in her father's mind. "When I go out to pray in bad weather, my reward becomes even greater," he replied, closing the door behind him.

Unknown to her well-meaning father, in that very moment a seed of doubt was planted in his daughter's heart. As she listened to his fading footsteps, Amira lay awake questioning why God would make life so difficult for people. Why would he afflict them instead of help them? Could bad deeds be forgiven only when outweighed by good deeds?

The shrill call for prayer from the mosque interrupted her thoughts. Quickly she got out of bed, rolled out her prayer mat, and knelt toward Mecca.

Despite his feelings about Christianity, for a time her father had a Christian friend. Twice a year, during special Muslim feasts like Eid ul-Adha, this man came to the house to visit. Curious, Amira tried to eavesdrop while the two men talked. Often the visitor was invited to stay for the festive holiday meal. And every time he left, she heard the same words from her father: "What a pity!"

"What do you mean, Dad? Why do you pity your friend?"

"I pity him because he's a Christian."

"But maybe he likes being a Christian—he could become a Muslim if he wanted to. Why should you pity him? Obviously he's quite happy."

"My friend doesn't deserve to go to hell. He has good values, but according to Islam, all unbelievers—including Christians—go to hell."

At thirteen, Amira enrolled in preparatory school. She was now wearing a djellaba—a long flowing dress—and a veil. To her dismay she was assigned a seat beside a Christian girl who wore jeans and a T-shirt. The girl also had a tattooed cross on her hand, which offended Amira every time she saw it. Her lifelong hatred of Christians surfaced.

"I don't want to sit next to an infidel!" Amira told her teacher. "Please give me another seat." Her large brown eyes flashed in disapproval. She was short for her age, but she knew what she wanted, and her strong personality more than made up for her small size. Still, the teacher was unmoved.

"Go back to your desk," she replied, "and try to be friends with her."

Amira decided to convert the girl to Islam by lecturing her on its supremacy as a religion. When her words didn't have the desired result, she adopted other measures. She tried her best to make the girl's life miserable, harassing her and insulting her. But no matter what Amira did, the Christian girl remained calm and friendly.

In their mixed school, Muslims and Christians went separate ways for their religious lessons and carried different sets of religious books. Increasingly impressed by her seatmate's humility, Amira put aside her father's stern warnings one day and asked to look at one of the girl's Christian books. The first picture she saw was of Jesus, surrounded by a crowd of people. The words printed below the picture pierced Amira's heart: "He went around doing good and healing all who were under the power of the devil" (Acts 10:38).

"So Jesus was always doing good things?" she asked.

"Yes," the girl smiled. "Jesus did nothing but good things."

When Amira got home that day, she asked her father to buy her a Bible. His response was a hard slap across her face. "I told you the Bible is a distorted book," he shouted. "How dare you ask me to buy you one!"

The small seed of doubt in Amira's heart had begun to germinate. The next week in Islamic class, the teacher was speaking about Muhammad's wives. Excuses were made for the prophet's many marriages, but Amira was not convinced. She wanted to ask a question, but the possible consequences made her nervous—so she softened what she had to say with several sentences before coming to the point: "If Muhammad was so concerned about the situation of these women, couldn't he have helped them without marrying them?"

Amira's teacher and father shared the same ideas about correction. The teacher slapped Amira's face and roughly escorted her to the director of the school, who reported the incident to her father. Shamed and angry, he made life miserable for his eldest child. Amira was afraid to cause any further problems. She decided to stop thinking about religion. There was no way for her to get answers to her questions anyway.

Searching for Truth

When Amira was sixteen years old, her parents divorced. Her mother left the house and all her children behind, and from that moment on, Amira's relationship with her mother was troubled, especially after she remarried. In her emotional turmoil, Amira sought solace once more in her family's religion, using the five pillars of Islam as her guide. She recited the creed, prayed, fasted, and gave alms. Although Amira was not yet able to make a pilgrimage to Mecca, she observed all the other Muslim requirements. More important, she lived to please God and sought Him sincerely. She dressed the strict Islamic way, covering everything but her hands and feet. As the eldest, Amira had to take on an entirely new role in her household, assuming the womanly responsibilities that her mother once held. Merging her new responsibilities at home with her studies was difficult, but Amira managed wonderfully and graduated from preparatory school with good grades. She wanted to enroll in a university.

At this time, in line with the general customs of her culture, one of her cousins asked for her hand in marriage. Although her father was elated by the proposal, Amira refused to accept it. She didn't want to be married at sixteen. She was determined to continue her studies. Her father promised that she could go to college if she agreed to be engaged to her cousin, but Amira turned down the deal.

By now Amira was beginning to feel rebellious. She started looking for a job. When she was offered a secretarial position in a Christian law firm, her father was furious, but Amira accepted the job anyway. It didn't take her long to notice some Christian books in the library at her workplace. When she spotted an icon of Jesus on the cross on her boss's desk, she instantly recalled the picture of Jesus she had seen during high school and the conversation about His doing good things.

"Why did Jesus have to be crucified?" she asked her boss. He was a nominal Christian who hadn't given much thought to specific beliefs. Startled by her question and afraid of the consequences of talking about it with a Muslim, he refused to answer.

During this time, clashes between Muslims and Christians were making headlines. Muslim terrorists were attacking Christian shops and stealing their goods. The boss's brother was one of the Christians who had been robbed. "Don't ever speak to me about religion again," he threatened, "or you'll be fired."

Amira's curiosity prevailed. Eager to find answers to her questions, she secretly began to read the Christian books she found in the library. She was drawn to what she read and became more and more convinced that Christianity held the truth. Nevertheless, her own thoughts and feelings scared her, so she sought guidance from a Muslim leader, the sheikh at a local mosque.

"Read the Qur'an every day," he told her. "Touching those Christian books is very wrong, so you need to repent and fast for three days. You'll also have to quit your job."

Amira did the first two things he told her. She went back to the Qur'an to find the truth; she fasted and confessed her sin. But her job meant too much to her, and she didn't want to give it up.

As she studied the Qur'an, both reading and listening to recitations of its ancient words, somehow her eyes were opened to a number of contradictions. She wrote these down in a notebook and thought about them carefully. The more she read, the more she was taken aback by the many verses that incited war and killing. So much in the Qur'an talked of bloodshed. Was God a cruel and violent God?

Amira was also shocked by the low value the text placed on women. It seemed to her that according to the Qur'an, women were second-class human beings. All these things increased her doubts further. How could she serve such a deity or obey his words? "Please, God," she prayed, sometimes in tears, "tell me what to do. What is the truth?"

Sad and confused because she had not found the God she so desperately longed to know, Amira took some time off work to think things over. Finally she concluded that her only option was to live without God. She'd tried that before, and once again it did not satisfy her.

She soon returned to work. After her disappointment with the Qur'an, she threw caution to the wind and started to read the Bible—the Old Testament, the Gospels, the Epistles. She couldn't stop reading, and everything she read was new and exciting to her. The more she learned, the more Amira realized the God who revealed Himself in the pages of this holy book was the real God, the One she had always wanted to believe in. She longed to follow Him because He was a God of love.

"It's written in the Bible that those who believed in Jesus were baptized," she startled her boss again one day. "I've read your holy book, and I believe in the Christian God. I want to be baptized. Please, can you help me?"

The man's face flushed. "I told you not to talk to me about religion! You're fired!" Her boss was determined to follow through on his previous threat, but Amira begged him to give her time.

"Please, just let me stay for a couple more months so I can try to find another place to work."

Although he was unwilling to say another word to her about Christianity, he did allow her to stay on the job a little longer. "But no more questions!" he warned.

One after another, Amira visited the Orthodox churches in her area. Everywhere she went, she got the cold shoulder. No one dared answer her questions, and every priest she spoke to was afraid to baptize her. "Go away," they told her. "Stay with your own religion."

She was disappointed, but she understood the priests' fear. Amira's middle-class, devoutly Muslim family was well-known and respected in the community. If a church took her in, it would pay a hard price.

Despite her feelings of loneliness and rejection, Amira knew that something was changing in her inner life. For one thing, she had stopped trying to fit in with her family. When they spoke badly about Christians and cursed them, Amira no longer joined in. And it didn't go unnoticed. Before long, her father was watching her closely. On Christmas Day he caught her watching a Christian sermon on television. He hit her and forbade her to go back to her job.

Amira no longer had access to the Bible or to any Christian books. All she had left were two pieces of paper on which she had copied some Bible verses, which she secretly read when she was in the bathroom. Five months of loneliness followed, months during which Amira could talk to no one but God in prayer.

"What about my future?" she cried out to him in tears. "What should I do?"

Amira started thinking about the story of Abraham, who had left his country and his family in obedience to God (see Genesis 12). She began to believe that it applied to her. "God," she prayed, "Abraham was already old when you spoke to him. You gave him a clear message. I am only twenty-one years old. Do you really want me to follow Abraham's example? Show me it's really you, Abraham's God, who has given me this new faith, and I'll obey you. But please, speak to me as you did to him."

Homeless and Alone

It wasn't long before Amira felt satisfied that God really was leading her. She left home. She had no idea where she was going, and she had no place to stay during the night, but somehow she clung to the firm assurance that she was obeying God. She had walked out of her father's house with a train ticket, her papers, some clothes, and the equivalent of roughly twenty dollars in local currency.

As her train rolled through towns and villages, she strained her eyes for any sign of a church. For hours she saw only the minarets of mosques. When she finally spotted a building that might be a Christian house of worship, she got off the train and walked in that direction. For the first time since her search began, a priest was kind to her. He sat quietly listening as she poured out her story.

"You are in danger," he said sadly when she had finished. "Officially conversion to Christianity is not prohibited, but you cannot receive new identification papers that reflect your new religion. You'll have to live your life as if you were still a Muslim, or you

279

could be charged with blasphemy. I hate to tell you this, but it would be safer for you to move to another country."

He gave her the address of a church in the nation's capital where she could go for help. She thanked him and went on her way. Tired, hungry, and confused, Amira arrived at the capital city, and at ten o'clock that night, Amira finally met one of God's special servants who gently and kindly opened the doors of the church for her. He was willing to help, but not without testing her first to see if her faith was real.

For a time Amira ended up sleeping in the street or in the courtyards of mosques. One night she sought refuge in a monastery but was treated so badly that she fled. She ate whatever she could find and sometimes went without food for days. The months that followed were full of suffering, but Amira's daily visits to the church kept her going. The kindhearted priest taught her more about the Christian faith, and once he was convinced that she was a true convert, he baptized her.

Before long she was included in a clandestine Christian meeting. The participants revealed that they too were Muslim-background believers, just like Amira. She was overjoyed and wonderfully encouraged that she was no longer alone. When the believers asked her to join their group, she accepted immediately. Her new friends helped her find a job and rent a flat. She began to regain a sense of belonging.

Ministering to Others

After this exciting turn of events, Amira started thinking that she might not have to leave the country after all. More and more Muslim-background believers were finding their way into the fellowship. Paul, the leader of the group, encouraged new converts to continue living with their families unless they were subjected to so much abuse that it was no longer possible. When they had to flee, the group provided two apartments—one for girls and one for boys. Before long, Amira was asked to help work with the girls.

The group of young women did not have an easy time of it. They had to relocate several times because of harassment. Some of them, including Amira, lost their jobs. But they continued to support each other and to grow in their Christian faith.

One of the girls who stayed with Amira was under eighteen years of age. While making a call from the apartment phone, she forgot that the line was monitored. The police discovered her whereabouts and informed her family. When Amira and the young girl returned from a dental visit, the girl's parents were waiting. The mother slapped Amira across the face as hard as she could. "I know who you are!" she shouted. "I know who your father is and where you're from. You took my daughter and made her a Christian. How dare you! You'll suffer for this."

The young girl's brother was a police officer, and he soon appeared on the scene too. He was a large man, and he started beating Amira mercilessly. In those terrible moments, she feared for her life. Then unexpectedly, a neighbor, who had been watching from a distance, came to her aid.

"Leave her alone!" he shouted, placing himself between the policeman and Amira. "Nothing bad has happened to your daughter. And there's no law against converting from Islam. If you work for the police, you ought to know that. Look at what you've done to her!" By now Amira was battered and bleeding.

The policeman retreated. The family left with their daughter. But it was clear that the girls' apartment was no longer safe for the girls, and they would have to move yet again. To make matters worse, now that her circumstances had been revealed, there were those who believed it was their religious responsibility to kill Amira. The fellowship quickly went into action. A group of them took her into their home, despite the risk to their own safety, until she was able to find another place to live.

Suffering for Christ

Amira was in great pain after her beating, but the greatest pain she suffered following her conversion came from her family. A couple of months after leaving home, she had sent to her family a letter confirming her father's worst fears. Deep down, he had known all along that his daughter had become a Christian. Tears filled his eyes when he read Amira's words, telling him that she loved him but that she'd had no other choice but to leave. "I hope to see you again," she wrote to him.

Despite his love for his daughter, the shaming of the family name enraged the man. How could his daughter, whom he had brought up in the strictest discipline of Islam, embrace another faith and become an infidel? If she continued on this road, she too would burn in hell. He needed to take action.

Amira had always been close to her youngest sister, Fatima. Even after leaving home, Amira had spoken to Fatima several times by phone. Unfortunately, the police had monitored some of those calls. Meanwhile they had physically abused one of the girls in the Christian fellowship, and in the process she had revealed information about Amira's activities. Amira had chosen a new name after her conversion, but by now her family and the police authorities knew very well who she really was. They also knew what she was doing and precisely where she lived.

In 1998, five years after her conversion to Christianity, Amira was so desperate to talk to her father and sisters that she picked up the phone and called them. She assured them of her love and told them she missed them. Her sisters were emotional, and her father friendly but distant. Nothing in his tone or what he said warned Amira about what he intended to do.

"Amira, you need to be very careful!" Fatima's voice broke with tears when she called her sister a few days later. "Father and our cousins intend to kill you. I heard them talk about a plan to kidnap you and force you to return to Islam. If you don't obey, they'll murder you. Please, Amira, this is serious. Hide!"

Honor killings are common across the Arab world. Amira knew that she had shamed her family and that her life was now at risk. She shared her predicament with the leaders of her fellowship, and they prayed for her and warned her to be very careful. It was also impossible for Amira to stay at home all the time.

At nine o'clock one Friday evening, she ventured out. Immediately she sensed a car was following her. When she stopped, the car stopped; when she walked, the car moved. Amira turned to catch a glimpse of the vehicle's passengers. In that very moment, she saw that one of her cousins was getting out of the backseat.

"You're coming with us," he growled, striking her and grabbing her by the hand.

"Where are we going?"

"That's none of your business. Just get in the car. Do as you're told."

Amira knew she was in serious trouble. This particular cousin was linked to a terrorist group and would show no mercy. She was forced into the car, and as the bright lights of the city streets faded away behind them, Amira's cousin called someone on his mobile phone. "We've got her," she heard him say. "We're leaving now; we'll be there in a few hours."

As they drove, the relatives in the car began to interrogate Amira, slapping her face and painfully yanking her hair when the answers she gave were unsatisfying. When at last they reached their destination, they beat her from midnight until five o'clock in the morning. Leaving her bleeding and in a heap on the floor, they locked her up in an empty apartment—no bed, no furniture, nothing to keep her warm, no food, nothing to sustain her. Injured, cold, and frightened, Amira knew that unless God intervened, there was no way she would survive.

The next morning her captors returned. Amira shivered with cold and fear when she heard their footsteps on the marble stairway leading up to her "prison." This time a sheikh was with them, and his appearance was intimidating. He had a thick black moustache, a long, crooked nose, and eyes that seemed to exude evil. He was in full Islamic dress.

"You have a choice," the sheikh told her. "Repent and return to Islam, or we will kill you."

Three days passed, during which Amira was not given any food, but at last she was given a meal. She was afraid, however, that the meat had been poisoned, so she ignored her hunger and refused to touch it. Fortunately, she was able to drink whatever water she wanted from the bathroom tap.

The sheikh was a brutal man who used many forms of mental and spiritual abuse to try to break Amira's will. But her cousins' physical abuse was even worse. For days they beat her. "Do you want to know what hell is like?" one of them taunted her. "We're going to show you." They tried to pull out her toenails; they stomped on her face; they set the sleeve of her shirt afire to show her what it would be like to burn in hell.

For days the interrogation and the torture continued. "Who taught you about Christianity? Who baptized you? Who supports you financially? What church do you attend?" On and on it went. Amira simply gave them her Christian name and told them why she was convinced that Christianity was the truth. Sometimes she didn't answer at all, which further infuriated them.

Finally her cousins concluded she was not going to recant. "You have two more hours to change your mind," they told her one evening at around seven. "We're leaving you here with the sheikh. This is your last chance. If you refuse, we'll kill you. We'll be back at nine o'clock."

Once he was left alone with Amira, the sheikh again repeated the urgency for her to repent. Then he changed the conversation to another subject—marriage. And almost before she realized what was happening, the sheikh was attempting to rape her. Amira fought him off with all the physical strength she had left in her. Lying on the floor, her flailing hand suddenly touched on a loose piece of ceramic tile. She grasped it, used it as a weapon, and pounded it against the sheikh's head until he began to bleed profusely. He tore off his caftan and rushed into the bathroom to staunch the bleeding and wash himself.

The keys, Amira remembered. *He has the keys!* She had seen him put the keys to the house in his caftan pocket. She reached for his robe and searched for her only hope to come out of captivity alive. She found a key ring that held several different keys.

"Please, Jesus, in your name," she whispered. "I don't want to die here." Trembling, trying not to make any jangling noise, she removed one key at random and returned the rest to the sheikh's pocket.

A few moments later her cousins returned. Trying to hide from his friends what he'd tried to do, the sheikh sat down on the floor with them.

"So did you think about what we told you?" one of the cousins asked Amira. "What have you decided?"

She shook her head. "I have nothing else to say. I'm tired."

"If you don't change your mind, it means you don't want to live. It's up to you. God will be pleased when we kill you. We're going to leave one last time, but we'll be back in an hour. This is your last chance." The three men left, locking the door behind them.

Ten minutes later, confident they were really gone, Amira mustered up enough courage to get up from the floor. She located the key that she had hidden in one of her pockets. She shivered as she tiptoed to the door and put the key in the lock. Amazingly, it fit. It really was a miracle.

In her bare feet, weeping as she went, she ran down the stairs. She knew she looked horrible. Her clothes were bloodied, her

285

shirtsleeve was half burned, and her face was bruised and covered in cuts. Her toenails were still bleeding, her hair had not been combed for a week, and she was weak with hunger. But she was alive.

Once she made her way out of the building and away from the house, she tried to collect her thoughts. She wanted to call somebody, but her cousins had taken all her money. She suddenly realized they had overlooked the gold ring she was wearing. She could sell the ring, take a taxi to the train station, and buy a train ticket to return to the capital. But whatever she did, she had to hurry.

Amira found a shop that exchanged goods for money, sold the ring, and finally found her way to the dusty train station. By then she realized that people were stopping to stare at her. *They must think I am either insane or dangerous*, she thought, but she didn't have the energy to care. More than anything else, she was filled with gratitude that God had spared her life.

At first, it seemed as if there were no train tickets available. But Amira prayed. All at once a man asked, "Would anybody like to buy my ticket? I've had to cancel my trip."

Amira leaped toward the man, almost grabbing the ticket out of his hand.

"You're an angel sent from God," she said as she handed him the money. Without further delay, she jumped on the train.

When she arrived at last in the capital city's central station at 1:30 a.m., the first thing Amira did was call Paul. His wife picked up the phone.

"Rachel, it's me, Amira."

When she heard Amira's voice, Rachel screamed. "Amira, where are you? We've looked all over for you. Oh, thank God! You're alive!"

"Yes, I'm alive, and I'm on my way to your house right now!"

After a tearful reunion with her friends, Amira told them what had happened. As they listened, they wept with her. They could see for themselves that she had been deeply wounded, both inside and out. They explained that they had been looking for her everywhere and had prayed for her day and night, wondering if she was in prison or with her family or worse.

Many hours during the time that she was in captivity, Amira had been unable to find words to pray. Now she learned that her Christian friends had been praying for her all along. Somehow they had been conscious of her pain, as if they were suffering with her. God had answered, and by his grace she had safely returned.

Carrying On the Battle

Today Amira continues her work among the Muslim-background believers in her country. She is healing from the past, she is focused on the present, and she is working hard to create a better future for her country.

Even before Amira left her family, she had been deeply disturbed by the discrimination against females that she had seen all around her. Her concern about this issue had only increased as years passed. In her desire to eliminate injustice toward girls and women, she has become politically active. And she makes special efforts to visit women in prison who have been placed there as converts from Islam.

Amira's apartment is always full of girls needing refuge and teaching, and her discipling ministry takes her all over her country and abroad. A network has been established between several Arabic-speaking countries to encourage and teach secret believers. Amira is very much involved with this network and has helped put together a teaching plan that is now used in several different countries.

None of this means that Amira's own problems are over. Sometimes she struggles with bouts of depression. She continues to get regular phone calls from the police—they watch her movements and tap her phone. Her freedom is limited, but she has learned to work within its boundaries. She longs to make things better in the land of her birth, and she is determined to stay there as long as she can. Although her family no longer harasses her, most of her close connections with them are broken. One day she wrote:

> I shake off my longings, my history, and my
>   dreams.
> I shake off my fears and love
> And run unhindered toward
> An adventure on blazing, untrodden tracks.
> The moment I flee my family
> Setting off on the first road
> Called Golgotha, I only seek the cross.
> I am mindful of the small foxes
> Slipping between my feet
> Attempting to trap and entice me without success.
> I shall remain planted in my Lord.
>
> We walk stridently on the Road
> Secure in the midst of the storm
> The earthquake and the splitting rocks
> To live, to love—is to be crucified.

Aware of the pain behind her and the battle still ahead, today Amira is determined to follow Jesus's steps, to keep walking in the way of the cross. She is at peace in the knowledge that she will never walk that road alone.

Thinking about God's Grace

1. What do you learn about God's grace in these passages?
   Romans 3:21–26
   2 Corinthians 12:9–10
   Ephesians 2:4–10

Titus 3:4–7

Hebrews 4:14–16

2. How do these passages affect your walk with God and your worship of God?

3. Contrast what the Qur'an teaches about Allah and what the Bible teaches about the grace of God. (You have learned a bit about the Qur'an in this chapter and others, so you should be able to answer this question.)

4. Read Hebrews 11. Was God sufficient for each of the people mentioned? Does God's sufficiency mean that we will always see things ending up "happily ever after" here on earth?

5. Read Romans 8:26–39, and use its teaching to help you pray for your suffering sisters.

12

How Can We Help?

After meeting the courageous women in these pages, I'm sure you've realized that in regions where the church is persecuted, Christian women and children are often the most vulnerable. Most persecuted men would agree with this. They realize that it's easier to go to heaven (like Fausto) than to be left alone in a refugee camp in Colombia, raising six children (like Marlene). This does not mean we downplay the hardships these men endure! Their persecution and suffering are very real, but for years, their wives have been forgotten and they have often had to suffer alone. At times you may have wondered if there are ways you can help strengthen and encourage them. Of course the first thing any of us can do is to pray for them.

As you continue to pray, you can get involved in advocacy efforts by writing to governments and local authorities to protest the treatment of our brothers and sisters. To do this, you need to be further informed about their situation. Open Doors will be happy to send you the information you need. If you contact your local Open Doors office (see the address list in the appendix), you will receive our monthly magazine. You can send cards and letters too. Our publications often feature stories of women, including some of those in this book, and you'll find their addresses available. They would love to hear from you. Go to the website: www.od.org, and click on "offices" to select the country. You can also stay informed by signing up for prayer emails.

You can involve yourself in our women's ministry by organizing a special event in your area or by participating in a prayer group. We need women to represent our ministry in local churches. Open Doors organizes special trips to visit women who are enduring persecution for their faith, to encourage them, listen to their stories, and pray for them.

Open Doors Projects

There are many Open Doors projects that you can help financially. Your gifts will help persecuted Christian women around the world. In many cases, help to women is included in projects that serve both men and women, for example, through training and support. Some projects from which women benefit are described in the following paragraphs. For security reasons, only general geographic and project descriptions are given. For more information, you can contact the Open Doors office in your country.

Africa

In some parts of Africa, married women who convert to evangelical Christianity from another faith are forced to either renounce their newfound faith or be divorced. If they are divorced, they are left without a home or an income. Preparing them for their life alone and protecting them must be a priority. That's why micro-saving and credit projects have been initiated to enable such women to become self-sufficient and trained in a specific skill. Training and encouragement are also offered to help them stand firm in their faith.

Pastors' wives receive specific training, and special help is provided for single mothers and orphans. Material aid is provided for families of prisoners. Literacy classes are set up and funded to help teach illiterate women how to read and write.

Open Doors sponsors various types of biblically based ministry seminars to support Christian family life and encourage the church to fulfill its role in teaching parents and children about their responsibilities as members of the body of Christ.

Middle East/Muslim World

Literacy classes sponsored by Open Doors give our teams access to women in cities and villages. These classes create an incentive for reading and studying the Bible. Other types of Christian literature are also provided to expand the women's knowledge and perspective.

Children's materials are printed and distributed in countries where there is little or nothing available for children, and a women's magazine can strengthen and encourage women.

We also help provide training in micro-enterprise efforts to enable women to learn a viable trade, such as sewing.

Women's conferences encourage fellowship, study, and worship, with the purpose of reconciliation between Christians from different backgrounds.

Asia

Open Doors training recognizes the valuable role of women in kingdom building and seeks to improve the life and ministry skills of

Christian women. These life-changing seminar-workshops empower women as they seek to understand their role in their family, society, and church. After attending these programs, many women have professed a renewed sense of purpose and an improved self-esteem.

As you have read in this book, a lot remains to be done to teach the relatively young Chinese church about biblically based marriage principles. For several years now, Open Doors has organized secret training seminars to address this need with couples.

Literacy classes for women and the training of teachers to conduct these classes are valuable parts of our ministry to the church in different countries in Asia. Micro-loans help persecuted believers set up small businesses. The money that is made can support female family members and allow them to be full-time teachers in literacy classes or to evangelize in rural areas.

Bibles and teaching materials are provided when the church expresses a need for these items.

Through the local church, we help support prisoners' and martyrs' families in various countries.

Latin America

Open Doors supports women's and children's ministry in areas where families have been displaced by violence. Also we offer specialized training programs that disciple, provide vocational training, and offer counsel from a biblical perspective, enabling women to cope with and survive their difficult situations. Livelihood equipment and materials are provided to families of prisoners and martyrs.

You Can Make a Difference

This list of projects is not complete, and it will continue to change as different needs arise. Ask God to speak to you as to how He wants you to be involved. Just remember what Brother Andrew taught me many years ago: in the measure we help carry someone else's burden, our own burden becomes lighter. It is my prayer that together you and I, by helping to carry their burdens, will make a real difference in the lives of our suffering sisters around the world!

One memorable Sunday in early 1968, Anneke van Olst and her boyfriend Johan Companjen heard Brother Andrew speak in a small church in their native town of Oldebroek in Holland. That afternoon she and Johan committed their lives to Christ, promising God that they would go wherever He wanted and do whatever He wanted them to do.

In May 1970 Johan and Anneke were married, and in September that same year, they started their studies at the Birmingham Bible Institute in the UK, preparing for missionary service. When a request arrived from Vietnam to come as soon as possible, they cut their studies short, and in December 1972 they left with their one-year-old daughter and one-month-old son to join the ranks of the Christian and Missionary Alliance in Vietnam. After language study, they were involved in church planting and evangelism in the coastal town of Quinhon, until the Communist takeover abruptly ended their missionary career.

While they were seeking the Lord and finding their bearings back home in Holland, Brother Andrew asked Johan to join the ministry of Open Doors. He foresaw that the church, which was left behind in Vietnam, would soon become a persecuted church. Sadly, he was right. While Johan began to travel the world with Brother Andrew, Anneke—who gave birth to another son in 1976— stayed home to take care of their young family. Johan kept her well informed about the worldwide ministry. Through prayer and giving hospitality, she remained very much part of Open Doors.

One day Anneke heard of the suicide of the wife of an imprisoned pastor in Vietnam. She knew the woman well, and this news deeply disturbed her. A burden grew in her heart to do something for the wives who were often lonely, isolated, and stigmatized when their husbands were imprisoned for their faith. When their youngest son went to college in 1995, Anneke was able to join her husband on many of his travels. Johan became president of Open Doors International that year, and as Anneke traveled with him, she saw firsthand the tragic toll of persecution. She talked to many of the wives and was gripped by their stories.

Anneke gave a voice to women throughout the Persecuted Church in her book *Hidden Sorrow, Lasting Joy*, published in 2000. The book, currently in two English editions and ten other languages, tells the stories of twenty women who have suffered because they, with their husbands, chose to follow Christ despite opposition and danger.

Anneke continues to travel to restricted countries to meet with these courageous women, with stories still untold. Through speaking engagements around the globe, she brings awareness to the free world, awareness of how these individuals pay a heavy price for their faith in Jesus Christ. Anneke's role with Open Doors continues to demonstrate to these women that their fellow Christians have not forgotten them.

Notes

1. Eberhard Mühlan, *Bevrijd uit Afghanistan* (*Story of the Shelter Now Prisoners*).

2. Anneke Companjen, *Hidden Sorrow, Lasting Joy* (Wheaton, IL: Tyndale, 2001).

3. In the West, when we hear stories like this, we immediately ask ourselves how such things could happen. The explanation lies in unbiblical teaching and faulty ideas that are still rampant among the Chinese house churches. Many Chinese house-church leaders believe it is a sign of giving in to the flesh for a believer to go directly home after being released from prison. It is said to be much more "spiritual" to go to the elders of the church first. A complete lack of understanding about the Bible's message on family life often causes deep marital problems among China's house-church community.

4. Soon Ok Lee, *Eyes of the Tailless Animals* (Bartlesville, OK: Living Sacrifice Book Co., 1999).

5. Ibid., 116.

6. For further reading on the SSIM, see Deborah Scroggins, *Emma's War* (Vintage, 2004).

7. *Burnt Alive: The Staines and the God They Loved* (Mumbai, India: GSL Publishing, 1999), 37.

8. S. David, *Christianity Today*, February 2003.

9. Pam Rosewell Moore, *Life Lessons from the Hiding Place* (Grand Rapids: Chosen, 2004), 114.

For More Information on Open Doors

For updated prayer points, or to learn about additional resources and involvement opportunities with the Persecuted Church, please contact your national Open Doors office.

Open Doors
PO Box 53
Seaforth
New South Wales 2092
AUSTRALIA
www.opendoors.org.au

Missao Portas Abertas
Rua do Estilo Barroco, 633
Chacara Santo Antonio
04709-011 - Sao Paulo, SP
BRAZIL
www.portasabertas.org.br

Open Doors
30-5155 Spectrum Way
Mississauga, ON L4W 5A1
CANADA
www.opendoorsca.org

Åbne Døre
PO Box 1062
DK-7500 Holstebro
DENMARK
www.opendoors.nu

Portes Ouvertes
BP 139
F-67833 Tanneries
Cedex (Strasbourg)
FRANCE
www.portesouvertes.fr

Offene Grenzen Deutschland
Postfach 1142
DE-65761 Kelkheim
Bundesrepublik, GERMANY
www.offene-grenzen.de

Porte Aperte
CP45
37063 Isola Della Scala, VR
ITALY
www.porteaperteitalia.org

Open Doors
Hyerim Presbyterian Church
Street No. 403
Sungne 3-dong
Kandong-gu #134-033
Seoul, KOREA
www.opendoors.or.kr

Open Doors
PO Box 47
3850 AA Ermelo
THE NETHERLANDS
www.opendoors.nl

Open Doors
PO Box 27-630
Mt Roskill
Auckland 1030
NEW ZEALAND
www.opendoors.org.nz

Åpne Dører
Barstolveien 50 F
4636 Kristiansand
NORWAY
www.opendoors.no

Open Doors
PO Box 1573-1155
QCCPO Main
1100 Quezon City
PHILIPPINES

Open Doors
Raffles City Post Office
PO Box 150
Singapore 911705
REPUBLIC OF SINGAPORE
www.opendoors.org/ODS/
index.htm

Open Doors
Box 990099
Kibler Park 2053
Johannesburg
SOUTH AFRICA
www.opendoors.org.za

Puertas Abiertas
Apartado 578
28850 Torrejon de Ardoz
Madrid
SPAIN
www.puertasabiertas.org

Portes Ouvertes
Case Postale 267
CH-1008 Prilly
Lausanne
SWITZERLAND
www.portesouvertes.ch/en

Open Doors
PO Box 6
Witney
Oxon 0X29 6WG
UNITED KINGDOM
www.opendoorsuk.org

Open Doors
PO Box 27001
Santa Ana, CA 92799
USA
www.opendoorsusa.org

Open Doors
Serving persecuted **Christians** worldwide

WANT TO LEARN MORE
about the PERSECUTED CHURCH?

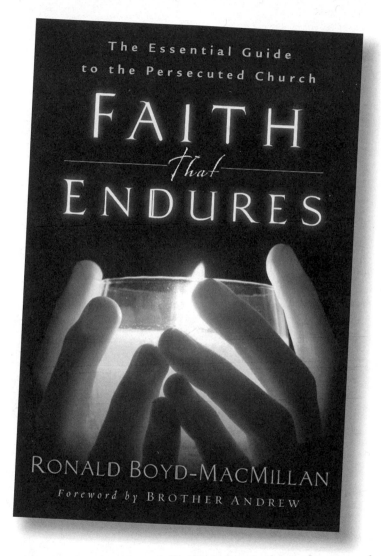

The Essential Guide
to the Persecuted Church

FAITH
that
ENDURES

RONALD BOYD-MACMILLAN

Foreword by BROTHER ANDREW

If the stories in *Singing through the Night* touched your heart, read more about the persecuted church and what you can do to help.

These are the stories you haven't heard on the news.
These are the people you will never forget.

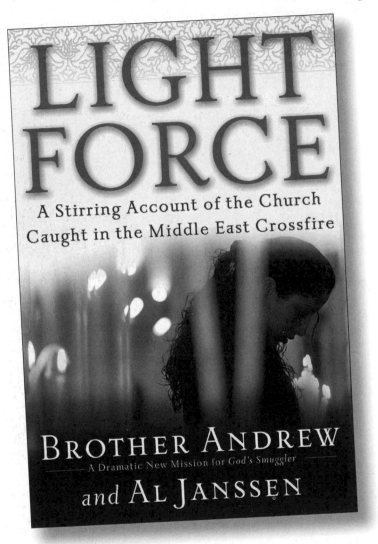

Be informed and get involved with

LIGHT FORCE:

A Stirring Account of the Church Caught in the Middle East Crossfire

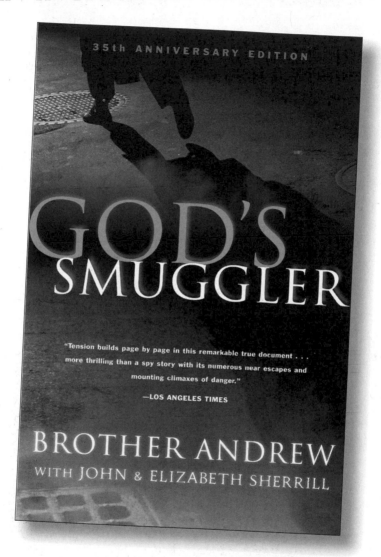